Design Thinking for New Business Contexts

"Yujia Huang and David Hands offer us a very accessible and straightforward insight into theory and practice of Design Thinking and beyond, this book will be useful for all who are looking for a guide to this topic and its application in all organisations."

—Professor Rachel Cooper OBE, *Director of ImaginationLancaster and Distinguished Professor of Design Management and Policy at Lancaster University*

"Most design and business scholars and strategists only grasp some aspects of Design Thinking, yet only few have a comprehensive understanding of its principles and applications. I herewith express my gratitude to Yujia Huang and David Hands for updating me and for sharing their expertise and insights to enable the sustainable transformations that we need in businesses as well as in society."

—Professor Cees de Bont, *Dean of School of Design and Creative Arts at Loughborough University*

Yujia Huang • David Hands

Design Thinking for New Business Contexts

A Critical Analysis through Theory and Practice

palgrave
macmillan

Yujia Huang
University of Dundee
Dundee, UK

David Hands
Lancaster University
Lancaster, UK

ISBN 978-3-030-94205-2 ISBN 978-3-030-94206-9 (eBook)
https://doi.org/10.1007/978-3-030-94206-9

Cover design by Yujia Huang

This Palgrave Macmillan imprint is published by the registered company Springer Nature Switzerland AG.
The registered company address is: Gewerbestrasse 11, 6330 Cham, Switzerland

Acknowledgements

This book is dedicated to the many hundreds of individuals drawn from both academia and industry who have shaped and informed the direction of discussions presented within the interrelated chapters throughout this textbook. Benjamin Franklin once remarked, "either write something worth reading or do something worth writing". As such, we aim to provide a fuller and richer account of design thinking as a maturing branch of design that demands closer attention by its vocal critics and also to curious minds as to the vast untapped potential of design as a driver for common 'good'.

Conversations, debates and the free sharing of ideas over countless years with many inspiring and thought provoking people has allowed Yujia and David to explore the emergence of design thinking as a recognised and invaluable agent for transformational change. In particular, Yujia would like to thank 'Design' for being so fascinating and meaningful that it keeps inspiring and driving her to discover and develop the world of endless possibilities and long-term sustainable futures. David would like to thank the amazing people he has worked within a variety of university settings; especially the students who he had the privilege to teach (yes even you Zunaira Mahmood!). Through the questioning of design, students have made us rethink our practice and understanding of design and of how it could be utilised in a diverse range of often unfamiliar contexts.

Furthermore, thanks to all the contributors for sharing their rich knowledge and detailed perspectives offered within their respective chapter contributions: In no particular order, we would like to extend our gratitude to—Dr Beatriz Itzel Cruz Megchun, Dr Xinya You, Dr Sotiris T. Lalaounis, Dr Bijan Aryana, Ir Ehsan Baha, and Dr Radka Newton. We would like to thank the Commissioning Editors at Palgrave Macmillan who have been continually patient in the development of this textbook. Without their support, this book would never have been possible. Final thanks go to all our readers of this book for being interested in design and using it as a way of reimagining desirable futures and also as an engine of creative practice for societal good.

You are the designers of an egalitarian future, committed to ensuring responsible business practice; shared and inclusive communities that values all individuals as equals; and importantly, custodians of our fragile and beautiful planet for generations to come.

Thank You

Yujia & David, 2021

Contents

List of Figures

List of Tables

Introduction

1

1.1 Introduction

"Time is not measured by clocks, but by moments" is a truism that reflects the essence of 'design for new business contexts' and the extraordinary conditions that shaped its development. With unforeseen events and changing circumstances occurring on a regular basis since early spring 2020, the world has dramatically changed, where the terms 'unpredictability' and 'uncertainty' have and will continue to feature heavily in our everyday lives. The origins of this book are rooted in a time and place where some sort of equilibrium was maintained; design thinking for business was incrementally gaining traction and organisations were slowly and comfortably moving into this newfound 'space'. The primary intention of the authors was to review, reflect and examine the rise of design thinking and its wider adoption throughout organisational life.

Due to the sudden and impactful nature of Covid-19 restrictions, the authors had to significantly reappraise content of the discussion over the subsequent chapters and the way in which they developed their ideas. Disruption was significant in both content and delivery of the final publication. This profound impact led the authors to consider the following two interrelated issues: if this change has had a huge impact on two authors regarding the way they conceive and structure a single textbook and the manner in which they produce it, how would multi-national organisations and businesses respond to this ongoing pandemic crisis? Mainly taking into account, their business operations span huge geographic and socio-cultural boundaries, with operational divisions and departments (let alone hundreds of thousands of employees to coordinate) responding to perpetual change and crisis brought about by Covid-19? Widely held practices, established orthodoxies and assumptions have been consigned to the waste bin of history within a matter of weeks as opposed to decades. We want to be explicit here; this book is not primarily about the pandemic, but examining its ongoing influence in the way that it is continually shaping the malleable contours of the organisational and business landscape. Agility and

Y. Huang, D. Hands, *Design Thinking for New Business Contexts*,
https://doi.org/10.1007/978-3-030-94206-9_1

resilience are terms increasingly discussed in business circles where the need for speed of response to unforeseen events are now featuring as integral elements of any proactive business strategy plans.

1.2 Background to Design Thinking for new Business Contexts

The origins of this book arise from three main areas of influence—industry practice, design research and teaching. What connects these three interrelated and complementary domains is the author's innate passion and curiosity surrounding the world of design. Design and designing are widely misunderstood outside of its disciplinary boundaries, regarded as a superficial activity 'often used to make things look good'. Or, 'design is simple and easy' not requiring much hard work and effort. On both accounts, these widely held assumptions are completely wrong; however, in order to dispel these common myths, the design profession has worked tirelessly to gain acceptance and recognition by its peers, both in industry and academia. Management guru, Peter Drucker famously once said, "You can't manage what you can't measure" and for many, this applies to design; however, you can measure the benefits and impact of design; the way design is 'valued' is one such means to measure it. For instance, a basic form of measurement could be to audit the return on investment (ROI), through the increase in sales of products/services; or improving market position whilst strengthening customer loyalty. Softer benefits could include reducing customer complaints on poorly performing products, and improving company image. Each of these benefits is of more importance to some companies as opposed to other—the value of design is relative to the particular context in which it is being used. However, as the world has moved considerably on over the last two decades, so has the role and influence of design.

Our research activities have taken us into new and unchartered areas of discovery. David has worked extensively in the emergent area of 'designing against crime' seeing how design can reduce (sadly not 'stop') opportunist crime such as theft and residential burglary. Design drawn upon in these contextually important situations is more concerned with behaviour change and raising awareness of particular behaviours that give rise to criminal opportunity. Meanwhile, Yujia has extensive industry experience, working on a wide variety of design and business strategy related projects. Now working in academia, she has identified the frequent misunderstanding and differing interpretations of design and design thinking between what goes on in industry practice and what academics critically debate. Regarding this ambiguity, both authors aim to provide clarity as to what constitutes design thinking for new business contexts whilst articulating the complexity of design thinking beyond simple definitions of its nature. Furthermore, both authors are also heavily involved in teaching, mainly at undergraduate and postgraduate levels, focusing upon design management, design for business and other closely connected themes where design is a central element to drive organisational competitiveness. We never ceased to be amazed by our students as to how they regard design and where it can be intelligently applied within the pursuit of business success and social 'good'. We hope this book offers the readership a set of distinct and diverse 'lens' to view and understand the world and how design can be a driver for equitable prosperity. It does indeed give rise to an interrelated set of questions 'who is leading change? Who are the beneficiaries of change' and 'what role can design play in leading this change?

1.3 Structure of Content

The following outlines key themes by each chapter, taking the reader through salient aspects of design for new business contexts.

Chapter 2: 'Evolution of The Relationship Between Design and Business' offers an expansive overview of the ongoing development of design thinking from its early origins in the late 1960s. It introduces the leading figures that were firm advocates for the value of design as an agent for transformational change. With the growing influence and recognition of design, businesses started to look towards design as a strategic resource to support the development of new and innovative products. The Harvard Business Review in 2015 dedicated an entire issue to design thinking, raising attention of design to the wider business community, lending further support to its adoption in industry. In addition to large multinational organisations, SMEs started to view and regard design as an integral element of company culture and planning activities. To raise awareness of design to the business community, design advocacy agencies (with the UK Design Council being one such notable example) began to offer design support programmes to provide specialist support and expertise to enable organisations to embed design within company culture. To date, national Design Councils are on the rise around the world, providing businesses and organisations vital skills and knowledge, in order to remain competitive whilst driving innovation in highly globalised markets.

Chapter 3: 'Crossing Boundaries: Design into Business and Management' provides a detailed account of the key differences between the way design and business programmes are devised and delivered within their own respective institutions and departments. It is time to explore contemporary design and business curricula that best prepare young graduates to compete in industry, and the critical skills do they need to flourish in their respective careers. Are higher education institutions keeping pace with fast moving developments in industry, and what are the skills and attributes that are required for workplaces of tomorrow? With the rise of digital technologies, these have afforded new ways to access learning and education provision. The growing ubiquitousness of online courses allows the upskilling of management executives to gain exposure to design thinking and the way it can inform and underpin their own practice within the workplace. In essence, critical design thinking skills and associated creative tools and techniques are featuring in numerous online courses far beyond the close confines of traditional design schools. It concludes by Dr Beatriz Itzel Cruz Megchun with a case study drawn from a leading business school in the USA reflecting on the challenges of implementing design thinking within established curricula.

Chapter 4: 'Organisational Complexity and Change by Design' explores the management of complexity of large organisations and how, if not managed effectively, can hinder the desired pursuit for long-term competitiveness. Organisations are re-appraising their existing structures, procedures and governance systems to manage efficiently their day-to-day operations. Set against recent events at the start of 2020, the global pandemic and ongoing environmental crisis has delivered a stern wake-up call to both governments and industries to prepare for, an accept instability, with market disruptions as a fact of corporate life. The chapter then turns its attention to the theme of 'change' and to the reason the process of change management is effectively implemented. It examines three established and widely used change management frameworks, highlighting their own respective strengths and weaknesses. Finally, it offers a designerly alternative approach to fostering change, through the guise of Richard Buchannan's work outlining the '4 Orders of Design' and how the fourth order of design can offer and effect comprehensive cultural change to a wide variety of organisational contexts.

Chapter 5: 'Business Thinking Through Design' contributed by Dr Beatriz Itzel Cruz Megchun at the University of Portland, USA, discusses how economic systems shape, direct and support business activity and lays down the foundations for innovation. It begins by examining the four mainstream economic systems that portray the whole economy with just one minimal image that reinforces a neoliberal narrative of the state and the domesticity of the household. However, there is an array of alternative economic systems that challenge the status quo, such as the sharing economy, circular economy, doughnut economy and social economy. Following this, the discussion introduces three main types of business and their basic forms, which are based around offering services to customers, merchandising business within the high street retail sector and manufacturing. It concludes with an extensive discussion on the way in which design thinking approaches can be embedded within these diverse range of business structures to accommodate long-term commercial success.

Chapter 6: 'Design Thinking for Sustainable Futures' takes an exploratory approach to a wide variety of interrelated themes that encompass the communication of organisational values and how these can be used as an effective means of competitive differentiation. The intertwined themes of sustainability and corporate social responsibility are taking prominence in policy development activities, company strategy formulation and consumers purchasing decisions; as such, many organisations are now meaningfully engaging with these ongoing and timely critical agendas. It then moves onto the emergent theme of social enterprises and how they place greater emphasis on 'purpose' as opposed to pure profit. In essence, they provide business solutions to social problems, whereby all profit is re-invested for the pursuit of greater social impact. Chapter 6 concludes with a comprehensive case-study discussion provided by Dr Xinya You at the University of Dundee, by examining young start-up companies within the local Gaming industry, and the manner in which design thinking methodologies and tools can be used within business planning activities to ensure their future survival.

Chapter 7: 'Design Thinking for Branding' Dr Sotiris T. Lalaounis, based at the University of Exeter Business School offers an extensive and highly detailed account of the contributions of design thinking to brand management by presenting a conceptual framework which explores the connections of the design thinking process with brand equity and its management. From a consumers' perspective, a brand is important because it provides consumers the ability to identify the organisation producing the product or delivering the service, and in consequence, assign responsibility to this organisation. Over time, consumers who purchase a brand develop their own brand knowledge, that is, their own brand meaning stored in their memory leading to trust towards the brand. Ultimately, design thinking provides the organisation immense power to balance brand consistency and brand relevance, and continuously manage and enhance brand equity. Most importantly, this is undertaken with a human-centred approach, placing the target consumers at the heart of the process to deliver products, services, experiences that they embrace and develop a relationship with.

Chapter 8: 'Design Thinking: Practice and Applications' is mainly focused on examining the application of design thinking in practice—the doing. It offers three diverse contexts where design thinking tools and processes are utilised to foster meaningful change within the organisation. The chapter starts with two detailed case examples provided by Dr Bijan Aryana and Ir Ehsan Baha who outline how both international companies demonstrated a strong commitment towards fostering closer end user relationships through a designerly approach. Here, the authors examine the design process and tools used within these processes to achieve the strategic aims of the companies under review. Dr Radka Newton provides an interesting case example where she led a team of academics to examine current student attitudes regarding their undergraduate studies. However, tried and tested approaches traditionally used by universities to glean student feedback were not sufficient as to the detailed and personalised information that she needed. To overcome this challenge, she looked towards the realm of design thinking and in particular the many differing tools at her disposal that she could draw upon. The discussion takes the reader through salient aspects of the research process that shaped her insights and recommendations for adoption by the university department.

Chapter 9: 'Design Directions and Future Trajectories' begins with a brief reflection as to the current state of design, especially its role beyond the traditional design studio and the limited confines of aesthetic application and promotional activities. However, design is increasingly playing a greater role in society, and one such initiative is the DESIS Lab network, founded by Ezio Manzini in 2009, an international network of design schools and related organisations working on initiatives in the design for social innovation and sustainability fields. It then turns attention towards the theme of participatory design as an inclusive approach to yielding detailed user insights, and how the designer would create a democratic framework for the meaningful inclusion of end-users in which to collect data throughout the design development process. Regarding data and data driven innovation, the discussion explores the exponential growth of the 'Internet of Things' (IoT) coined by British entrepreneur Kevin Ashton in 1999, referring to the billions of physical devices that are connected to the internet, sharing and collecting data in real-time. With IoT offering the huge potential to disrupt established markets, companies now need to radically re-think their business models and operating procedures to exploit fully this new technology.

Chapter 10: 'Summary' provides a succinct overview of the themes raised and debated throughout the chapters. It concludes by offering a set of alternative futures as to the direction of design and its growing influence in many and often unexpected areas of activity. It presents five dimensions of design thinking that has been identified and critically debated through the chapters, offering an alternative understanding of design thinking as a powerful tool to re-imagine new and desirable organisational futures.

1.4 Using the Book: A Reader's Guide

Design thinking for new business contexts is the primary focus of the author's intentions to illustrate the way in which a 'designerly' thinking approach can be drawn upon to engage with critical and emergent organisational challenges. These challenges can be viewed from a diverse range of dynamic forces from within the organisation or external macro forces beyond organisational boundaries affecting business activities, or both. At the time of writing this book, a whole of industry sectors and organisations around the world are struggling to adjust their operations and planning activities set against a backdrop of Covid-19 pandemic restrictions. Profound change is being brought about through the continual and ever-changing restrictions that frequently change on a daily basis. As such, the authors aimed to identify and discuss these challenges within and throughout the overall book, highlighting how design can support the organisation to respond to these challenges. Each chapter is based around critically exploring distinct themes and sub-themes closely connected to the main area of particular focus. The themes explored are not exhaustive, arguably a small selection of the many emergent areas of business activity that we are currently witnessing.

When viewed in entirety, we aim to offer a kaleidoscopic portrait of design and design thinking in action, with the overall intention to build an open-ended awareness on what design thinking represents. It is anticipated that the reader can draw upon these multiple perspectives to inform and develop their own critical understanding of design thinking relative to their own field of enquiry or disciplinary background. Each chapter starts with a list of keywords, affording the reader a brief glimpse of themes explored within that particular part of the book. You may wish to read the book from beginning to end or consult specific chapters based on both time and need; we have aimed to accommodate both approaches when structuring the overall narrative and discursive flow of the chapters.

To conclude each chapter, we have included extra elements to aid your understanding of what was discussed. These learning aids include 'Review questions' that invite you to reflect upon specific topics discussed. In a way, these questions serve the purpose of deeper introspection as to your understanding of the discussion at hand. Then, 'Project questions' form the basis of potential projects that could be developed as part of your educational studies (be it undergraduate or postgraduate) based on time availability and suitability to your subject area. To complement these, 'Chapter tasks' are more practical in nature, whereupon you could turn a project idea into one with more tangible outcomes. Set against Covid-19 travel restrictions and available access to libraries, both authors had to heavily consult online resources to overcome these limitations; these can be found in the 'References' section.

Evolution of the Relationship Between Design and Business Activities

2

Learning Objectives

- To develop an understanding of the scope, nature and role of design in a variety of dynamic business contexts;
- To introduce the reader to the origins of design thinking as a business asset that can also assist within strategic planning activities;
- To introduce and develop an understanding of the role of design in achieving organisational goals and strategic vision;
- To examine the role of design as an interventional and propositional business tool through established design process models.

2.1 Introduction

A common question designers frequently get asked is "what is design thinking"? Whereby, a straightforward and digestible answer could be returned that would encapsulate its entire essence and meaning in one single sentence. However, design thinking is far too a broad holistic term that requires greater scrutiny in terms of its value and relevance within its wider application; be it either within a commercial context or the not-for-profit sector. Rather than asking, "what is design thinking" we propose to re-frame the question to "how does design thinking work"? As such, it allows a different interpretation and discussion to its inherent value whilst also removing its vagueness towards a more meaningful definition.

The leading design theorist, Richard Buchanan, raises an interesting point, arguing, "in general, design is continually evolving and the range of products or areas

Supplementary Information The online version contains supplementary material available at [https://doi.org/10.1007/978-3-030-94206-9_2].

Y. Huang, D. Hands, *Design Thinking for New Business Contexts*, https://doi.org/10.1007/978-3-030-94206-9_2

where design thinking may be applied continues to expand" (Buchanan, 1995, p. 25). With the changing remit of design in terms of its relevance, it is now being utilised and drawn upon in diverse environments far beyond the development of new products. Since the late 1990s, design and management literature have presented the concept of 'design thinking' as a path for innovation and growth. Likewise, design organisations and European innovation policies include design as a way to improve businesses, add value and gain competitive advantage. Design thinking has been presented as a method to develop business strategies (Drews, 2009; Fraser, 2009; Lockwood, 2009, 2010; Clark & Smith, 2010). It is defined as a user-centred, problem solving, collaborative approach influenced by the ways designers think and work, involving a combination of divergent and convergent thinking, rapid prototyping, testing and iteration, visualisation techniques and acceptance of constraints to discover needs, find new opportunities and creating effective solutions (Martin, 2007; Brown, 2009; Lockwood, 2009; Norman, 2013).

Consequently, design thinking has been recognised as a strategic resource mainly in large, global corporations developing design-led organisations such as Apple, Google, IBM, Barclays, Samsung and Pepsi (Brown, 2015; Ignatius, 2015; Kolko, 2015; Yoo & Kim, 2015); in small and medium-sized enterprises [SMEs] there are some barriers and the concept is not widely known yet (Cox, 2005; Acklin, 2013; Gulari & Fremantle, 2015). European design organisations have been creating awareness and measuring the benefits of design when is used on a strategic level (McNabola, 2014; Micheli, 2014; Melander, 2015; N&WRA and CIRCA Group, 2015). Accordingly, design programmes in the UK have been created to support the incorporation of the strategic role of design in businesses of all sizes, with an emphasis on SMEs (Ward et al., 2009; Design Council, 2012a, 2012b). However, the results of the programmes do not discuss the SMEs' context, the criteria for eligibility of SMEs, further development of the programmes or how to reach more SMEs.

Given the importance of SMEs for the European economy (European Commission, 2015), the aim of this chapter is to identify the aspects that must be considered for the incorporation of design thinking as a strategic resource in organisations, such as context specific characteristics, opportunities, challenges and obstacles. By exploring how design thinking principles are applied in similar size companies—small design firms—key aspects are identified about the design process as a way to inform and set strategic decisions in 'non-design' SMEs as well as opportunities and barriers for the design sector to better demonstrate the value of design.

In order to understand design thinking as an intellectual field of enquiry, perhaps it would be beneficial to pause for a moment and identify the origins of the term and its subsequent evolutionary development. It could be argued (and many have convincingly done so) that the origins of design thinking can be traced back to the American Economist and Political Scientist Herbert Simon and his seminal book *The Science of the Artificial* (1996) where he argues "everyone designs who devises courses of action aimed at changing existing situations into preferred ones" (Simon, 1996, p. 55). This sentiment provided a seismic shift in the understanding of design as a professional activity, in particular the role of design within the architectural design and engineering professions. With careful reading, the second and third editions of his book (Simon, 1996) offers a comprehensive shift away from the use of design within a limit range of professions, through to designerly 'practice' being embedded within a diverse range of activities. The following chapters discuss this development of his thinking and understanding of the role of design in greater detail.

It is worthwhile to note here another contemporary of Simon, namely that of Professor Bruce Archer, who led the Department of Design Research [DDR] at the Royal College of Art until 1978. Archer was an instrumental figure in the development of critical enquiries into design and its relationship to science. However, Archer's systematic approach to design methods was not without its critics; John Christopher Jones challenged the methods and rigidity of conventional design methods offered by Archer. In 1970, he published the seminal book *Design Methods* that offered an alternative to establish design theory put forward by his contemporaries. Over subsequent editions of the book, Jones provides numerous design methodologies to assist the designer with emphasis on the user and the thoughts that precede the designed outcome, in essence, moving focus away from the product to the processes and methods that led to the product.

It is noteworthy to say, the emergence of academic journals focusing upon design research and methodologies, in particular 'Design Studies' (1979); 'Design Issues' (1984) and the 'Journal of Design Management' (1990) by the North American based Design Management Institute happened at this point. In 1972, Rittel and Webber presented their seminal academic paper Dilemmas in a General Theory of Planning, at the Institute of Urban and Regional Development, University of California, who identified 10 'Wicked' problems in urban planning and design. These wicked problems required new approaches and forms of understanding that traditional science and engineering based methodologies were unable to address. It may be worthwhile Rittel and Webber did not first use pointing out here that the term 'wicked' problem, they borrowed the term from the Austrian-British philosopher Professor Karl Popper, and as such, popularised its usage within the realm of design theory and practice.

The wicked problems raised by the authors included:

1. There is no definitive formulation of a wicked problem.
2. Wicked problems have no stopping rule.
3. There is no immediate and no ultimate test of a solution to a wicked problem.
4. Every wicked problem is essentially unique.

For a fuller and exhaustive discussion of these wicked problems, refer to their academic paper that was published a year later (Rittel & Webber, 1973). Buchanan (1992, p. 5) raises an interesting point regarding the concept of design thinking in his seminal paper, suggesting that:

> Despite efforts to discover the foundations of design thinking in the fine arts, the natural sciences, or most recently, the social sciences, design eludes reduction and remains a surprisingly flexible activity. No single definition of design, or branches of professionalized practice such as industrial or graphic design, adequately covers the diversity of ideas and methods gathered together under the label.

Having acknowledged the breadth of its application and scope (which negates reduction), Buchanan raises the primary challenge of its adoption and value given that it can be used "to remarkably different problems and subject matters".

Followed by publications in the 1980s by design researchers (Rowe, 1987; Schön, 1983), design thinking attracted wider acclaim by 2009, probably due to the affirmations by Tim Brown (2008) on how thinking as a designer transforms organisations and leads to innovation. However, it has been argued that there are different definitions of 'design thinking' according to the context where the term is used. Johansson-Sköldberg et al. (2013) make a distinction between the management and the design realms. In a similar way, Kimbell (2011) presents the origin of the term in design research and its adoption by the management discourse in business schools. To gain a comprehensive understanding, this chapter critically discusses the concept of design thinking from both perspectives.

2.2 Design Thinking and Design[ing]

Although Simon never used the term design thinking, his definition of design as devise "courses of action aimed at changing existing situations into preferred ones" (Simon, 1996, p. 111) by the creation of artefacts, is one of the first contributions towards a cognitive approach of design. Another key point is the diverge-and-test notion or what he calls the 'generator test cycle' where a series of alternatives are generated and tested, informing the impact of each cycle. Rowe (1987) provides a description about the process of designing in architecture introducing the activity of design as a combination of rational enquiry and 'impulses' where the nature of the problem-solving process shapes the solution. Rowe introduces a simplified version of the Archer's model of design. In a similar way, Schön (1983) presents design as a process of reflection-in-action, enabling a constant improvement of the professional practice and solutions. Such process is described as the essence of the design process in which reflection-in-action is applied, tested and developed with the purpose of finding possible solutions to problematic situations. In other words, both, the problem and solutions might not be clear from the beginning, but they are defined and redefined during the process. Lawson (1997) draws attention on the design process as a combination of convergent and divergent thinking. Convergent thinking refers to a rational and logical approach while divergent thinking is intuitive, imaginative and focused on seeking alternatives. In these terms, designers need to develop the perfect balance between convergent and divergent skills (Fig. 2.1).

Cross (2006, 2011) adopts the term "designerly ways of knowing" and on a case-based approach aims to develop an understanding of the nature of design ability and what designers do when they design. Cross refers to a model based on three steps: (1) clarifying the task, (2) searching for concepts and (3) fixing the concepts. Lastly, from the cognitive sciences, Norman (2013) defines design thinking as the process in which an original problem statement is taken as a suggestion to later think about the issues underlying the problem statement might really be. It is the search for the real problem, and once found, the development of a wide range of potential

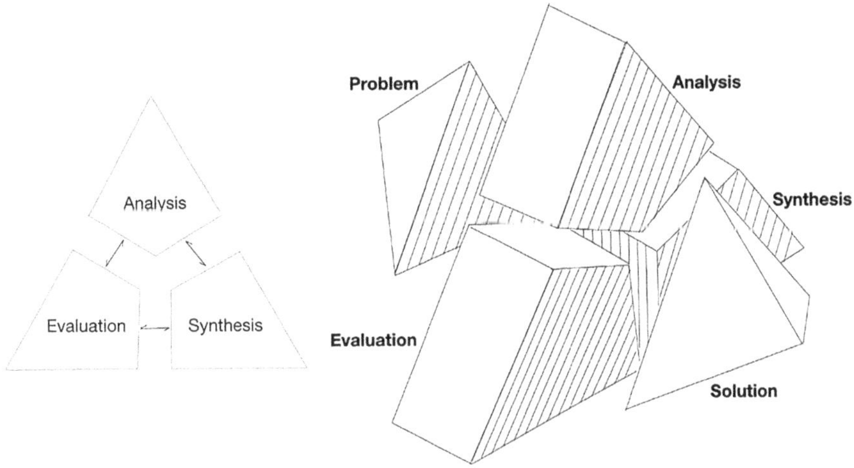

Fig. 2.1 Lawson's design process (adapted by authors)

solutions. Norman (ibid) argues that Human Centred Design (HCD) and the Double-Diamond Model of Design—developed by the UK Design Council—are two of the powerful tools of design thinking.

The focus of HCD is on solving the right problem and doing it in a way it meets human needs. These two aspects give rise to the two phases of the design process. The first phase is to uncover the right problem; the second is to find the right solution. The HCD process takes place within the double-diamond process containing four activities: (1) observation, (2) idea generation, (3) prototyping and (4) testing. Norman (ibid) explains that it is not only practiced by designers, but by all great innovators. The reason it is attributed to design firms is that designers pride themselves on their ability to innovate and be creative. Norman's work focuses on design and the way humans interact with it, however, it is important to notice that he also reflects about the role of design in the world of business by discussing how the HCD process describes the ideal but in the reality, businesses are forced to act in a different way, often because of time and budget constraints.

2.3 Design Thinking and Business Planning Activities

Martin (2007) reflects about the tension between business and design to state that is precisely the integration of both types of thinking, analytical and intuitive, the definition of design thinking. Such balance is necessary for an optimal business performance and for gaining competitive advantage (Fig. 2.2). Based on an interview with Martin, Dunne (Dunne & Martin, 2006) synthetises three aspects of design thinking:

1. Cognitive: Design thinking is an on-going cycle of generating ideas (abduction), predicting consequences (deduction), testing, and generalising (induction);

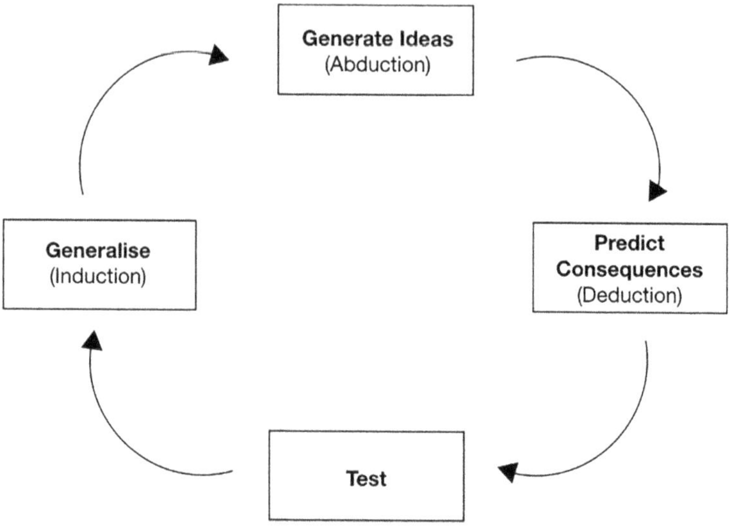

Fig. 2.2 The cycle of design thinking (adapted by authors)

2. Attitudinal: Instead of considering constraints as barriers for the implementation of ideas, embrace them as triggers to find creative solutions;
3. Interpersonal: Encourage collaborative kills to learn to understand other people and their reasoning.

Based on IDEO's practices, Brown (2008, 2009) articulates the framework of design thinking using an extensive amount of examples and case studies as a discipline that applies the designer's skills and methods to match people's needs considering what is feasible, desirable and viable in order to get customer value and market opportunity. The key aspects include:

1. A combination of divergent and convergent thinking as a way of problem solving where the convergent phase drives towards solutions and the divergent thinking multiplies options to create choices;
2. 'Building to think' or the 'power of prototyping' to generate better results by quickly seeing limitations and possible directions;
3. Empathy and a human-centred approach, based on finding the needs of users using field observations, prototyping and visual storytelling;
4. Acceptance of constraints, which should be seen as an opportunity for innovation;
5. Collaborative work, drawing attention in the importance of multidisciplinary and interdisciplinary teams.

Brown raises two interesting points: the first one is to make the designers' skills accessible to professionals from a non-design background in order to accomplish innovative results. "Design thinking can be practiced by everybody" (Brown, 2009,

p. 149). The second, that design thinking should move into the organisations, the service sector and the public sphere since it has the potential and tools to embrace global issues. Also with an IDEO background, the Hasso Platter Institute of Design at Stanford (headed by IDEO's founder, David Kelley), commonly known as the 'd.school', developed their 5-stage design-thinking model. This model takes first on the definition of the problem and then the implementation of the solution considering the needs of the user at the core of concept development. The process is focused on finding needs, understanding, thinking, and doing by a bias towards action. It is cyclical and iterative since continuous testing is key to improve the initial ideas (Hasso Plattner Institute of Design at Stanford, 2010) (Fig. 2.3).

Similarly to Brown, Lockwood (2009) argues that the term design thinking is referred as the application of a designer's sensibility and methods to problem solving, no matter what the problem is, turning out to be a methodology for innovation and enablement. He defines design thinking as a human-centred innovation process that emphasises observation, collaboration, fast learning, visualisation of ideas, rapid concept prototyping and current business analysis, influencing innovation and business strategies. In essence, it is a tool to imagine future states and to bring products, services and experiences to the market. The key attributes are:

1. Deep understanding of the user by using ethnographic methods;
2. Collaboration, with users and involving multidisciplinary teams;
3. Accelerate learning through visualisation, hands-on experimenting and prototyping;
4. Visualise, by becoming tangible the intangible;
5. Business analysis integrated during the process.

It is key the combination of creative ideas with more traditional management aspects in order to have a comprehensive point of view. One of the most useful contributions by Lockwood is the differentiation between design thinking and design management. He argues that design thinking is an innovation process related to

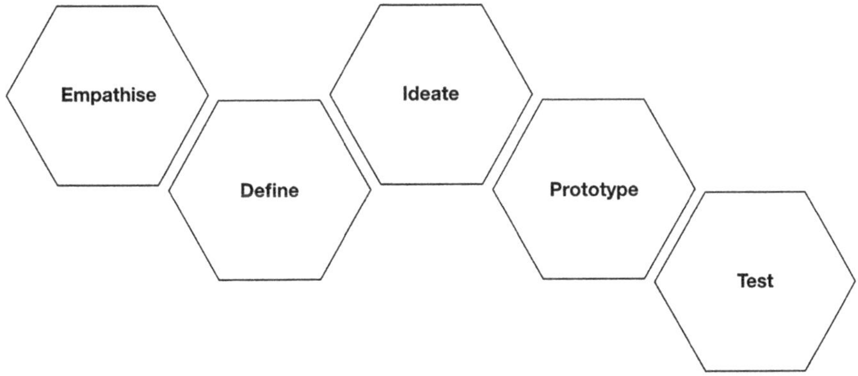

Fig. 2.3 IDEO design thinking process (adapted by authors)

discovering needs, opportunities and creating new solutions, while design management lies in the integration and improvement of design into business. A key aspect stated by Lockwood is the incorporation of design thinking as a strategy method because design thinking helps to reframe problems and to connect people and business.

Introducing the Design Council Double Diamond Process Model

"The double diamond diagram was developed through in-house research at the Design Council in 2018 as a simple graphical way of describing the design process" (Design Council, 2019). As discussed earlier, despite how the concept of design thinking is used according to the context, it could be argued that all the models regarding the process of design agree on four similar stages, well represented on the model developed by the Design Council in 2005. The model was further tested against the results of a study conducted in 11 leading global companies with the purpose of understanding their design processes, the key elements involved and how these processes take a product or service from an idea through implementation (Design Council, 2018) (Fig. 2.4).

This model identifies four stages: Discover. The first stage is about exploring issues, gathering insights and identifying user needs by, for example, asking questions, posing a hypothesis or analysing market data. It is phase of divergent thought where keeping a wide perspective is key to develop a broad range of ideas. Define. The second quarter represents the phase in which all the possibilities found in phase one are refined to formulate the problem to be addressed. In a strategic level, it refers to the interpretation and alignment of the needs with the business objectives. Develop. This stage indicates the period where solutions are developed, iterated and tested. Feedback from each round of development informs improvements as well as additional considerations arise. Deliver. The last quarter represents the time when the resulting outcome is finalised, produced and launched. It also includes the final testing and evaluation of the impact by collecting data from diverse sources to inform future projects. ◀

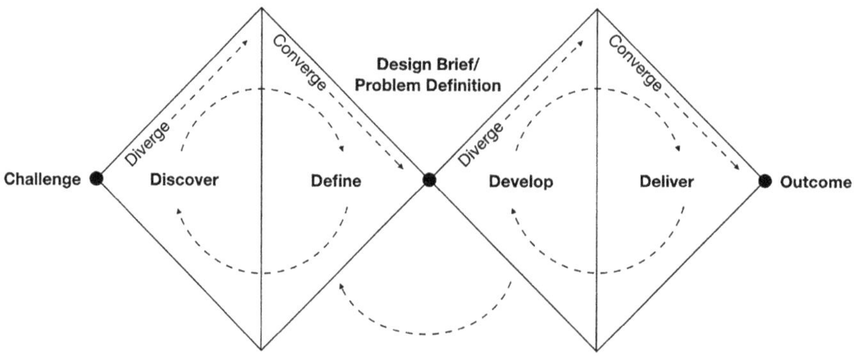

Fig. 2.4 Double-diamond model (adapted by authors)

2.4 Design Thinking and Business Strategy

One aspect surrounding the controversy of design thinking as a business strategy is given by Gianfranco Zaccai, President and Chief Design Officer of Continuum. He explains that this 'phenomenon' occurred probably because executives started to look for other ways to look at their businesses since they realised the pragmatic, linear, analytical and quantitative approach was not having the expected results (Lockwood, 2010). Zaccai articulates design as "a way of thinking that creates insights that inform what and how you execute, as well as how you communicate, market, support, and service once the product is introduced" (Lockwood, 2010, p. 18). Thereby, design informs the whole business strategy. However, the decision by an organisation to become more design centric depends on the personality of the company leadership. Zaccai suggests that a gradual implementation of design-driven approaches could be the first move. If it is first applied in one part of the business, it could learn from the mistakes and lately transfer it into the entire organisation (Lockwood, 2010).

Fraser promotes a formal framework (2009) introducing design as a path to understand stakeholder needs, a tool for visualising new solutions and a process for translating novel ideas into effective strategies. Fraser proposes a methodology called "The Three Gears of Business Design":

- Gear One: It refers to get a deep user understanding where new opportunities are revealed. This helps reframe the business challenge through the eyes of the end user and set a human context for innovation and value;
- Gear Two: This the phase of development where there is a broad exploration of possibilities to meet the needs found in gear one; New solutions are generated and visualised through prototyping.
- Gear Three: This phase aligns the new idea with the proposed future by designing the business itself (Fig. 2.5).

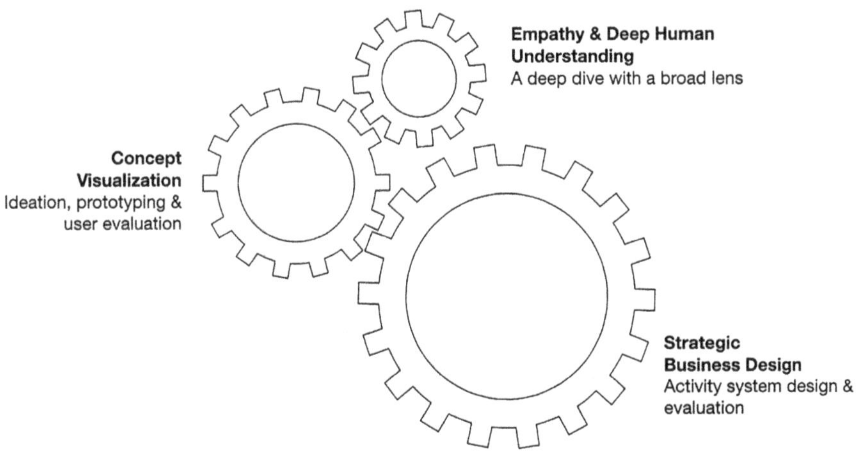

Fig. 2.5 3 Gears of business design framework (adapted by authors)

It is about exploring what it takes to take the idea to the market, identifying the strategies that will drive success and prioritising the activities the organisation must do. The final step is the integration of the new concept into the current operation as well as the identification of the barriers and how they will be surmounted. In addition to this methodological framework, Fraser proposes a mindset for the individuals in the organisation consisting of: (1) mindfulness, (2) open-minded collaboration, (3) abductive thinking, (4) permission to risk early failure, (5) imperfection and iteration early in the process, (6) creative resolution of trade-offs and constraints. The combination of both is what drives breakthrough strategies for enterprise success.

In a similar perspective drawn from a series of interviews, Drews (2009) articulates the nature of design thinking as a mindset pointing out three key points: (1) consumer-centricity, (2) orientation towards the future and (3) challenging the form. One of the advantages of design thinking discussed by Drews, is that visualising and early prototyping engage stakeholders since having something to look at facilitates discussion and allows the idea to evolve. It also helps to decrease the high-risk factor of radical ideas. Likewise, Fraser, Drews (2009) presents the value of design thinking in a way businesses can understand their customers and their future choices, ensuring the company has the capacity to manage the innovation of their products, services and ways to do businesses.

Business people and educators might find a common point of interest with design thinking when they want to create something new and discover new opportunities. "Design thinkers are good not only at finding the answers but also at asking the right questions" (Drews, 2009, p. 41). Clark and Smith (2010) offer the term 'innovation intelligence' to describe design thinking to an executive audience. They argue that the type of intelligence, which supports innovation and provides an organisation with multiple ways to solve problems, drives design thinking. At the end, it allows to discover the best possibility that best delivers competitive advantage. Lockwood (2009) approaches design thinking in a similar way. Design thinking is defined as an innovation process. They key value of design in business lies on the discovery of the right problems and solving the problems for both, customers and businesses. It is about the process, the final solution and the design outcome. More recent perspectives illustrate design thinking as a well-established practice in global corporations, generating the terms 'design-driven' organisations and 'design-led' cultures.

The September 2015 issue of the Harvard Business Review reflects about the evolution of design thinking. In the article Design for Action, Brown and Martin (2015) explain how design thinking can help strategic and systemic innovators to build new futures. The best way to build strategy is by having an iterative interaction with the decision maker. By building on empathy with the decision maker and discussing the ideas in progress, the final step of introducing a new strategy becomes easier. Kolko (2015) argues that large organisations and professional are working on the development of design-centric cultures. There are five key aspects:

1. Focus on the user's experiences, especially the emotional ones;
2. Create models to examine complex problems;

3. Use prototypes to explore potential solutions;
4. Tolerate failure;
5. Exhibit thoughtful restraints.

The same edition makes reference to Samsung and Pepsi as organisations that turned design thinking into corporate strategy. The case for Samsung shows the progress of several years where a corporate design centre was established to work on future design: visualise the distant future and develop new business concepts (Yoo & Kim, 2015). The case for Pepsi highlights the relationship between design and innovation and the facts for design to thrive: (1) having a leader with a holistic approach of design; (2) sponsorship from the top; (3) external endorsements such as business leaders, design/business magazines and awards; and (4) quick wins (Ignatius, 2015). Regarding the challenges still to be faced by organisations, Drews (2009) argues that one of the reason of design thinking has not reached its full potential is the well-known gap between the quantitatively business people and the qualitative creative ones.

The gap is attributed to a system education focused on 'right' and 'wrong' answers, which confronts the science students against the 'arty' ones. The result is professionals who love to measure ideas as soon as possible, opposed to others who avoid limits and challenge the problem they were asked to do in the first place. The key will be to overcome the hierarchies between both areas in order to get the designer's ideas incorporated into successful business propositions and the business people open to learn their minds to perceive unseen opportunities. Another important argument is that design thinking might not be the answer to every business challenge, but is an excellent approach for the some of the business issues related to setting markets, sustainability and re-shaping of the economic system. In times when reinvention seems a 'must have', design thinking is a skill for doing it.

2.5 Design Thinking in SMES

Several case studies show evidence that design thinking was deployed as a strategic force, transforming the vision of large and global organisations. There is no doubt about the success of innovative companies such as Google, IBM, Samsung and Pepsi. Even Brown (2015) reflects whereas design thinking is a competitive advantage when everyone is doing it. While such statement might be valid for large corporations, for owner-managers of small businesses the incorporation of design thinking entails a different context. "The category of micro, small and medium-sized enterprises (SMEs) is made up of enterprises which employ fewer than 250 persons and which have an annual turnover not exceeding EUR 50 million, and/or an annual balance sheet total not exceeding EUR 43 million" (Article 2 of the annex to Recommendation 2003/361/EC European Commission, 2015). SMEs represent over 99% of all businesses in the UK and in Europe. Thus, they are an important part of European economy as a source of employment, economic growth, entrepreneurial skills, and recognised as a key role in innovation (European Commission,

2015). Given their importance to the European economy, SMEs have become a focus of European innovation policies that recognise and encourage the value of design as a driver for growth and competitiveness. Commission of the European Communities (2009) emphasises that companies that invest in design tend to me more innovative, more profitable and grow faster. However, some of the barriers relate to both, design companies and non-design SMEs.

Barriers for SMEs

1. SMEs often have little experience of design, do not know how to find professional help or integrate design into their innovation processes.
2. SMEs located in small cities might not have access to quality design advice since large design consultancies are concentrated in big cities.
3. SMEs often lack the resources, expertise and methods to evaluate the risk and the rate of return on design investment.

Barriers for Design Firms

1. The average small size of design companies weakens their influencing power in governments and the reach of new markets into a wider circle.
2. Many designers do not have sufficient business knowledge and skills necessary to be better integrated into the business and innovation community such as strategic design, design management and design-driven innovation.
3. Designers have not organised themselves as a profession resulting in a low levels of networking, coordination and influence.

The Northern and Western Regional Assembly and CIRCA Group (2015) highlight the importance of design-driven innovation for SME competitiveness and propose a change of attitude towards a design-driven approach. Alongside the report offering the benefits of design thinking and that introducing design thinking can influence positively on economic growth, productivity, competitiveness and employment in Irish SMEs, the research shows similar barriers compared with the report by the EU Commission: (1) SMEs do not understand the value of design and take new ideas on board slowly. (2) Few graduates entrepreneurs undertake basic courses on design processes. (3) The design industry is fragmented and not doing a good job at promoting itself. Moreover, Acklin (2013) concludes that the use of design as a strategic resource entails a learning process by SMEs on how to manage such new knowledge and minor attention has been given on the way the companies with little or no design experience build capabilities to execute design management.

Similarly, Gulari and Fremantle (2015) point out that SMEs' design needs and design capabilities are different from large enterprises. For example, SMEs avoid taking risks, probably due to lack of capital, insufficient human resources and limited time. In this way, a design thinking approach through experimentation, iteration and cheap prototyping is relevant and can help them build innovation capabilities. In contrast, SMEs often have a good understanding of their customers since they use their close relationships with their clients and observations to generate new ideas.

However, the knowledge used for innovation and growth is tacit and shared by a reduced number of people; therefore, the innovation methods should support SMEs to externalise such knowledge. Lastly, whereas design has a positive impact in an organisation when it is embedded in its culture, a design-led culture drives a cultural change that requires organisations to go out of their comfort zone, adopt new ways of thinking, commitment to action over the long term, and inspirational leadership.

The Danish Design Centre developed in 2001 the Design Ladder, a tool to measure the level of design activity in Danish companies. It is centred upon the premise that the idea of a positive link between settings design in a strategic position in the company and obtaining higher earnings (Melander, 2015) (Fig. 2.6).

The highest stage represents design used as a strategic medium to accomplish business objectives, which could be understood when 'design thinking' is applied thoroughly. It became a reference to present the progression of the incorporation and use of design in an organisation (McNabola, 2014).

Case Study: Design Support Programmes for SMES in the UK

Organisations in the UK have been facilitating a link between designers and SMEs and launching design support programmes. The Design Council, the UK's national strategic organisation for design championship, has extensively researched about the role of design in UK businesses and is the main advocate about the value of design (Design Council, 2012a, 2012b). Ward et al. (2009) review the results of 'Designing Demand', a programme undertaken by the Design Council, between 2006 and 2010. The reasoning behind the programme is that the skills that designers have used to create successful products, communications and services can also be applied to the design of businesses themselves.

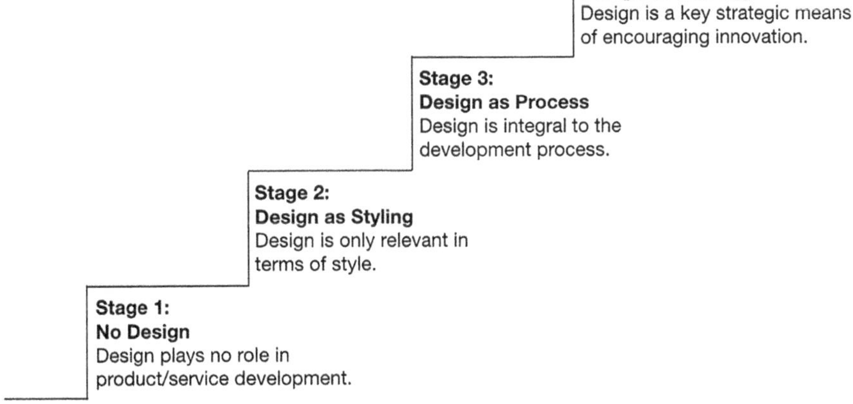

Fig. 2.6 Danish design ladder (adapted by authors)

In this way, the programme connected experienced designers with SMEs to guide them through the process of investing in design and innovation strategically and using it effectively. Additionally, the programme brought design thinking into the company and their staff through games, workshops and team tasks.

One of the conclusions is that 'vision and strategy' is a key area where design adds value. "If design thinking can help companies put the strategy into their vision, it can also help them put the vision, or more explicitly, the visual, into their strategy" (Ward et al., 2009, p. 80). The programme continued under the name Design Leadership Programme (Design Council, 2012b) and the report shows:

1. Businesses grew. For every £1 invested in design, businesses can expect over £20 in increased revenues, over £4 increase in net operating profit and a return of over £5 in increased exports.
2. Design helped businesses to identify their biggest strategic challenges and create new opportunities to overcome them by using design effectively.
3. Design changed the way businesses work, resulting in an improvement of organisational cultural and performance.
4. Businesses became clearer about the integral role of design and that it should not be sidelined for other strategic requirements.
5. Businesses showed that once they have been exposed to design tools and good design management practice, they are equipped to do it again themselves.

The Design Council continues giving support to businesses through design consultancy by way of 'Business Growth Service' as well as by providing online resources such as case studies, guides and reports. UK Research and Innovation (2021) developed an innovation strategy placing design at its core as a methodology that can be applied for creating better products, services, processes and business models. The document points out the lack of awareness by businesses in exploiting the value of design as a strategic scoping and planning tool. The key argument is that by using the design process as a framework, the creative process allows businesses to progress 32 Design Thinking in SMEs from a contextual understanding towards new propositions and development opportunities. This innovation strategy includes business of all sizes and no specifics considerations are presented for SMEs.

Design for Europe (2021) is a three-year initiative to support design driven innovation across Europe. In general, it brings together information about user-centred design thinking and the application of design tools and methods in services, systems and organisations that enable business-model and other forms of innovation. Whereas there is not a section addressed to SMEs, the platform collects a set of resources available to businesses such as case studies, tools, design toolkits, guides, articles, reports, links, and events. However, there is no evidence if they are used, thereby measured or how to get feedback. Past initiatives worth of being highlighted are 'Design Service Programme' in Northern Ireland run by Invest Northern Ireland between 2008 and 2015 and 'Service Design Programme' in Wales run by the National Centre for Product Design and Development Research (PDR) between 2010–2013. Both worked on delivering support for strategic design. The programme in Northern Ireland focused on providing four service elements: awareness, advice, capability and support, while the Welsh programme worked at a strategic level with 90 companies to support the development of service design in industries in the manufacturing sector and expertise in the design companies (N&WRA and CIRCA Group, 2015). Overall, it is suggested that the support to SMEs is given through a specialised consultancy and/or online resources. Nevertheless, the programmes reports do not evidence the discussions about SMEs' context, the process on how SMEs incorporated design knowledge or how they were reached. As Cox (2005) expressed, "experience shows that smaller companies do not respond well to generalised awareness programmes…. SMEs need to be reached on a local basis, with active support and a practical demonstration of the benefits on offer". ◀

▶ **Chapter Summary** This chapter has established the status of design thinking as a vital tool (or a philosophical approach) for organisations to draw upon in these uncertain times. It is by no means a definitive account of the subject area as its growing complexity is testament to its vibrant nature as a leading change agent, be it within or beyond the organisation, or as a subtle means to change people's perceptions and behaviours.

The authors introduced a series of design thinking frameworks and models that have been widely adopted and applied when developing business development strategies. If unfamiliar with these commonly used frameworks, there is a dearth of literatures freely available that critiques the effectiveness and value of these process models. The Design Council Double Diamond model is premised on two basic aspects: first, the four differing stages of idea development, beginning with discovering the opportunity, then taking the ideas to fruition in phase four. The second element is based around modes of creative thinking, that is, divergent and convergent approaches to problem solving and solution development. This generic model is comparable to Fraser's 'The Three Gears of Business Design' but features a stronger emphasis on the end-users as opposed to business strategy development which lies central to Fraser's model. Even though they are similar, there is a distinct nuanced difference between the two process models, which is not that explicit to readers unfamiliar with these two systems. Finally, when exploring the Danish Design Ladder in terms of application, this is quite different to the other two process models. Here, the Design Ladder is intended for use by the organisation to establish 'how and where' they currently use design (be it for superficial styling activities or more pronounced at a strategic level of application). Having established where the company is positioned on the Ladder, they can then implement strategies for further design 'augmentation' within the organisation. All the process models and design positioning frameworks discussed within this chapter are highly malleable in nature, thus being able to be applied in contexts that are broad and far reaching in nature. For instance, if a design process model was tailored to a specific industry or organisational set-up, then its wider applicability would be greatly reduced; hence the generic nature of the models examined within this section.

Set against global challenges and macro-economic uncertainty, it is worthwhile to critically debate and explore the role and value of design thinking as a meaningful agent of change. Its gradual journey towards maturity is relentless and carefully orchestrated with industry practice informing current academic theory—and vice versa. It does indeed give rise to an interrelated set of questions 'who is leading this change? Who are the beneficiaries of change' and 'what role can design thinking play in leading this change?

Review Questions

1. The role of Design Thinking has many different definitions as to its value and application within contemporary industry practice; how would you define the unique value of Design 'Thinking'?
2. What would you consider the key attributes of Design Thinking that makes it distinct from other established problem solving techniques?
3. The Design Council Double Diamond model is widely acclaimed as a leading design thinking process model—what would you consider its limitations in terms of wider application?
4. Fraser proposes a methodology called The Three Gears of Business Design—would you suggest that another gear be added and if so, what would the focus of the fourth gear be?
5. What are the common barriers to design adoption by the organisation, in particular to SMEs?

Project Questions

1. Design can make a meaningful contribution to the company in a wide variety of ways; could you identify and list three key areas where design can add real value?
2. Design thinking as a problem solving approach is subject to fierce debate within the design profession; as such, create a taxonomy of leading design thinking process models that outlines their similarities and differences. Following this, could there ever be one successful generic design thinking model?
3. If you could expand upon or refine the Design Council Double Diamond model, what, where and how would you modify it to be of value to organisations beyond the commercial sector?
4. On the Danish Design Ladder, identify four leading companies that you consider to be located at each of the four stages of design maturity?
5. The Cox Report (2005) was regarded as a comprehensive report into the value of design; now in the 2020s, what aspects of it would you update or include to reflect current industry developments?

Chapter Tasks

1. Public Sector organisations and departments are now embracing design thinking, how can it be used to improve end-users 'experiences' in the delivery of public services?
2. Can you identify a series of Design Support Programmes in your country and outline their strengths and weakness in terms of value and appropriateness to the organisations that they are targeting?
3. The Danish Design Ladder has 4 primary elements—if you had to add another level at the top (5) what would it focus upon?
4. Outline the primary aims and objectives of an internal design audit within a product-based SME identifying their current strengths and weaknesses regarding design.
5. How can designers or design thinking activities contribute to the corporate strategy development process? Where and how does design meaningfully contribute to long-term commercial 'vision?'

References

Acklin, C. (2013). *Design Management Absorption in SMEs with Little or No Prior Design Experience*. PhD thesis, Lancaster University, UK.

Brown, T. (2008). Design Thinking. *Harvard Business Review, 86*(6), 84–92.

Brown, T. (2009). *Change by Design: How Design Thinking Transforms Organizations and Inspires Innovation*. HarperCollins.

Brown, T. (2015). When Everyone Is Doing Design Thinking, Is It Still a Competitive Advantage? [Online]. *Harvard Business Review*. https://store.hbr.org/product/when-everyone-is-doing-design-thinking-is-it-still-acompetitive-advantage/h02axx?sku=H02AXX-PDF-ENG

Brown, T., & Martin, R. (2015). Design for Action. [Online]. *Harvard Business Review*. https://hbr.org/2015/09/design-for-action

Buchanan, R. (1992). Wicked Problems in Design Thinking. *Design Issues, 8*(2), 5–21.

Buchanan, R. (1995). Wicked Problems in Design Thinking. In R. Buchanan & V. Margolin (Eds.), *The Idea of Design*. MIT Press.

Clark, K., & Smith, R. (2010). Unleashing the Power of Design Thinking. *Design Management Review, 19*(3), 8–15.

Commission of the European Communities. (2009). Design as a Driver of User-Centred Innovation. Brussels. [Online]. https://ec.europa.eu/docsroom/documents/2583/attachments/1/translations/en/renditions/native

Cox, G. (2005). *Cox Review of Creativity in Business: Building on the UK's Strengths*. HM Treasury.

Cross, N. (2006). *Designerly Ways of Knowing*. Springer.

Cross, N. (2011). *Design Thinking: Understanding How Designers Think and Work*. Berg Publishers.

Design Council. (2012a). *Designing Demand Executive Summary*. [Online]. London: Design Council. http://www.designcouncil.org.uk/sites/default/files/asset/document/Designing%20Demand_Executive_Sumary_Final.pdf

Design Council. (2012b). Design Delivers for Business. A Summary of Evidence from the Design Council's Design Leadership Programme. [Online]. Design Council. https://www.designcouncil.org.uk/sites/default/files/asset/document/DesignDelivers%20for%20Businesspercentage20briefing.pdf

Design Council. (2018). The Design Economy 2018: The State of Design in the UK. [Online]. https://www.designcouncil.org.uk/sites/default/files/asset/document/Design_Economy_2018_exec_summary.pdf

Design Council. (2021). Design for Europe. [Online]. https://www.designcouncil.org.uk/what-we-do/design-training-and-education/design-europe

Design Council Double Diamond Design Process. (2019). [Online]. https://www.designcouncil.org.uk/news-opinion/double-diamond-universallyaccepted-depiction-design-process

Drews, C. (2009). Unleashing the Full Potential of Design Thinking as a Business Method. *Design Management Review, 20*(3), 38–44.

Dunne, D., & Martin, R. (2006). Design Thinking and How It Will Change Management Education: An Interview and Discussion. *Academy of Management Learning & Education, 5*(4), 512–523.

European Commission. (2015). User Guide to the SME Definition. [Online]. Publications Office of the European Union. http://ec.europa.eu/DocsRoom/documents/15582/attachments/1/translations/en/renditions/native

Fraser, H. (2009). Designing Business: New Models for Success. *Design Management Review, 20*(2), 56–65.

Gulari, M. N., & Fremantle, C. (2015). Are Design-led Innovation Approaches Applicable to SMEs? [Online]. https://rgurepository.worktribe.com/output/248810/are-design-led-innovation-approachesapplicable-to-smes

Hasso Plattner Institute of Design at Stanford. (2010). An Introduction to Design Thinking PROCESS GUIDE. [Online]. https://dschool.stanford.edu/groups/designresources/wiki/36873/Design_Process_MiniGuide.html

Ignatius, A. (2015). How Indra Nooyi Turned Design Thinking Into Strategy. *Harvard Business Review, 93*(9), 80–85.

Johansson-Sköldberg, U., Woodilla, J., & Çetinkaya, M. (2013). Design Thinking: Past, Present and Possible Futures. *Creativity and Innovation Management, 22*(2), 121–146.

Jones, J. C. (1970). *Design Methods: Seeds of Human Futures*. John Wiley.

Kimbell, L. (2011). Rethinking Design Thinking: Part I. *Design and Culture, 3*(3), 285–306.

Kolko, J. (2015). Design Thinking Comes of Age. *Harvard Business Review, 93*(9), 6671.

Lawson, B. (1997). *How Designers Think*. Architectural Press.

Lockwood, T. (2009). *Design Thinking: Integrating Innovation, Customer Experience and Brand Value* (3rd ed.). Allworth Press.

Lockwood, T. (2010). Design Thinking in Business: An Interview with Gianfranco Zaccai. *Design Management Review, 21*(3), 16–24.

Martin, R. (2007). Design and Business: Why Can't We Be Friends? *Journal of Business Strategy, 28*(4), 6–12.

McNabola, A. (2014). Introducing Design for Europe. [Online]. Design Council. http://www.designcouncil.org.uk

Melander, C. (2015). The Design Ladder: Four Steps of Design Use—DDC. [Online]. DDC. http://ddc.dk/en/2015/05/the-design-ladderfour-steps-of-design-use

Micheli, P. (2014). Leading Business by Design. Why and How Business Leaders Invest in Design. [Online]. Design Council and Warwick Business School. http://www.designcouncil.org.uk

Norman, D. (2013). *The Design of Everyday Things* (2nd ed.). Basic Books.

Northern & Western Regional Assembly and CIRCA Group Europe. (2015). Design-Driven Innovation: Why It Matters for SME Competitiveness. [Online]. https://dbei.gov.ie/en/News-And-Events/Speeches/Launch-of-Design-DrivenInnovation-Why-it-Matters-for-SME-Competitiveness.html

Rittel, H., & Webber, M. (1973). Dilemmas in a General Theory of Planning. *Policy Sciences, 4*(2), 155–169.

Rowe, P. (1987). *Design Thinking*. MIT Press.

Schön, D. A. (1983). *The Reflective Practitioner*. Basic Books.

Simon, H. (1996). *The Sciences of the Artificial* (3rd ed.). MIT Press.

UK Research and Innovation. (2021). About Innovate UK. [Online]. https://www.ukri.org/about-us/innovate-uk/

Ward, A., Runcie, E., & Morris, L. (2009). Embedding Innovation: Design Thinking for Small Enterprises. *Journal of Business Strategy, 30*(2/3), 78–84.

Yoo, Y., & Kim, K. (2015). How Samsung Became a Design Powerhouse. *Harvard Business Review, 93*(9), 72–78.

Crossing Boundaries: Design into Business and Management

3

Learning Objectives

- To understand the relationship between strategic design adoption and commercial competitive advantage.
- To examine common elements of university design degree programmes and their influence on transferable skills development.
- To develop an understanding of the challenges of implementing design thinking within business school curricula.
- To introduce the rise of online executive design thinking programmes to support continuing professional development.
- To critically examine the introduction of a design thinking programme within a leading North American higher education institution.

3.1 Introduction

Over the last decade, we have witnessed practitioners and academics from the realm of business and management valuing design as an invaluable means of dealing with complex innovation challenges. Design in its broadest sense, is a multidisciplinary activity that transcends traditional disciplinary boundaries, moving into areas of critical engagement that were unthinkable during its formative stages of continual development. The eclectic nature of design is a broad church of ideas, diverse attitudes, and different agendas; when viewed in entirety, the dynamic interrelationships of these elements are embedded in the way organisations develop new products, services, systems and interactions in order to enrich the lives of the

---

Supplementary Information The online version contains supplementary material available at [https://doi.org/10.1007/978-3-030-94206-9_3].

Y. Huang, D. Hands, *Design Thinking for New Business Contexts*,
https://doi.org/10.1007/978-3-030-94206-9_3

peoples 'experiences.' With this inherent agility and wider applicability, design humanises scientific and technological advances, which continually shapes our lives. The quest for continual innovation drives business vision in the relentless search for differentiation and competitiveness in highly challenging marketplaces.

Business leaders of tomorrow need to be equipped with the skills and ability to inspire, motivate and encourage employees to achieve visionary goals, of the individual and the organisation. When we look at the world's leading brands, often you find a key individual central their success; Tim Cook (Steve Jobs predecessor) at Apple, Huateng 'Pony' Ma, elusive entrepreneur who created the technology company in China—Tencent, and Marrisa Mayor, CEO and President of Yahoo as notable examples. Training and developing visionary business leaders for tomorrow takes us to one single point of discussion: education. Where and how do we equip business leaders with the abilities to lead and deliver projects, encourage initiatives, build a sense of common purpose, and empower others? This chapter aims to contribute to the ongoing debate of critically examining the role and nature of business schools and their teaching curricula in best preparing graduates for leadership positions in industry. Having set the scene as to how design can offer many strategic benefits to the company, we turn our attention to exploring the strengths and weaknesses of current business/management education, set against the need for continual change in both teaching planning and delivery.

The discussion explores the differences and similarities between design and business curricula currently on offer in a wide variety of degree programmes, illustrating how critical thinking, problem solving and teamwork skills are developed within the students. Current debate in business/management schools shows the many parallels between design and business pedagogy and how the primary elements of these two disciplines could be embedded within teaching practice. If successful, a future thinking curricula would provide business educators with a number of important designerly concepts, tools and methods that could be directly integrated into existing courses. Design Thinking is an engaging way for students to learn about customer development, problem solving, product-solution fit, creativity, divergent and convergent modes of thinking, iteration, failure, resilience and teamwork. It allows students to develop their creative confidence and shift their beliefs about what skills they need in order to become business leaders of tomorrow. The chapter concludes with a guest contribution in the form of a small case study from Dr Beatriz Itzel Cruz Megchun, Assistant Professor of Design & Innovation at Pamplin School of Business, University of Portland, USA. Here, Dr Cruz argues that design thinking principles and practices can both enrich and complement existing business programmes and the many benefits far outweigh the risks of significantly re-designing tried and tested teaching curricula.

3.2 Design for Business: The Critical Imperative

It is widely acknowledged that design can add many benefits to business profitability and overall long-term success (Nomen and BCD Barcelona Centre de Disseny, 2014; Cox, 2005; The Design Council, 2015; Kotler & Rath, 2013). Thomas Watson Jr,

Table 3.1 The contribution of design to business success

Design activity	Design as process	Design as strategy
Develop innovative products and services	85%	86%
Develop higher quality products/services	83%	86%
Differentiate products and services	73%	86%
Penetrate into new markets	65%	84%
Provide more added value to customers	81%	80%
Make better decisions based on customer insight	61%	74%
Support the marketing of products/services	59%	74%
Build a brand and image	61%	70%
Achieve cost reduction	53%	66%
Accelerate the innovation process	59%	64%
De-risk the innovation process	60%	56%
	% of company respondents interviewed	

the second Company President of IBM, famously remarked, "good design is good business" which still holds true today. Businesses can draw upon the full power of design in a wide variety of ways, ranging from graphic design right through to organisational change (based on research findings by Cooper et al., 2016). Table 3.1 identifies how and where design can contribute to increased business success.

As we can see from Table 3.1 the wide variety of applications that design can take and the impact that it can provide. Design can offer far more benefits than anticipated; however, design is still largely misunderstood by business in terms of what it can offer. There is a commonly held assumption by businesses that design is mainly used for aesthetic purposes such as logos and simple graphics—which sadly, still prevails today. In order to raise its value as a strategic business asset, design councils/associations such as the Danish Design Centre (DDC) in Denmark right through to Korea Advanced Institute of Science and Technology (KAIST) in South Korea are continually working with businesses and organisations to communicate the many benefits of design that it has to offer. Referring to Table 3.1., design can play a significant role at a strategic level through:

- *The development of innovative products and services*: design connects creativity to innovation which can lead to the creation and commercialisation of innovative products/services. New markets could be opened-up to the company or new market segments could be exploited within existing markets. This is turn, can lead to sustainable business growth through design.
- *Developing higher quality products/services*: design would enable the company to reposition its present product/service offerings, either by enhancing product attributes via adding design value to ensure premium status; or alternatively, offering the product to a mass market audience at a lower price position.
- *Differentiate products and services*: to establish a clear difference between company offerings against rival products. Design is an excellent means of differentiation and can be a powerful tool to secure market share.

The consideration and application of design at a strategic level requires senior levels of support and authority in order to be effective. As such, this takes design into the highest echelons of corporate decision making which is now becoming a strategic asset. To adopt this approach towards the use of design, senior managers and CEO's need to have a good understanding of design in order to unlock its full potential. However, an interesting question arises here; how do senior decision makers in business gain exposure to the many benefits of design? It would be sensible to assume that design, design management and design leadership would feature within business and management school curricula (either as a core or as an elective optional module). Sadly, that is not the case; design thinking within business schools is still a relatively rare phenomenon, often only touched upon a superficial level if at all. Formosa and Kroeter (2002) based at Parsons School of Design, New York undertook a review of 19 top-tier American MBA programmes and found that "not a single one addressed or incorporated design into its curricula in any significant way. Even in those programmes focused on marketing and branding, curricular attention to the principles or theories of design is cursory, at best". Which is odd, given that the world's leading brands use design throughout every aspect of application, such as Louis Vuitton (superior product quality); BMW (precision design engineering); Disney (design experiences); Taobao (user experience design) and so forth. Many of these companies are cited as excellent examples of business success, but yet the way they use design is predominantly overlooked in the majority of teaching within management/business schools. These visionary companies (amongst many others) operate in highly complex and competitive postmodern marketplaces where design is vital to their ongoing success.

The world of business and commerce is undergoing radical transformation, with social and technological changes relentlessly disrupting traditional business models on a daily basis. Set against this turbulent backdrop, it has left numerous business schools teaching outdated curricula and pedagogic practices that do not respond to these dynamic and emergent challenges of the third millennium. However, a growing number of business schools have acknowledged shortcomings in their curricula and teaching provision (Glen et al., 2014). With this in mind, design orientated modules or short courses could provide business students with exposure to creative problem solving techniques through cultivating confidence via new types of learning activities. Matthews and Wrigley (2011) argue, "Australian universities show some early experimentation with design thinking, often with in units on innovation where interest in design thinking may be of longstanding interest. Within Australian business schools there is some recognition are realising the area of design thinking in business is a growing and necessary field and some initiatives have begun". Carefully considered and taught within a business school setting, design thinking can meaningfully contribute to a number of core business modules/programmes of study. For instance, the commonly featured modules management and strategy, are heavily weighted towards 'process' that rely on rational planning and analysis type activities, leaving considerable room for the adoption of design thinking. Furthermore, marketing lies in having a deep understanding of customers and end-users needs which is consistent with empathic design which could significantly benefit from tools and techniques such as user journeys, empathy maps and personas—the basic elements of design thinking. In addition, these designerly techniques would allow students to explore and understand business principles outside of a traditional classroom setting (i.e. 'chalk and talk') and learn from real business world problems, connecting theory with contemporary industry practice. One common approach to connect classroom learning to industry practice is through work placements or internships; however, internships often would not engage with or gain exposure to design thinking practices.

3.3 Teaching Design in Design Schools

In order to understand as to how design thinking could be embedded within management and business schools, let us briefly turn our attention to design schools and their approach to delivering design and creativity skills. Firstly, due to the large number of design degree courses offered, there will be a large amount of variation between each university course—even though basically they will be teaching the same subjects, that is, interior design, fashion design and so on. However, the following elements of curricula and learning principles generally remain consistent throughout the design education sector.

Entry onto design degree programmes: virtually all design courses will require the applicant to demonstrate their creativity and suitability for study onto their respective course; this is predominantly demonstrated by a creative portfolio of work (be it the large traditional A0 black portfolio or an online portfolio of work that is widely used now). There needs to be a significant body of work that aligns with the particular degree course that the applicant is applying to, such as product design which demonstrates three dimensional thinking and so forth. In the UK, a general Art and Design foundation course is a preparatory course where the applicant can over the duration of their studies, build a comprehensive portfolio of work in order to apply for higher study. More often than not, this entry route onto a design degree is commonplace across the West.

Types of design courses: traditionally there used to be two types of design degree courses—2 dimensional design that covered—graphics, illustration and publishing type disciplines; and 3 dimensional design that focused upon—interiors, products and fashion. However, with the rise of digital, we are now witnessing the increasing amount of courses that teach web design, gaming and design interactions; hence now becoming the third aspect of design study. We have omitted architecture from this discussion, even though regarded 3D design, it has its own specialist requirements in terms of teaching and learning outcomes that are regulated by professional statutory bodies such as the Royal Institution of British Architects (RIBA).

Teaching Methods: This is the key difference that separates design education to comparable courses in more traditional disciplines and the sciences. Design courses are heavily orientated to skills development in a practical sense, with lesser emphasis on formal lectures and seminars. Rather than the main element of learning in the lecture theatre, greater attention is paid to learning in the (design) studio, where the tutor(s) would have greater contact with the students through learning 'on the job.' In practical workshops, students learn and become familiarised with the different types of methods commonly used within their discipline. Furthermore, the use of formative design presentations and subsequent critical feedback ('crits') from tutors and peers forms a continual basis of learning that reflects industry practice. Lectures do feature on design degree courses, mainly used to develop the students understanding of historical movements in design and critical contextual studies that underpins contemporary design discourse. Finally, skills development regarding the use of software and digital technologies is increasing in prominence on design courses, thus reflecting the move towards digitisation in studio practice and industry. Guest lectures from external design experts are frequently commonplace in teaching, thus affording real world insights from leaders drawn from their own respective disciplines.

Transferable Skills Development: Are an integral part of the majority of degree programmes, and design is arguably one of the most critical disciplines where skills is fundamental to its professional development. There are two types of skills developed; firstly—subject specific for instance where a fashion design student would learn in the workshop, skills in making and crafting garments; or industrial design students using specialist tools, techniques and equipment to create prototypes and physical models. Secondly, the development of transferable skills is as important to subject specific skills. Due to the broad range of skills developed over the duration of study, transferable skills are developed that are critical to the design discipline that they wish to enter into; but also to careers outside of design. Main transferable skills achieved during design study include: (1) problem solving; (2) creative thinking; (3) communication; (4) project management; (5) teamwork; (6) independent research abilities.

Postgraduate Specialism: Following on from undergraduate design study, a student may wish to specialise further within their own discipline or use postgraduate study to explore a complementary study to that of their first degree. Postgraduate degrees can be roughly divided into two distinct camps—(1) PGT 'taught' which are generally more structured, with a large dissertation/research project at the end which allows specialism within its own subject area. (2) PGR 'research' that requires the student to undertake most of the study independently via research, often supervised by one or two academics in support over the study period. This study route is an excellent means of preparation if the student wishes to continue their research study to Doctoral (PhD) level. Alongside these standard postgraduate courses, there are also highly specialised master's programmes, professions for which by law you need to be properly qualified to practice, for example, medicine, dentistry, law and social work.

Regarding postgraduate design courses that feature a strong orientation towards business and management themes, these vary, but predominantly sit within the realm of design management and strategy, design for business, design and branding and so forth. Loosely speaking, these types of courses strongly feature on process for developing new products or services, however, with the advancement of design touching upon many other related disciplines, the breadth and content of these courses has advanced significantly over the last decade. As touched upon earlier, even though universities offer the same types of courses, the variation between them is often quite significant. For instance, Lancaster University offer a postgraduate design management course that develops modes of thinking critical to the challenges design managers face across a range of real-world situations. It explores design management from a range of future-oriented perspectives, including service design, design for sustainability, right through to design policy development. Birmingham City University, have a long established MA Design Management course that focuses heavily upon creative skills development to support entrepreneurial and business capabilities through design. Although these types of courses are quite diverse in nature, there are some common elements or themes that run throughout them. These would often include:

Creative research methods: that develops an understanding of a range of design research methods and their application within real world contexts. The focus would be to develop analytical and creative design thinking through theoretical investigation and practical activities. This type of module introduces and develops research approaches, methodologies and tools used to inform design research, as well as ideas about how and when to deploy these research tools appropriately, frequently within a business setting.

Critical and contextual studies: exploring the complex relationship between design and business and explores this relationship in both historical and contemporary contexts. Usually a core module of this nature, considers how design can contribute to sustainable and commercially viable propositions and the resultant relationship to organisational agendas.

Design for business: would focus on the origins of design management/design leadership, its past, present and emerging forms; its functions and purposes; and its relationships with policymaking. It would provide the historical and practical context for design management in general and the role of the design manager in particular. Furthermore, topics and themes would explore the meaning of designing versus managing and the many ways design managers can contribute to organisations.

3.4 Teaching Business Management in Business Schools

In this section, we turn our attention to examining common elements of curricula that features in a wide variety of business management schools. For the sake of brevity, this discussion only focuses upon postgraduate study as opposed to undergraduate, mainly due to the wide breadth of undergraduate courses offering business management studies. Furthermore, postgraduate courses tend to be more specialised, offering a narrower range of taught modules, which allows easier comparison across the higher education landscape. We have identified common modules where and how design thinking could make a significant contribution to learning outcomes; currently though, design is rarely mentioned nor featured in the taught elements that we highlight.

Entry onto business degree programmes: Generally speaking, entry into the majority of postgraduate courses requires a set of strong qualifications that feature (in particular) Mathematics and English. The undergraduate degree should be complementary to associated disciplines that sit with business and management (i.e. finance, accountancy, marketing etc.). Like the majority of postgraduate courses, a comprehensive personal statement that covers evidence that you have an enthusiasm for the subject, ideally supported with evidence of work experience/voluntary work and additional reading and research around contemporary business themes are required.

Types of business management courses: Alongside general business management courses such as Master of Business Administration (MBA), specialist areas of study often include International Business Management, Accounting and Finance, Business Analytics, Marketing Communications, and Charity Marketing and Fundraising. These in a way, demonstrate the breadth of business management courses on offer and their rich variety of disciplinary specialisms.

Teaching methods: Mainly take place in the form of traditional lectures and seminars. Seminars are smaller interactive workshop type sessions where discrete learning groups are formed to allow exchange of ideas and concepts. Due to emphasis on team working, much of the learning takes place via group projects and assignments, often working with companies drawn from industry. In order to provide industry insight and relevance, it is not uncommon to see guest lectures from leading academics and business leaders sharing personal insights based on their own experience.

Elements that could feature design thinking: common modules (or learning units) that could benefit from the inclusion of design thinking to afford a series of alternative perspectives, include:

1. *Corporate strategy*—where design could greatly contribute to the formulation of business strategy development. For instance, corporate strategy is predominantly deployed to identify, plan and achieve long-term business objectives and goals. A designerly approach would yield a solution-based means of solving problems via the inclusion of end-users or developing a deeper understanding of users' needs and values. Furthermore, this approach could also raise the value of design as an invaluable way of increasing efficiencies within the product planning process through the reduction of time and resources on poorly defined ideas and concepts.
2. *(International) Marketing*—is arguably the closest business function to design, but yet design is rarely touched upon in this core element of learning. The relationship between design and marketing is becoming increasingly more strategic

and business-driven, with primary emphasis on understanding user needs. This symbiotic relationship covers areas ranging from consumer behaviour to marketing research, customer relationship management right through to marketing communications. In addition, internationalisation and evolution of markets have created opportunities for companies to focus on marketing from a global perspective and central to this is the role of design that can make universal product offerings country specific.

3. *Digital Innovation*—or put simply, the application of software technologies to existing business problems or practices. With the rise of digital, companies are re-orientating their business strategies to increase their online operations; design provides an enhanced series of user experiences that reinforces brand values. Also, design can be an ideal means of differentiation in highly competitive markets; as such, its prominence as a strategic resource in corporate strategy and decision making should be widely promoted within business school curricula.
4. *Entrepreneurship*—in an unpredictable world, innovative minds are constantly searching for new commercial opportunities. Thinking and acting entrepreneurially is as valuable in a large organisation as it is to a new start-up venture. Both leading companies and start-ups must develop new ideas, products and services that create real value for the customer. Primary aspects of the entrepreneurial process include creativity, opportunity recognition, sales, finance, leadership and effective communication—design influences and embraces all these interrelated activities, transforming ideas into tangible products for marketization.

However, embedding design and creative thinking within business school curricula is not as straight forward as one would first imagine. There is a considerable cultural divide between the two disciplines that in some aspects are diametrically opposed to one another. However, this clash of cultures could create a contested space between the two disciplines, whereby design thinking connects decision makers to creators. It is widely acknowledged that curricula in business management school are tightly bound, with many conflicting demands placed upon the students. Adding more modules to an already packed curriculum could present challenges to the educators, given that if something extra is added, something needs to be removed from the teaching programme. One quick and effective way of introducing design into business schools is through offering design thinking as an optional module that could arouse curiosity and an opportunity to explore something novel within the student learning journey. If enrolment on design orientated modules proves successful, these optional modules could then become a permanent core feature of the curricula. As discussed earlier, with the emphasis on soft skills (i.e. communication, teamwork, problem solving) that strongly feature in design practice, these attributes could influence and inform (creative) teaching practices on other business management centric modules. Over time, with the increasing recognition of design, more design focused modules could be offered or the inclusion of a distinct design management programme to existing curricula. This would allow modules to be shared across the suite of courses, whilst a distinct stand-alone course in its own right. Interestingly enough, one of the early pioneers of design management in the UK was Peter Gorb, who introduced design management to the London Business School in 1976, which then later was formally established as a Design Management Unit in 1982. Seminal papers arising from work undertaken at the DMU formed the iconic design management publication in 1988, titled *Design Talks*! (Gorb & Schneider, 1988)

3.5 Academia and Industry: Design Alliances

With the rise of online learning gaining a foothold, we are witnessing an increase of executive education aimed at management professionals who can undertake short courses (usually between 6–8 weeks) based around design thinking/strategy related themes. There is a wide variety of formats that these courses take; some are a combination of academic institutions and business partners; alternatively, a select number of courses offered solely by leading businesses such as IBM, and other partnership programmes a mixture of both. Below is a range of common examples of short design thinking courses currently on offer:

(1) London Business School (2021) (UK): Innovation through Design Thinking [Duration: 6 weeks online; 4–6 learning hours per week]. This short course introduces the student to the basic principles of design thinking that could be applied to creative challenges within their own workplace. Learning units include the importance of innovation to the organisation; understanding customer needs; problem framing within an organisational context; idea generation and creative thinking techniques; prototyping and developing ideas. Case examples to aid learning are drawn from real life industry examples based on themes of new product development and service innovation.

(2) Rotman School of Management (Canada): Business Design Thinking: From Insight to Innovation (Rotman School of Management, 2021) [Duration: 6 weeks online; 4–6 learning hours per week]. This intensive short programme introduces a 4-step framework to frame and solve business problems via a designerly approach to innovation. Key elements of learning include defining business problems through sense-making; effective multi-disciplinary team working; navigating the four stages of innovation and mastering design thinking tools and techniques. What is interesting about this programme is the diverse learning strategies that are on offer. These include live webinars, interactive workbooks and peer review sessions that take learning distinctly away from traditional lecture based format.

(3) MIT Management Executive Education (USA): Mastering Design Thinking—Create Value through Systematic Innovation (MIT Management Executive Education, 2021) [Duration: 12 weeks online, 6–8 learning per week] This ambitious programme confidently states that on completion of study, the learner will have mastered design thinking. To support this bold statement, study takes place over three months, navigating the vast terrain of new product development with specific emphasis on defining for and developing solutions based on user-centred needs. Ten course specific modules are offered, each one focusing upon a key component of design, creativity and NPD.

(4) IBM Design Thinking: IBM's Enterprise Design Thinking Framework (IBM, 2021) is a free online resource where individuals can draw upon and utilise design thinking resources to aid design thinking in their own respective organisation. Three main principles form the core of this expansive framework—(1) a focus on user outcomes; (2) restless reinvention; (3) diverse empowered teamworking. On successful completion of the study units, participants can earn digital 'badges' that demonstrate that they have achieved learning outcomes from completing their suite of online courses. Recently, IBM (2020) announced, "what started out as a simple idea to attract talent has turned into the most influential IT credential program in the world. Now, IBM has issued its three millionth badge and hosts about 2,500 activities where badges are issued".
(5) IDEO & Tsinghua University. *Lead a Creative China 2030* (ideo.cn, 2021) is a joint venture between IDEO and Tsinghua University through its PBC School of Finance and Academy of Arts & Design. It is a 12-month executive programme aimed at leading decision makers in China, with the ambitious aim to transform China's national economy through a design thinking mindset. Drawing heavily on the work and tools developed by IDEO, the programme covers business strategy, organisational design, industry analysis and technological innovation. Notable contributors to the course has included—Masayuki Kurokawa, a Japanese architect and industrial designer; David Kelly, the founder of Stanford d. school; Jake Knapp, the inventor of Sprint; and Liu Guanzhong from Academy of Arts and Design of Tsinghua University.

Case Study: Embedding Design Thinking Into Business School Curricula

The following case study offered by Dr Beatriz Itzel Cruz Megchun, Assistant Professor of Design & Innovation at Pamplin School of Business, University of Portland, USA.

This section will briefly introduce an example of how design thinking can be embedded within business school curricula and its value to developing student's creative problem-solving skill sets. It will start by discussing the shifts in business school activities to understand the integration of design as an agent for transformational change. It will start by offering a descriptive overview of the classroom setting, intended learning outcomes, teaching methods and subsequent transferable skills. Finally, it will conclude with a reflection on the challenges of implementing design thinking within a business school context.

Across the world, academic institutions have struggled to offer programs that reflect on (or challenge) the politics of the time, the social fabric, the fluctuating state of the economy, and the environment's increasing devastation. In addition, they need to integrate the skills and competencies that are critical to face the challenges imposed in the twenty-first century. A report detected a gap between the skills that people learn and the skills people need to thrive in this new economy (WEF, 2015). It is vital to enhance new forms of learning, using existing and emerging pedagogical approaches (project-based, experiential, inquiry-based) with adaptative learning methods. It requires collaboration among policymakers, educators and education technology providers to implement an instructional system that could help close the twenty-first century skill gaps. Business schools in particular have a bond with wider industry. It affords them to regard their curricula, global business contexts (globalisation, leadership and innovation), the ethical practice of management and the development of graduates' responsibilities.

Management education emerged alongside educational institutions, as it was not regarded as being properly academic. Its materialisation occurred in the late eighteenth century and early nineteenth century in Portugal—the School of Commerce in Lisbon 1759, France -École supérieure du commerce de Paris, 1819, and Germany—Cameralism. Business schools flourished after World War II, preparing managers with scientific and analytical components and skills that had proven useful and relevant in administering post-war corporate enterprises (Khurana & Spender, 2012). They concentrated on implementing higher standards and the development of rational-analytic problem-solving abilities coupled with analytical tools. This over-emphasis of analytic techniques, led managers to divert their attention away from social aspects such as reticence to other perspectives, become detached from other actors, and fail to appreciate the impact that business decisions have on people's lives (Baker & Baker, 2012; Starkey & Tempest, 2009). The current business education system does not always prepare future business leaders and managers to address complex issues that often lack definitive solutions, such as the diversity of stakeholders, climate change, inclusion and equity. This situation leaves future professionals ill-equipped to deal with uncertain and risk situations where the process is unknown and the ends to be sought, unclear. Likewise, there has been an increasing demand for professionals with high cognitive and interpersonal skills as they are more effective in processing information and conveying what that information means. These individuals train to speak about the desirability, viability, and feasibility of new ideas, bringing together multiple information streams, distil key trends, and identify new opportunities. Furthermore, business schools need to confront the challenges businesses and society faces to orient their programmes and research accordingly. Datar et al. (2011), argue, "business schools need first to reassess the facts, frameworks, and theories that they teach (knowing). Second, focus on developing the skills, capabilities, and techniques that lie at the heart of the practice of management (doing) and the values, attitudes, and beliefs that inform managers world views and professional identities (being)."

Over the past decades, the importance of design thinking in management (Boland & Collopy, 2004; Brown, 2008; Dunne & Martin, 2006; Martin, 2009; Liedtka, 2018) and management education (Beckman & Barry, 2007; Kimbell, 2011; Liedtka & Ogilvie, 2011) has been widely acknowledged. Many pioneering business schools have integrated design thinking as a much-needed approach to deal with complex, ill-defined problems through the ability to think critically, decide wisely, communicate clearly and implement effectively. Design has a long research tradition complete with fundamental concepts, methodologies, and distinct epistemological assumptions that can assist business schools in addressing and connecting the knowing, doing, and being within their curriculum. Johansson-Sköldberg et al. (2013) divide the design field into five discourses: design as the creation of artefacts (Simon, 1969); design as reflective practice (Schön, 1983); design as a problem-solving activity (Buchanan, 1992); design as a way of making sense (Kruger & Cross, 2006); and design as a meaning of creation (Krippendorff, 2006). The design process involves an iterative cycle of synthesis, generation, analysis and evaluation through which design requirements and specification co-evolve along with the solution (Johnson et al., 2007; Johnson, 2001; Dorst & Cross, 2001). People that use design thinking are able to think via three different dimensions: (1) thinking of (e.g. imaging, visualising, ad dreaming up); (2) thinking about (e.g. consideration of, reflection on, and deliberation about), and (3) thinking through something (e.g. understanding, grasping and figuring out) (Cooper et al., 2009). Bringing design pedagogy into business schools is not new however, as Herbert Simon (1969) argued for such integration over four decades ago. He argued that professional schools concern with "what ought to be", and pure science focus on explaining "what is", and thus the business curriculum should integrate both a discipline-based science as well as practitioner orientation. In the twenty-first century, Findeli (2001) proposed creating design programmes that taught design as a meta-practice concerned with humanistic values within complex systems. He proposed a discipline centred on the practice of design as a process, as a way of knowing based on processing an intervention. Design courses are consolidating capabilities and skills from multiple disciplines related to design practice and processes—artistic techniques, scientific principles, and social theories- to promote humanistic values.

Design Thinking Curriculum Design in the University of Portland, USA

The University of Portland (UP) is a private Catholic, non-profit teaching-based institution with various competitive majors at the undergraduate and graduate levels. It has a cohort of around 3741 full-time undergraduate students and 350 graduate students per academic year. The University has five schools: the College of Arts and Sciences, the Dr Robert Pamplin, Jr. School of Business (PSOB), the School of Education, the Shiley School of Engineering and the School of Nursing. PSOB was founded in 1939, and it is one of five business schools in Oregon accredited by the Association of Advanced Collegiate Schools of Business (AACSB). The school offers undergraduate majors and graduate programmes (MBA and MS) and executive programmes. Its graduates work in global organisations such as Daimler, Providence, Intel, Adidas, Nike, US Bank, Columbia, Boeing, among other organisations. UP serves the thriving community of Portland and states located on the West Coast of the United States, also known as the Pacific Coast. It has cities such as Los Angeles, San Francisco, Seattle that attract industries based on technology, healthcare, creative work and athletic/outdoor apparel (Fig. 3.1). Portland is considered a strategic location as it offers relatively low energy costs, accessible resources—north-south and east-west interstates, international air terminals, extensive marine shipping facilities, and west coast intercontinental railroads. It hosts multiple local and global

Fig. 3.1 West coast industry (developed by author)

organisations in the athletic, creative, education, healthcare and technology sectors. The Portland metro area has become a business cluster for tech companies, athletic/outdoor gear and breweries. These businesses have access to multiple education providers from state and private education institutions, such as Portland State University, Oregon State University, University of Oregon, Oregon Health and Science University, Portland Community College, Reed College, Pacific Northwest College of Art, and so on. Most of these institutions offer postgraduate courses, executive education and research programmes that strengthen collaboration with industry in different areas of activity.

PSOB identified design as an opportunity to enhance their value proposition on the West Coast. They wanted to increase the number of courses that best prepare students with integrated decision-making skills relevant to industry. They aspired to follow the steps of Ivy League institutions and renowned institutions that offer joint design programmes in their college of engineering and school of business. Across the US, there are twelve academic institutions with MBA or MS joint programmes which are focused on design, innovation, business design, leadership and integrated design, business and technology (Fig. 3.2). The largest number of programmes (seven) are on the East Coast, then followed by three programmes hosted by a state on the West Coast and two programmes in another state on the Midwest. The programme directors and academic leaders from Carnegie Mellon University, Massachusetts Institute of Technology, Northwestern University, Stanford University and the University of Pennsylvania have joined efforts to promote the IDI degree. It is a collaboration of graduate programmes that bring together design, engineering and business through a human-centred design process approach. Each programme has its own identity, but all apply an integrated design innovation process and mindset at the heart of the teaching philosophy. They provide highly immersive opportunities for students to work on a wide range of projects in studio-based environments. In addition to the five programmes, they have collaborations with related programmes and individuals in the US and around the globe. Projects can vary from 24-hour design hacks to multi-semester projects and thesis work that focus on real-world challenges. Another avenue that professionals have for career development is the certifications provided by continued education providers. In the US, there are seven universities, Stanford University, UC Berkeley, Northwestern University Segal Design Institute and SDI at the McCormick School of Engineering, TUFTS, Parson and Cornell University, offering (executive) certificates. The last avenue is professional certifications from consultancies such as IDEO, Park + Grow, LUMA Institute, DMI workshops, SMART design, and Fjord.

In 2017, PSOB appointed a design academic to the entrepreneurship and innovation management department. The mandate for the academic was to develop innovative learning experiences in current classes, design new courses at both undergraduate and graduate levels and build connections with the local industry community in Portland. First, there was an analysis by PSOB and university core competences, capabilities and infrastructure that were available. Then, it was defined design and its potential implementation at undergraduate

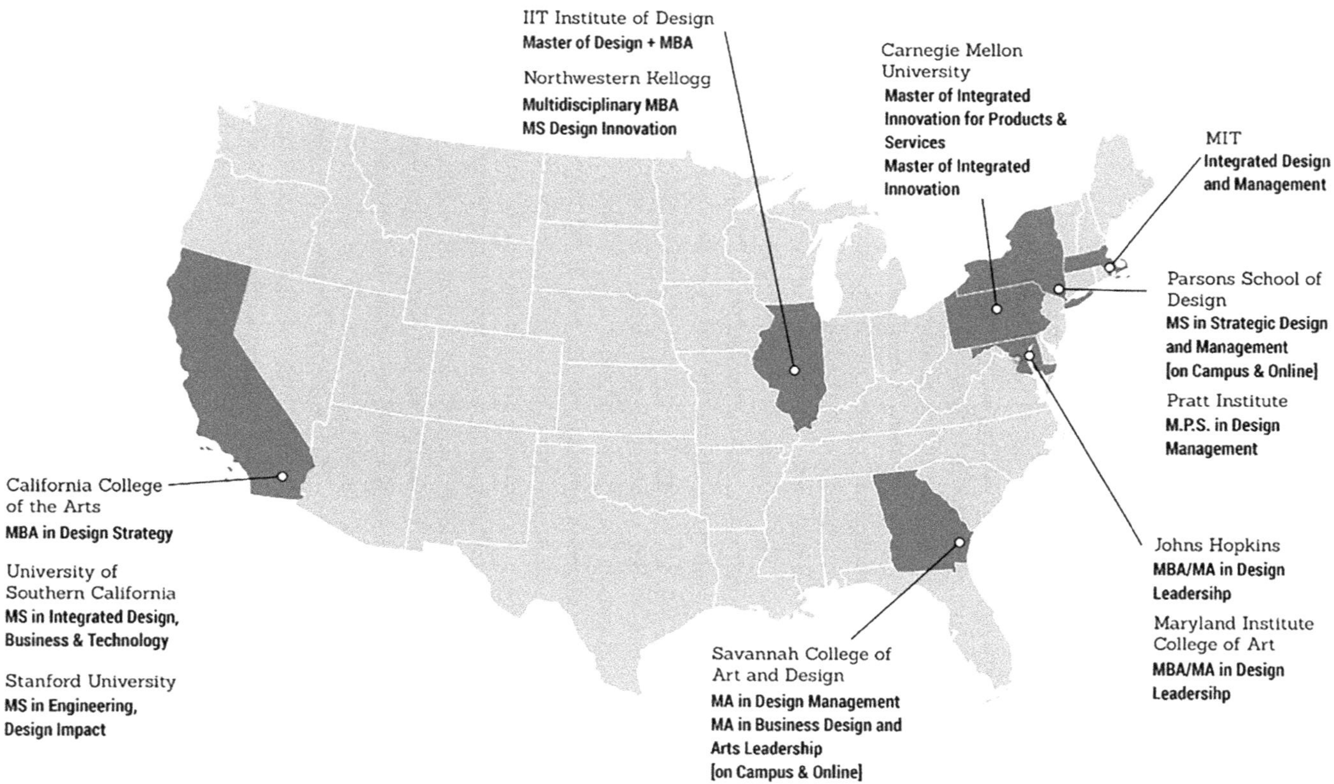

Fig. 3.2 Educational institutions offering join programmes (developed by author)

and graduate levels in the business school (and other schools). The academic then analysed the business context and the academic offerings of other educational institutions in the metropolitan area and wider west coast. The outcomes identified multiple areas of opportunity. The academic started designing a comprehensive series of classes and devised courses as early interventions until they could be embedded into the curricula and assess their impact on the innovation (and entrepreneurship) minor and marketing majors. PSOB integrated into the curricula seven design classes: brand design, design management, innovation, design thinking, design in business and society, creativity, innovation and design, designing innovative brands, service marketing and design thinking in healthcare. These classes aimed to provide students with the opportunity to acquire knowledge, capabilities and skills to undergo an approach to deal with complex, ill-defined problems through the ability to think critically, decide wisely, communicate clearly and implement effectively in their respective fields. The nature of the courses offered the possibility of implementing experiential learning by integrating support systems—standard and assessments, instruction, professional development, and learning environment—that encouraged foundational literacies, competencies, and character qualities (Fig. 3.3). The courses were designed to address and exercise how students apply core skills to everyday tasks (foundational literacies), how students approach complex challenges (competencies), and how students approach their changing environment (character qualities). They used high-impact practices through different assignments that allowed students to share common intellectual experiences, collaborative assignments/projects, writing-intensive work, co-designing with learning communities, and diversity and global learning projects. As a result, they were able to apply ethnographic and design methods, information and technology application, work in

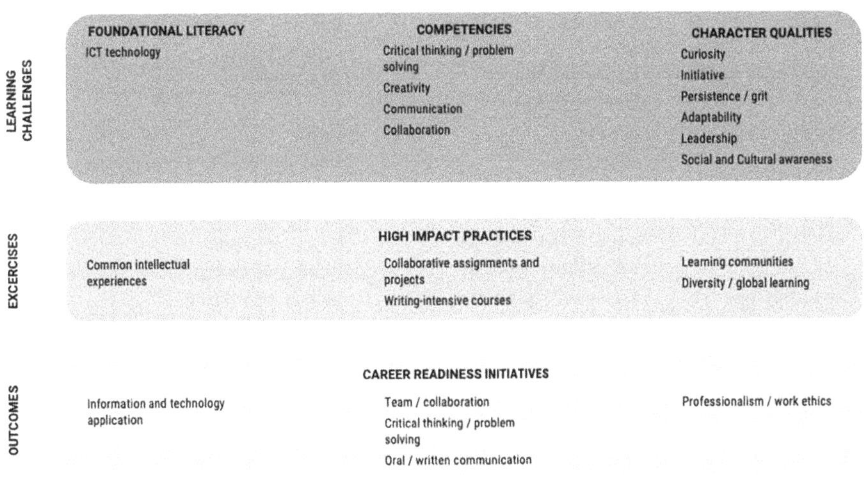

Fig. 3.3 Twenty-first century skills for a new vision of education (developed by author)

teams and collaborate, use critical thinking and problem-solving approach, pursue oral and written communication and focus on ethical approaches.

A multidimensional approach, allows designers to explore spaces of possibility, use emergence, co-evolve with their artefacts and their sciences, create a new order, engage in collaborative development, and utilize creative cognitive processes to explore, generate, and evaluate hypothetical possibilities (Alexiou et al., 2010; Buchanan, 1992). This perspective contrasts with the structured and focused business approach based on history, business rules (learning and implementation), facts and delivery. The implementation of design thinking in marketing creates collaborations that unveil users' behaviours, habits, and desires to achieve outcomes that address functional, social and emotional dimensions. It also assists brands in collecting, analysing and inferring data that will inform their positioning strategies. Design thinking in innovation focuses on generating, managing and introducing technologies that benefit wider society. It also broadens cross-functional skills and negotiation strategies necessary to be a responsible and ethical innovative leader in a contemporary global business environment. Teaching followed a generic design thinking process to map design activities and outcomes that benefit students' learning goals and experience (Table 3.2). The process guides students to understand their actions, identify where they are in the process and define the outcomes that they can obtain. The design activities featured observation, contextualisation, definition, conceptualisation, prototyping, implementation and post-assessment. The results would depend on the design activity, and these can be tangible or intangible -artefacts, activities, knowledge source and core values. Artefacts refer to the tangible outcomes of the design activity. Activity regards the processes that designers undergo to understand the

Table 3.2 Twenty-first century design activities and outcomes

<table>
<tr><th>Design activity</th><th>Outcomes (innovation)</th><th>Outcomes (marketing)</th></tr>
<tr><td>Observe</td><td>Artefacts
Noun
Representation
Objects/things</td><td>Artefacts
Representation
Objects/things</td></tr>
<tr><td>Contextualise</td><td rowspan="2">Activity
Question
Business process
Puzzle like process
Image make process
Serendipity process</td><td>Activity
Industrial and business process
Puzzle like process</td></tr>
<tr><td>Define</td><td rowspan="2">Knowledge source
Research activity
Inquisitive process
Social engineering</td></tr>
<tr><td>Conceptualise</td><td rowspan="2">Knowledge source
Research activity
Inquisitive process
Social engineering
Problem solving</td></tr>
<tr><td>Prototype</td><td rowspan="3">Core value
Interdisciplinary
Multidisciplinary
Myth</td></tr>
<tr><td>Implementation</td><td rowspan="2">Core value
Discourse
Multidisciplinary
Myth</td></tr>
<tr><td>Post assessment</td></tr>
</table>

phenomenon that they need to deal with in their project work. Knowledge source considers the different capabilities and approaches to comprehend the socio-technical paradigm. Students study and apply design as a medium to question how they know the world (epistemology), what the world is (ontology) and how they practice (methodological). It is more important than ever that prospective professionals consider different worldviews, critique knowledge and have the appropriate instruments to works towards creating desired futures.

The inclusion of design thinking is an elective class open to all majors hosted in PSOB. It offers an introduction to working with human-centred design to address business challenges, social problems and complex systems. Students were able to learn to use a set of tools that they could apply in their workplace (or everyday activities), as they might collaborate and communicate with clients, stakeholders, and co-workers to reimagine and solve problems or generate new ideas. They used experiential learning to combine theoretical knowledge with social and emotional proficiency skills to respond to real-life scenarios. This learning approach allowed students to become familiar with learning, reflecting, experiencing, thinking and doing.

The learning goals concentrated on:

- integrating cross-functional knowledge to solve concrete business problems;
- becoming an effective and professional communicator;
- recognising opportunities, problems and risks;
- making and defending decisions in structured or unstructured contexts; and
- making ethical and socially responsible choices in business and community settings.

The course featured four sections that provided students with theoretical foundations of design thinking, its critical role, and in particular, the context of use. The first section (introduction) introduces students to design and the intrinsic relationship between design thinking (DT), human-centred design (HCD), innovation and creativity in contemporary business contexts. It explores how DT supports the design of new solutions that are tailor-made to respond to people's needs. The second element (looking) concentrates on providing a series of instruments, tools, and techniques that help students understand a given problem or need. They observe, engage and empathise with people to understand their experiences, needs and motivations. Then, they immerse themselves in the physical environment to gain a deeper personal understanding of the challenge at hand. The third section (understanding) helps students collect the data to facilitate its subsequent analysis and synthesis. The information assists them in identifying core problems and in generating ideas, as they will have become familiar with the users and their latent needs. The fourth section (deliver) introduces students to different tools and instruments to translate ideas into tangible outcomes, be it, products, services or entirely new systems.

Every semester, a different challenge and partner organisation was selected. New students were able to learn about design thinking throughout the semester via introducing its theory and praxis in a natural context. Furthermore, they were able to draw upon and use multiple instruments, methods, and frameworks based on design, ethnography, marketing and business considerations to negotiate solutions that will benefit multiple stakeholders. The goal was to utilise business knowledge competencies, problem recognition, prioritisation, decision-making competencies and relationship management in both real and hypothetical learning scenarios. The semester project featured three main stages: (1) immersion, (2) inspiration and (3) articulation, which facilitated the introduction of different methods (Fig. 3.4). Firstly, students were immersed into the challenge; then they contacted the community, organisations, and other stakeholders who were involved in the decision-making to document and appreciate different perspectives. Finally, the students established user profiles of the stakeholders to understand their needs, motivations, behaviours and habits (activity map). Once they reframed the challenge(s), they adopted a five human factors methodology that included 'people, objects, environments, messages, and service' (POEMS) to build a deeper emotional engagement with the users. The second stage (inspiration) focuses on learning methods to collaborate and co-design with different actors to create a diverse and inclusive dialogue. The utilisation of POEMS and brainstorming (Fig. 3.4) were to address biases and transform abstract ideas into realisable actions. The third section (articulation) concentrated on devising a plausible set of solutions that included and benefitted the diverse range of stakeholders. Students developed one idea sheet to define their concept/idea/proposal to create an action positioning strategy. The project employed multiple learning activities and assignments to ensure that students achieve each learning outcome throughout the duration of the project.

These included:

1. The use of a new human-centred approach that enhances innovation activities in terms of value creation, process performance, and market impact;

   To understand innovation beyond the design and development of new products, services or systems to other fundamental sources of value creation;
2. To use various forms of research to explore problems from different perspectives and including various stakeholders;
3. To develop individual and collaborative capabilities to identify customer needs to create sound concepts and hypothesis, to collect appropriate data and to develop prototypes that allow meaningful feedback in a real-world environment; and
4. To translate broadly defined opportunities into actionable innovation possibilities and recommendations for client's organisations.

The introduction of design (and design thinking) within the business school, provided students with an educational experience that allowed them to develop foundational literacy, competencies, and character qualities required in the twenty-first century. Educational institutions need to facilitate experiential learning by creating dynamic learning spaces, pedagogical content, and learning instruments to foster the integration of creative problem solving methodologies.

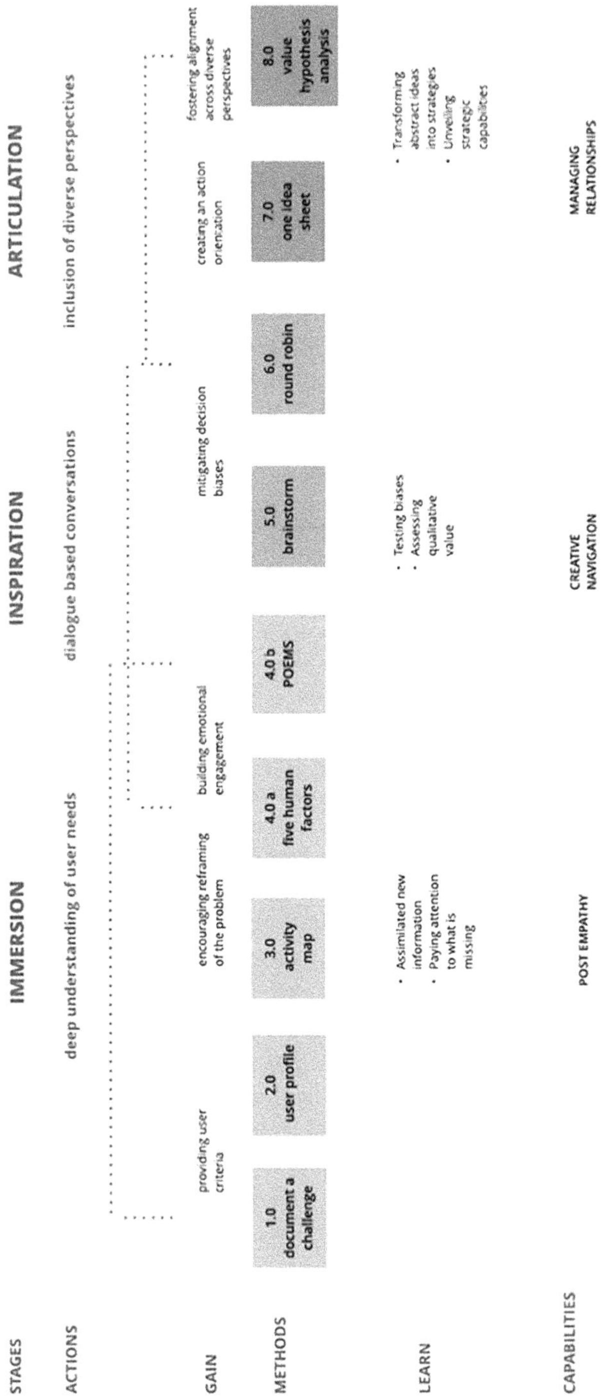

Fig. 3.4 Design thinking—semester overview (developed by author)

Integrating an interdisciplinary approach facilitates building a growth mindset to embrace new challenges, try new things, learn from mistakes, be accountable and develop an ability to negotiate and empathize regarding ethics and social decisions. The second change deals with developing competencies and character qualities that allow students to be critical thinkers, creative, collaborative, and communicative, and also, curious, persistent, flexible, and socially and culturally aware. The third change concerns a deeper understanding of the intrinsic relationship between business and community networks to achieve sustainable development. ◀

Chapter Summary In order to best prepare visionary business leaders of tomorrow, we need to reappraise our teaching practices in higher education; none more so than in business and management schools. To develop risk-taking, entrepreneurial minds who have the innate ability to inspire teams and individuals alike, the way we view current teaching curricula and delivery needs to adapt in order to produce leaders who will be operating in highly challenging and complex markets and industries. One strategy at achieving this is to critically examine core aspects of creative teaching methods and tools in traditional design schools, and see the transferable elements that could be adopted into other disciplinary contexts. This chapter has raised the issue of how and where design schools teach creativity and design thinking methods and map them against established business school curricula. The case example offered by Dr Beatriz Itzel Cruz Megchun goes some way in illustrating how design thinking can form an integral part of business school activities and how these new approaches can inform the development of business leaders of tomorrow. Chapter 4 takes an expansive overview of organisational structures and dynamics, and of how organisational systems need to change in order to become more agile and responsive in times of uncertainty.

Review Questions

1. Design can offer the organisation many benefits; identity where and how design can make a meaningful contribution to business competitiveness.
2. It is widely acknowledged that design is an invaluable source of differentiation; how can design enable this?
3. Potential employers are demanding that applicants demonstrate that they have a broad range of transferable skills, what 'soft' skills are developed within design education?
4. What are the unique benefits of executive design thinking programmes offered by joint education and industry partnerships?

5. Referring to the design thinking programme within the case study discussion, what other aspects of design thinking would you consider needs to be included within the teaching schedule?

Project Questions

1. Identify a particular product differentiation strategy where the company could distinguish their product from competing products.
2. Name three leading brands where they have successfully used a product differentiation strategy; how has this made their offerings unique in their respective marketplaces?
3. IBM Skills is a comprehensive programme of skills development. What other short courses do you think they could provide to attract new users?
4. The creation of user personas are a common feature of design thinking activities, as such, devise a persona based around the lifestyle characteristics of a Generation Z customer.
5. Identifying latent user needs is a core element of design thinking. Identify a set of tools that could enable the identification of undiscovered user needs; what makes them suitable for this type of research activity?

Chapter Tasks

1. Take a simple household washing detergent as an example and devise a differentiation strategy to make it unique as compared to a rival product; list the value-added benefits that it could offer to customers.
2. List three transferable skills that design education focuses upon, how does a design approach make these distinct from other non-design teaching methods?
3. Make a list of traditional marketing methods which are not successful in attracting the attention of Generation Z consumers.
4. Select two common examples of creative problem solving techniques; use these to solve a problem of your own choice. Identify and list elements that worked and also aspects that were not so successful.
5. In a group setting, identify a series of formalized design thinking process models, then rank the attributes that unifies them and also the elements that makes them markedly different.

References

Alexiou, K., Johnson, J., & Zamenopoulos, T. (2010). Embracing Complexity in Design: Emerging Perspectives and Opportunities. In T. Inns (Ed.), *Designing for the 21st Century Interdisciplinary Methods and Findings* (pp. 87–100). Gower.

Baker, D. F., & Baker, S. J. (2012). To "Catch the Sparkling Glow": A Canvas for Creativity in the Management Classroom. *Academy of Management Learning & Education, 11*, 704–721.

Beckman, S. L., & Barry, M. (2007). Innovation as a Learning Process: Embedding Design. *Thinking California Management Review, 50*, 25–56.

Boland, R., & Collopy, F. (2004). *Managing as Designing*. Stanford University Press.
Brown, T. (2008). Design Thinking. *Harvard Business Review, 86*, 84–92.
Buchanan, R. (1992). Wicked Problems in Design Thinking. *Design Issues, 8*, 5–21.
Cooper, R., et al. (2016). *Design Value: The Role of Design in Innovation.* http://imagination.lancaster.ac.uk/update/design-value/
Cooper, R., Junginger, S., & Lockwood, T. (2009). Design Thinking and Design Management: A Research and Practice Perspective. *Design Management Review, 20*(2), 47–55.
Cox, G. (2005). *Cox Review of Creativity in Business: Building on the UK's Strengths.* https://webarchive.nationalarchives.gov.uk/ukgwa/20130129110402/http:/www.hm-treasury.gov.uk/d/Cox_review-foreword-definition-terms-exec-summary.pdf
Datar, S., Garvin, D., & Cullen, P. (2011). Rethinking the MBA: Business Education at a Crossroads. *Journal of Management Development, 30*(5), 451–462.
Dorst, K., & Cross, N. (2001). Creativity in the Design Process: Co-evolution of Problem–Solution. *Design Studies, 22*(5), 425–437.
Dunne, D., & Martin, R. (2006). Design Thinking and How It Will Change Management Education: An Interview and Discussion. *Academy of Management Learning & Education, 5*, 512–523.
Findeli, A. (2001). Rethinking Design Education for the 21st Century: Theoretical, Methodological and Ethical Discussion. *Design Issues, 17*(1), 5–17.
Formosa, K., & Kroeter, S. (2002). Towards Design Literacy in American Management: A Strategy for MBA Programs. *Design Management Journal, 13*(3), 46–52.
Glen, R., Suciu, C., & Baughn, C. (2014). The Need for Design Thinking in Business Schools. *Academy of Management Learning and Education, 13*(4), 653–667.
Gorb, P., & Schneider, E. (Eds.). (1988). *Design Talks! London Business School Design Management Seminars*. The Design Council.
IBM. (2020). IBM Awards its Three Millionth Digital Badge. [Online]. Retrieved May 11, 2021, from https://www.ibm.com/blogs/ibm-training/ibm-issues-its-three-millionth-digital-badge-and-disrupts-the-labor-market-in-the-process/
IBM. (2021). Enterprise Design Thinking. Retrieved May 8, 2021, from https://www.ibm.com/design/thinking/
ideo.cn. (2021). *Lead a Creative China 2030*. Retrieved May 8, 2021, from https://ideo.cn/en/news/tsinghua-ideo-lead-a-creative-china-2030
Johansson-Sköldberg, U., Woodilla, J., & Çetinkaya, M. (2013). Design Thinking: Past, Present, and Possible Futures. *Creativity and Innovation Management, 22*, 121–145.
Johnson, J., Alexiou, K., Creigh-Tyte, A., Chase, S., Duffy, A., Eckert, C., Gascoigne, D., Kumar, B., Mitleton-Kelly, E., Petry, M., Fen Qin, S., Robertson, A., Rzevski, G., Teymur, N., Thompson, A., Young, R., Willis, M., & Zamenopoulos, T. (2007). Embracing Complexity in Design. In T. Inns (Ed.), *Designing for the 21st Century Interdisciplinary Questions and Insights* (pp. 129–149). Gower.
Johnson, J. H. (2001). The 'Can You Trust It' Problem of Simulation Science in the Design of Socio-Technical Systems. *Complexity, 6*(2), 34–40.
Khurana, R., & Spender, J. C. (2012). Herbert A. Simon on What Ails Business Schools: More than "a Problem in Organizational Design". *Journal of Management Studies, 46*, 619–639.
Kimbell, L. (2011). Rethinking Design Thinking: Part 1. *Design and Culture, 3*, 285–306.
Kotler, P., & Rath, A. (2013). Design: A Powerful but Neglected Strategic Tool. In R. Cooper, S. Junginger, & T. Lockwood (Eds.), *The Handbook of Design Managament* (pp. 87–95). Bloomsbury Publishing.
Krippendorff, K. (2006). The Semantic Turn: A New Foundation for Design. *Artifact-Routledge, 1*(11), 51.
Kruger, C., & Cross, N. (2006). Solution Driven versus Problem Driven Design: Strategies and Outcomes. *Design Studies, 27*(5), 527–548.
Liedtka, J. (2018). Why Design Thinking Works. *Harvard Business Review, 96*(5), 72–79.
Liedtka, J., & Ogilvie, T. (2011). *Designing for Growth: A Design Thinking Toolkit for Managers*. Columbia Business School.

London Business School. (2021). *Innovation Through Design Thinking*. Retrieved May 8, 2021, from https://online.london.edu/innovation-through-design-thinking

Martin, R. (2009). *The Design of Business: Why Design Thinking Is the Next Competitive Advantage*. Harvard Business Press.

Matthews, J., & Wrigley, C. (2011). Design and Design Thinking in Business and Management Education and Development. In K. Voges & B. Cavana (Eds.), *Proceedings of the 25th Annual Australian and New Zealand Academy of Management Conference: The Future of Work and Organisations* (pp. 1–19). Australian and New Zealand Academy of Management.

MIT Management Executive Education. (2021). *Mastering Design Thinking: Create Value Through Systematic Innovation*. Retrieved May 8, 2021, from https://executive-ed.mit.edu/mastering-design-thinking?

Nomen, E. and BCD Barcelona Centre de Disseny. (2014). *€Design Measuring Design Value: Guidelines for Collecting and Interpreting Data*. https://beda.org/wp-content/uploads/2019/01/GUIDELINES-FOR-COLLECTING-AND-INTERPRETING-DESIGN-DATA.pdf

Rotman School of Management. (2021). *Business Design Thinking: From Insight to Innovation*. University of Toronto. Retrieved May 8, 2021, from https://execonline.rotman.utoronto.ca/business-design-thinking?utm_source=Google&utm_medium=c&utm_term=%2Bdesign%2Bthinking%2Brotman&utm_location=1007321&utm_campaign=B-365D_WW_GG_SE_RDT_Brand&utm_content=Rotman_Design_Thinking&gclid=Cj0KCQiAubmPBhCyARI

Schön, D. A. (1983). *The Reflective Practitioner: How Professionals Think in Action*. Basic Books.

Simon, H. A. (1969). The Business School: A Problem in Organizational Design. *Journal of Management Studies, 4*, 1–6.

Starkey, K., & Tempest, S. (2009). The Winter of Our Discontent: The Design Challenge for Business School. *Academy of Management Learning & Education, 8*, 576–586.

The Design Council. (2015). The Design Economy. https://www.designcouncil.org.uk/resources/report/design-economy-2015-report

WEF. (2015). New Vision for Education: Unlocking the Potential of Technology. [Online]. Retrieved May 20, 2021, from http://www3.weforum.org/docs/WEFUSA_NewVisionforEducation_Report2015.pdf

4 Organisational Complexity and Change by Design

Learning Objectives

- To develop an understanding of the complex nature of organisations and traditional management structures;
- To explore a range of contemporary issues in the management and governance of large organisations and their strengths and weaknesses;
- To examine external forces and unforeseen challenges that impact upon the organisation and the rise of unpredictable socio-economic environments;
- To introduce to the reader the role of change management and commonly used change management frameworks;
- To develop an understanding of design beyond traditional disciplinary boundaries whilst acting as a means for organisational change.

4.1 Introduction

The contemporary business environment is witnessing considerable change and uncertainty; as such, regardless of size and market activity, organisations have become increasingly vulnerable to external forces and market disruptions. Furthermore, set against the backdrop of Covid-19 and the massive challenges that it has presented to organisations and society, a radical reappraisal of established business models and organisational systems is urgently required. Many organisations, as well as national governments, swiftly realised that they were not prepared, reactively having to improvise due to their crisis response capabilities being too

Supplementary Information The online version contains supplementary material available at [https://doi.org/10.1007/978-3-030-94206-9_4].

Y. Huang, D. Hands, *Design Thinking for New Business Contexts*, https://doi.org/10.1007/978-3-030-94206-9_4

rigid and inflexible. Alongside this unprecedented event, globalisation, deregulation of trade and global markets have equalised organisational competitive environments in terms of access to human resources, information, and technological expertise. In order to remain competitive in these unpredictable times, organisations have to continually reinvent themselves through reappraising their structures, systems, and strategic objectives. Organisational agility and resilience are the new mantra influencing boardroom decision-making activities, where contingency and adaptability need to be woven into the fabric of the organisation. This chapter explores four interrelated key themes:

1. Managing complexity and the organisation, where in today's unpredictable marketplace, the need for constant innovation and consumer insight is critical in delivering meaningful value to ever demanding customer audiences. In order to achieve this aim, organisations have to create and implement the most effective frameworks and governance systems to manage effectively their day-to-day operations.
2. Following this, it focuses attention on managing uncertainty in order to be proactive and agile in responding to unforeseen challenges that may lie ahead. Recent events regarding global pandemics and environmental crises have delivered a wake-up call to organisations and governments alike to prepare for, and accept instability and market disruptions as a permanent fixture of strategic planning activities.
3. One such route to achieving this involves organisational change management and the ability to instigate and effect cultural change. Change is critical in ensuring that the organisation remains competitive in turbulent business environments. Three widely used change management frameworks are critically debated as to their relevance and applicability in today's hyper-connected business environment.
4. Finally, it offers an alternative approach to fostering organisational change, introducing design thinking and the plethora of creative tools and techniques that it beholds to the commissioners of change. Richard Buchannan's 4 orders of design is introduced as an alternative lens of view to that of the traditional management approaches commonly applied to change management. The chapter concludes by offering a series of review questions and exercises that draw upon many of the themes raised within this section.

4.2 Managing Complexity and the Organisation

As we move into an era of uncertainty, organisations of complexity are operating under extremely turbulent and dynamic market forces—many of which are beyond the control of the organisation. We are witnessing an ever-increasing pace of technological and market developments, coupled with increased customer demands and expectations. In today's increasingly crowded marketplaces, organisations (regardless of size) cannot be complacent in the delivery of their products and services—competitiveness and agility is now a commercial imperative and a prerequisite for long-term survival. It is widely acknowledged that the best route to commercial success is offering consumers both products and services that exceed their expectations, and at the heart of this—is the creation and delivery of added value products driven by innovation. These products and services that are offered to the consumer, are the end result of a set of complex and interrelated processes intelligently managed by the organisation.

In turbulent environments, in which organisations are currently functioning, and undoubtedly will be functioning for the foreseeable future, design remains the last valuable opportunity for the inspiration of creativity and the ability to formulate quick responses to latent market challenges. Central to the issue of organisational agility to respond to unforeseen market dynamics is that of size. At one end of the spectrum, SMEs can usually function with a single manager at the top, directing resource and vision in response to shifting market demands. At the polar opposite of the spectrum are large multinational organisations whereby the divisions of functions and human resource sit beneath many layers of hierarchy and decision making. Consequently, senior managers and decision makers in large organisations are often far removed from the point of delivery—be it a product or a service; or frequently, both. Furthermore, they are likely to have limited understanding of day-to-day operational issues, customer needs and quality difficulties, unless they make a specific point of gaining first-hand experience of customer interactions. Another limitation of hierarchy and division, is the frequently cited issue of fragmentation and miscommunication within the decision making process. The centralisation of these primary activities is often the barrier for organisational change.

Morgan (1988) describes these large bureaucratic organisations as 'machines' that are slow moving, cumbersome entities that are resistant to change and are slow to embrace and enact change. Research undertaken by Aronowitz et al. (2015) offers a bleak outlook for machine organisations when trying to accommodate change:

> When machine organisations have tried to engage with the new environment, it has not worked out well for many. A very small number of companies have thrived over time; fewer than 10% of non-financial S&P 500 companies in 1983 remained in the S&P 500 in 2013. [...] 82% of them went through a re-design in the last three years. However, most of these re-design efforts fail—only 23% were implemented successfully.

Another area of consideration is that large organisations are not homogenous entities per se, but complex systems comprised of many sub-parts, each with their own individual culture and identities. When an organisation expands its business operations, the variation amongst these smaller sub-groups; these sub-groups may include—production, marketing, sales, HR and so forth. Furthermore, clear lines of communication are important between these interrelated functions, especially within the development of products and services; sadly, often, as these functions increase in size, they move apart as opposed to becoming more closely aligned and integrated. Consequently, as information flows from outside the organisation into the relevant departments, it becomes more opaque and ambiguous, leading to the occurrence of unsound data and information having a detrimental impact on the design development process. Ghobadian and Gallear (1997) identify a series of insights as to the inherent limitations of large organisations when compared against SMEs. A select range of examples includes:

Structure

- Hierarchical with several layers of management—which in turn, leads to inefficiencies within the decision making process, as agreement and authority moves up through managerial levels of responsibility.
- Multi-sited and possibly multinational—poses significant challenges, in particular if new product/service introductions are desired in unfamiliar market territories. Furthermore, senior managers may be unfamiliar with market requirements when penetrating new market segments.
- Normally slow response to environmental changes—reminds us of the old analogy, 'Speedboats versus Supertankers' where more agile and responsive leaner organisations can adapt quickly to unforeseen external events and challenges; one such example are global pandemics, which as we are witnessing, causes huge problems and challenges to established business models.

Procedures

- System dominated—which often hinders innovative activities if the system cannot accommodate the desire for organisational creativity and creative individuals. One only needs to look towards Google, Facebook and Squarespace for leading examples of truly innovative companies.
- Rigid and unadaptable processes—where bureaucracy and superfluous procedures frequently hinder the effective flow of information within and throughout the organisation. This is particularly acute when there are significant geographical distances between each site and area of operation.
- Fragmented decision makers—who are often far removed from points of sales or contact with their customers. This is particularly prevalent in highly vertical/siloed organisations.

Behaviour

- Mostly bureaucratic—where the free flow of information between functions is reduced through paperwork and chains of decision-making. This could be exacerbated by a combination of points as above.
- Strongly departmental/functional mindset—is a mindset present when certain departments or sectors do not wish to share information with others in the same company. This type of mentality will reduce efficiency in the overall operation, reduce morale, and may contribute to the demise of a productive company culture.
- Cultural inertia—established organisations have developed their own cultural identity and practices, which over time could lead them to becoming more hostile to change and reticent to embrace new ideas and market opportunities. There

> is strong evidence that some organisations have cultures that are maladapted to their environment, and that this is reflected in their performance. Carrillo and Gromb (2007) point out, "Since homogeneity locks organizations in their current culture, there is an interesting trade-off between flexibility and gambling. On the one hand, organizations may decide to remain flexible enough to adapt to any environment change. This is achieved by allocating agents to both cultures. On the other hand, organizations may bet on whether the new environment will build on one of the existing cultures and screen all agents to fit in that culture"

However, it is worthwhile to point out here that not every type of large organisation is bureaucratic in nature. Alongside the continually changing social landscape, organisations are also changing in their structural configurations, morphing and adapting to the macro economic environment in order to become more profitable. Furthermore, with highly competitive markets and greater uncertainty, gives rise to the post-bureaucratic organisation, in particular, organisations operating in typical new industries such as IT, services and pharmaceuticals as opposed to traditional manufacturing. However, what connects the two organisational types, are the common themes of—division of labour, authority, and control. Bolin and Härenstam (2008) argue, "All workplaces have an organizational structure, as work tasks are carried out in a production process somewhere, and by someone, and have to be coordinated and controlled. Organizational structure provides a regularity that makes organizations independent of specific individuals and means that they are more than the sum of their individuals."

Division of Labour: In essence could be distilled as the specification of particular roles within the organisation and where they are assigned (i.e. located within specialised functions) in order to take place. Specialisation within this context refers to the production process that is then sub-divided into discrete areas of activity, regardless of how employees are assigned or associated to job specific tasks. However, it is worthwhile to point out here the distinct differences between the two types of organisations; in predominantly bureaucratic organisations, division of labour is more specialised in nature. Within post-bureaucratic organisations, it is more concerned with horizontal integration across business functions.

Authority: refers to the decision making structure within the organisation, be it centralised with the responsibility assigned to top management; at the opposite end of the spectrum, decentralised decision making is often delegated to specific functional teams, individuals or projects. Each approach has their own merits and weaknesses depending on the organisational type. When we turn our attention to creative organisations, it is so often the case where individual control of the decision making process encourages creativity, which in turn could lead to the development of innovative new ideas and concepts. Carrier (1996) adds, " Such a [decentralised] management structure would promote the entrepreneurial process, as employees would be able to vouch for their ideas without being hindered by unnecessary hierarchical levels. In addition, this structure would consequently mean a more informal relation between the top management and employees and enable a faster recognition of feasible ideas".

Control: In other words, it is the degree to which jobs and procedures within the organisation are controlled by standardisation of behaviour and how a task is carried out (Robbins & Barnwell, 2002). While adhering to rules is crucial in strongly bureaucratic organisations, personal discretion and the ability to make decisions independently are defining aspects of post-bureaucratic organisations. In sum, bureaucracy is characterised by specialisation, centralisation, and formalisation, while integration, decentralisation, qualitative and quantitative measurement of results and goal fulfilment characterise post-bureaucracy. (Bolin and Härenstam, ibid.)

Organisational Structures: A Brief Overview

Having outlined key characteristics of large organisations, it is now time to identify and discuss other common forms of business structures. The main objective of developing a business structure is so that employees know where they sit within an organisation and who to report to in terms of line management. Different organisational structures are shaped by the industry in which they operate, although they will vary considerably because every business is unique in terms of their own particular culture and values.

Flat Organisation—In essence, in a predominantly flat organisation, everyone is equal, where viewpoints and values are shared democratically amongst the employees. Often these types of organisations are referred to as 'self-managed' organisations where there are no hierarchy, seniority or job titles. However, in terms of scalability, this structure is often best suited to smaller companies, then over time, introducing more levels of management as the company grows in size—regarding practicalities of governance and operation, large organisations are not best suited to this type of structure. One such benefit of this structure is that the decision making process can be accelerated due to the lack of management hierarchy and chains of command.

Functional Organisation—which takes us back to the bureaucratic organisation, based on functional specialities and domains of knowledge. Common functional elements frequently include HR, Production, R&D, Marketing and so forth, where each department and function has a clear identity and reporting structure. Regarding the development of new products (especially where speed to the market is critical) often the decision-making process is hindered through achieving agreement between key individuals within each of the functions. In terms of ownership of ideas, as an example, if a new product concept is based on market pull factors (where a gap in the marketplace has been identified) usually the marketing function would lead on a project of this nature. At the other end of the spectrum, if the R&D function has identified new technologies that feature strongly within a product, this would be classified as a 'technology push' type of project, where they would be instrumental in leading it. A frequent source of tension that occurs is miscommunication between each of the functions when developing new products—at worst, leading to poor performance and sales when introduced to the market. Stringer (2000) argues, "most large firms are poorly equipped to implement a growth strategy based on radical innovation because most large firms are 'genetically' programmed to preserve the status-quo". In other words, these large firms do not have the right organisation, culture, leadership practices or personnel, to implement radical innovation. Over time, companies revise their organisational structures to accommodate growth and changes in the external environment.

Divisional Organisation—often refers to multinational organisations operating across international boundaries; however, divisions could also refer to specific market segments or particular consumer groups. This type of structure allows the large organisation to compartmentalise significant areas of business operation into tightly bounded groups. Furthermore, these groups would have distinct autonomy from the parent company, being able to manage their own operations based around products and or services that they offer. However, there are some inherent challenges associated with divisional structures; firstly, with a diverse range of organisational divisions, each one could (and often does) compete for resources from the parent company that may impede overall strategic objectives. In addition, to be successful, divisions must be well managed. Executive leadership is the single most important determinant of success for a company using a divisional structure. Secondly, the duplication of resources, where each division requires the same organisational functions—as in marketing, HR and so on, increases the cost of operations across all the divisions. It is not uncommon, for example, for a firm to adopt a functional structure in its early years. Then, as it becomes bigger and more complex, it might move to a divisional structure, perhaps to accommodate new products or to become more responsive to certain customers or geographical areas.

Matrix Organisation—is primarily a complex organisational configuration where employees report to a number of line managers. Often, this type of organisation is best suited to the management and delivery of large projects, where different specialisms are working closely together on a daily basis. In relation to the design and development of new products, the primary functions of marketing, R&D, Design and production, would form teams combining and drawing upon expertise from the varying departments at different stages of the project. Within this structure, employees would be usually report to the team leader and their line manager from their respective function. However, the drawback within this arrangement is that matrix teams are difficult to manage and diversity has been known to contribute to poor performance. In a research study undertaken by Oertig and Buergi (2006), they point out, "In the matrix setting, there was a tendency for project team representatives to listen more to their line function management than to the project team leader. It was important that the project leadership managed the influence of line functions by networking with higher-level line managers and lobbying as necessary. As an example, a project leader reported going to the line function head to ask for someone to be allowed to attend a face-to-face meeting abroad"

Organisational Attributes

In essence, an organisation is a dynamic system that a company (regardless of size) can use to create an authority and communication structure for their employees that supports the fulfilment of corporate goals. Having introduced the basic types of organisational structures, other key considerations need to be taken into account when selecting the most appropriate framework for the company. These include:

- *Levels of Management*—The majority of organisations consist of layers of management and or reporting structures. The top managers or CEO's occupy the most senior area of responsibility for the organisation, mainly creating overall strategic vision and goals. Sitting beneath these are Middle managers who report to top managers and allocate resources across the company. Furthermore, they are often responsible for actioning corporate strategies and directing their effective implementation throughout organisational strata. Then we come to first line managers who focus on day-to-day operational activities such as supervising employees and coordinating projects. The job titles vary considerably but include such designations as manager, group leader, office manager, supervisor, etc.
- *Macro Business Environment*—organisations need to configure themselves so that they are best prepared and most suitable to the conditions of the external environment in which they are operating. Businesses operating in highly dynamic market sectors need to be able to respond to highly fluid changes in the marketplace—high street retailing is one such notable example. Francesca Cassidy (2019) argues, "many high streets across the country are working towards this reinvention, making themselves "places to be". Others continue to struggle with 2018 seeing a slew of large retailers going into administration. The public wants more than a retail destination; they want a location to meet, eat and drink, a place for services and experiences, as well as shop. Retailers that can successfully reinvent themselves will reap the rewards through more customers and higher sales".
- *Growth Stage of the Organisation*—is a key driver in determining the structure of the organisation. Smaller start-ups often adopt a leaner more agile approach to the management and governance of their operations. Growth potential companies, who are more established, would need to move to a more stable structure that allows expansion and stability in order to move to the next stage of their life cycle successfully. Churchill and Lewis (1983) writing for the Harvard Business Review argue, "a company's development stage determines the managerial factors that must be dealt with. Its plans help determine which factors will eventually have to be faced. Knowing its development stage and future plans enables managers, consultants, and investors to make more informed choices and to prepare themselves and their companies for later challenges. While each enterprise is unique in many ways, all face similar problems and all are subject to great changes".

4.3 Managing Uncertainty in Unpredictable Times

Change is inevitable and as such, the organisation needs to be proactive and agile in order to respond to unforeseen challenges that may lie ahead. In stable, predictable market environments, change is incremental and can be accommodated for; however, 2020 witnessed seismic change that fundamentally transformed the business landscape—the global pandemic Corona Virus Disease (Covid-19). Widespread shutdown of commercial enterprises, restrictions in the movement of people both within and beyond national borders has affected virtually every sector of organisational and industrial life. Established business models and organisational practices have undergone dramatic re-appraisal in how we work, consume and lead our daily lives. Emerging from the ongoing chaos of Covid-19, it has necessitated innovations in the development, delivery and consumption of products and services. Anderson et al. (2021) based in the influential Pew Research Center, USA, undertook a research study to anticipate life following Covid-19, to consider what life will be like in 2025 in the wake of the outbreak of the global pandemic and other crises in 2020. Some 915 innovators, developers, business and policy leaders, researchers and activists responded. Their broad and nearly universal view is that people's relationship with technology will deepen as larger segments of the population come to rely more on digital connections for work, education, health care, daily commercial transactions and essential social interactions. A number of respondents described this as a 'tele-everything' world. Seetharaman (2020) points out, "the hospitality industry, world over, has faced a significant negative impact because of the lockdown measures many countries adopted, as it forced consumers to stay away from restaurants and cafes. While hotels and homestays are primarily meant for leisure and therefore, not considered essential, food is by itself an essential resource. Through the lockdown, restaurant regulars have shifted their preferences towards off-premise dining, drive-through food pickup, ready-to-eat meals, etc." The scale and extent of the uncertainty that business organisations are currently facing in this crisis is considerable; especially given the limited information about Covid-19 and its long-term impact. As such, this uncertainty is demanding that established operating models must contain a high degree of resilience and flexibility as situations evolve. Due to the severity of the global pandemic, the economic damage to businesses throughout the globe has exceeded early predictions by many leading business analysts. Now, the 'new normal' is continuous uncertainty and fluidity. Due to the severity of this crisis, many organisations are in a continuous struggle for their very existence. The severity and speed of the crisis are reflected in the International Monetary Fund's (IMF) projections for US GDP growth. After an estimated GDP expansion of 2.2% in 2019 (year-on-year), the US economy, in the IMF's view, was expected to grow at a rate of 2.1% in 2020 (forecast of October 2019). With the onset of the pandemic, the IMF quickly shifted its estimate into contraction, of −5.9% in April 2020, revised to −8.0% in June. The latest estimate (October 2020) is less severe at −4.3%, but this would still be the worst result in many decades. The forecasting institution foresees the world economy shrinking at a rate of −4.4% in 2020, after having grown 2.8% in 2019 (estimate). (imf.org, 2020).

In addition to global pandemics, there are more subtle and discrete changes that are continually arising (for some these are opportunities, others—distinct threats), namely that of the rise of IoT product systems that are transforming established marketplaces. Many leading companies have developed and strengthened their business models over many decades, but the shift to IoT is often more challenging for them. From tennis rackets to coffee machines, IoT has the potential to create endless disruptive innovations, often in a plethora of unforeseen business segments. Tony Shakib, Global IoT Business Acceleration Leader, at Microsoft Azure believes that we're at an inflection point where some companies are taking investment in IoT infrastructure seriously, allowing them to capture meaningful data, and integrate it into their workflow management systems. He points out, "Gradually we're crossing from the experimental phase to mass adoption", *he explains.* "Once we get there, we'll see real change. Once you start connecting devices and using data intelligently, the amount of innovation you can do becomes exponential." (IoT Business News, 2020). History can provide us with many examples of organisations and commercial enterprises that had failed to keep pace with market developments, the same could happen again to organisations that fail to embrace the digital revolution. IoT does not discriminate to any organisation, regardless of their expertise, prestige and heritage; it enables companies to provide the tools to shift away from traditional manufacturing to the fertile landscape of interconnect devices, services and holistic systems.

Alongside IoT offering many unique opportunities and threats to the organisation, the emergence of the circular economy should not be overlooked. Since the birth of the Industrial Revolution, circa eighteenth century, companies and their customers followed a linear path of consumption. Starting with extraction and manufacturing, then through to commercialisation and use, followed by disposal by the user. This model has been in operation for over 250 years, informing and shaping businesses and manufacturing operations in unison. In essence, the circular economy is an economic system aimed at reducing waste and the continual use of finite resources, often referred to as 'take-make-dispose'. On 4 March 2019, the European Commission adopted a comprehensive report on the implementation of their Circular Economy Action Plan (EU, 2019). It was an ambitious programme of Europe wide activities that covered the whole lifecycle of products, from manufacture through to consumption and subsequent disposal. In 2012, the average European used 16 tons of materials—and only 40% of that was recycled or reused. In terms of value, material recycling and waste-based energy recovery captured only 5% of the original raw-material value. Even recycling success stories such as steel, polyethylene terephthalate (PET), and paper involve the loss of 30 to 75% of the value of the materials during the first use cycle. On average, European businesses and households use materials only once (McKinsey, 2016).

Due to the harmful environmental impact caused by excess waste and the overuse of harmful non-biodegradable materials (in particular plastic waste), there is a fast growing cohort of consumers who are becoming more ethically minded regarding climate change and environmental care. Extensive market research identifies millennials as a growing body of customers who are demanding environmentally friendly products that are sustainable which heavily informs their purchasing decisions. In 2018, as part of its New Plastics Economy initiative, the Ellen MacArthur Foundation announced at the World Economic Forum in Davos, that the list of leading brands, retailers and packaging companies working towards using 100% reusable, recyclable or compostable packaging by 2025 or earlier has grown to 11. These included Amcor, Ecover, Evian, L'Oréal, Mars, M&S, PepsiCo, The Coca-Cola Company, Unilever, Walmart and Werner & Mertz—together representing more than six million tonnes of plastic packaging per year (Ellen MacArthur Foundation, 2018). As such, organisations need to radically re-think their business offerings, moving away from the traditional linear model of business practices, including risks associated with the use of scarce and non-renewable resources; prioritisation and sales of products produced with virgin resources; the failure to collaborate; and failing to innovate or adapt. These are all factors that will negatively affect the ability of organisations to continue business as usual; in an era of uncertainty, the need for change is an organisational imperative.

4.4 Organisational Change Management

Having acknowledged the need for change, there are many strategies that the organisation could adopt in order to effect meaningful change within the company. Change is critical in ensuring that the organisation remains competitive in fast moving environments. However, this process is not as straightforward as first anticipated. Balogun and Hope Hailey (2004) report a failure rate of around 70% of all change programmes initiated. It may be argued that this poor success rate indicates a fundamental lack of a valid framework of how to implement and manage organisational change as what is currently available to academics and practitioners is a wide range of contradictory and confusing theories and approaches (Burnes, 2004). In essence, change management is the effective implementation of a clearly delineated plan of activities and associated tools to lead the people side of change in pursuit of corporate objectives. In traditional management literatures, the organisation can draw upon numerous established change management models for adoption. The next few sections outline a number of common frameworks that are widely used in industry; each one with their own particular strengths and weaknesses. The following commonly known models for review include:

- Kurt Lewin's Change Management Model
- Kotter's 8 Step Change Model
- The McKinsey 7-S Model

Kurt Lewin's Change Management Model

Kurt Lewin was a German-American psychologist who first introduced his 'Three Steps Change' model in 1947, that featured three distinct areas of activity—(1) unfreezing, (2) changing, (3) refreezing (Lewin, 1947). Although simplistic in nature, it is still equally as relevant today as when it was first offered in 1947. The three simple stages can be developed in greater detail of application based upon the particular organisational context in which it is being used.

- *Unfreezing*: the first and arguably most important stage. Here, preparation for change is introduced to the department/organisation, and most importantly, to the employees who will feature heavily within this process. Lewis acknowledges that resistance to change is inevitable, so for change to be effective there is a need to replace organisational behaviours and attitudes to reinforce it (this is what Lewis called 'force field analysis'). In short, force field analysis is accepting and understanding the many different factors for and against making any planned changes. Although not actually a formal part of the model, the particular set of actions within the unfreezing stage may include—identifying what needs to be changed; ensuring buy-in from senior management/board of directors; and then, creating the need for change. Throughout this early critical stage, it is important to communicate the drivers for change and the benefits that change has to offer. Having now 'unfrozen' the established status quo, the model then moves on to stage 2 'Changing.'
- *Changing*: this is where the transition occurs, and the delicate implementation of change commences. Due to transitioning, employees could become resistant to change at this critical stage, therefore clear communication and leadership are important elements to alleviate their concerns. Furthermore, referring back to leadership, the encouragement of employees to participate within change implementation is vital.
- *Re-freezing*: the third and final stage 'Re-freezing' is to establish and embed the new sense of order achieved through the change process. What is important here is to create a new culture that fosters and supports new processes and systems that are in place. In addition, mechanisms should be in place to support change in the long-term; very easily old practices and mindsets could revert back to the pre-change culture, rendering the whole exercise redundant.

Although since its first introduction, the world has moved on considerably, but many aspects of the model provides an intuitive and fundamental understanding of how changes occur, in context of the social behaviours observed at an individual and collective level within a group or larger organisation (Fig. 4.1).

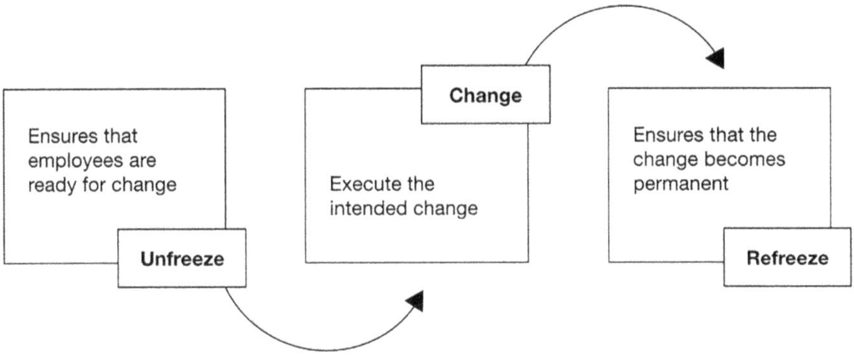

Fig. 4.1 Kurt Lewin's change management model (adapted by authors)

Kotter's 8 Step Change (1995) Model

Kotter is the Konosuke Matsushita Professor of Leadership, Emeritus, at the Harvard Business School, USA. Drawing upon his academic expertise in the complementary domains of business administration and the management sciences, Kotter pioneered his 8-step change model to full effect. What characterises his model to other change models is that the emphasis here is on senior management directing change as opposed to more of an employee perspective. Furthermore, it places heavy emphasis on the speed of implementation. The 8 component elements of the model include:

- *Step One*: Create Urgency: all effective change is a response to a problem and the first step is to identify a strong sense of urgency and the need for the implementation of organisational change. This 'messaging' is vital in ensuring that employees being a part of the change process understand the reasons that underpin this course of action. Common themes that drive the need for change may include one (or more) of the following forces—(1) shifting market demands; (2) increased competition from their nearest competitors or new market entrants; (3) changes in technology that may present either new opportunities or threats.
- *Step Two*: Form a Powerful Coalition: whereby senior business managers/leaders combine to drive the momentum for change. This in a way, signals a sense of urgency and agency to move change into a positive direction. Furthermore, managers could be coalesced from business units or functions such as marketing, HR, production and so on that reinforces the messaging from senior management.
- *Step Three*: Create a Vision for Change: Through the coalition of leaders driving the change management project, a strong and compelling vision for the post-change organisation needs to be clearly articulated to all stakeholders. In addition, the new core values arising from change need to be clearly understood and effectively implemented throughout the organisation; ambiguity and or mixed messages need to be avoided at all costs, which could have a detrimental impact to the overall process.

- *Step Four*: Communicate the Vision: The new vision needs to be integrated into activities of all individuals across the organisation, so if any one individual does not accept it, then it can lead to issues with synchronisation and cooperation. Kotter (1996) adds, "some key elements to effectively communicating the vision include repetition, explanation, the use of multiple forums, and leading by example".
- *Step Five*: Remove Obstacles: by removing the many obstacles that may hinder the process, these centres around the employees who are the ones primarily instrumental in the success of the project. This would involve identifying those most resistant to change and working with them to alleviate their fears or concerns.
- *Step Six*: Create Short-Term Wins: the introduction of a series of short-term achievable goals ensures momentum whilst supporting motivation amongst employees. Incentivising quick wins builds morale and shared vision throughout the organisation. Without short-term wins to celebrate, leaders and employees can easily get tired of the change process, become complacent and lose that all-important urgency.
- *Step Seven*: Build on the Change: based on Kotter's consultancy experience, he was a keen advocate to encourage the organisation to move beyond early successes and consolidate change. This could be achieved through establishing more ambitious targets and milestones thus ensuring continued momentum of change implementation.
- *Step Eight*: Anchor the Changes in Corporate Culture: The final and arguably the most difficult stage of the entire process is institutionalising the new organisational culture—in essence, embedding new behaviours, processes and habits that reflect and embrace the change[d] process. Following 'completion' of the change management process, it is imperative that the newly introduced management system aligns with the future direction and strategic growth of the organisation (Fig. 4.2).

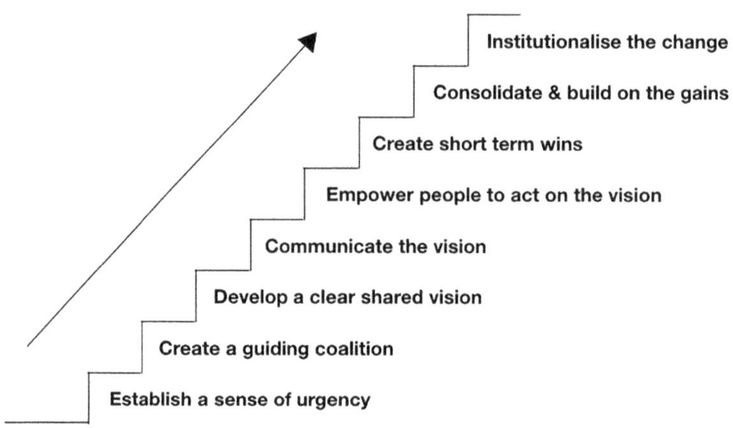

Fig. 4.2 Kotter's 8 step change model (adapted by authors)

The McKinsey 7-S Model

It was devised in the 1970s by Tom Peters and Robert H Waterman who are former consultants at McKinsey and Company. In essence, this framework provides a holistic understanding of how organisations function and enables the different elements to align to foster strategic transformation, in short—'Change.' Even though it has been over 30 years since the development of the model, it is equally as relevant today as it was then in the late 1970s. All the seven elements of the model have to be equally addressed, as the elegance of the model is that it needs to be understood and applied across all seven ['hard' or 'soft'] interrelated areas of consideration. These include:

- *Style*: in a way refers to leadership 'style' or as to how things are done in the organisation. Leadership informs and effects behaviours and attitudes, which in turns shapes the business towards a particular set of values.
- *Skills*: indicates the skills and skills deficits within the organisation; does the business have in place the right skills, knowledge and competencies to achieve corporate strategy.
- *Systems*: are the operational elements of the organisation; mainly focused upon and around procedures and processes. These would form an important part of any change management project.
- *Structure*: directly relates to the management structure, as discussed earlier, is the existing structure hierarchical or flat and so forth. Furthermore, is line reporting and the levels of authority clear to the employees as to who they report to.
- *Staff*: this is quite straightforward, it relates to employees and their general capabilities; plus, the number of staff and the diversity needed in each area to optimise organisational capability and capacity.
- *Strategy*: corresponds with the dynamic external forces, which may affect the organisation; does it have the right strategy in place to withstand external market changes and threats via competition.
- *Shared Values*: are the central focus of the model as these affect the other six elements of the change management process. Shared values centre on what the company believes in; what is its core mission and so forth (Fig. 4.3).

These three diverse change management models have their own unique strengths and weaknesses according to where and how they are used. There are many more comparable changes management models in existence, but these are arguably the most commonly used and understood. Turning our attention away from established models drawn primarily from the management sciences, we now focus on design and on how it can provide an alternative perspective when fostering organisational change.

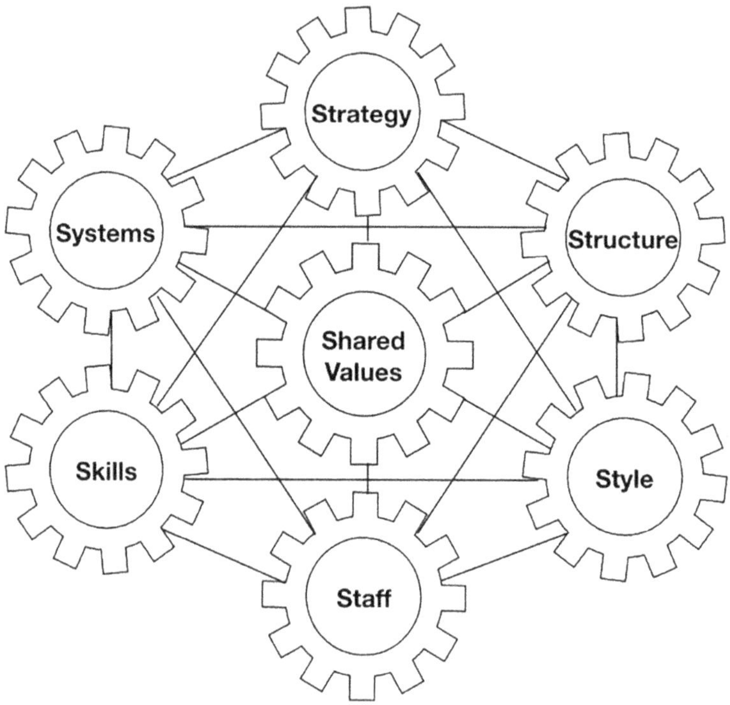

Fig. 4.3 The McKinsey 7-S model (adapted by authors)

4.5 A Designerly Approach to Organisational Change

As previously discussed, classic change management models offer a high-level framework for transformational change. However, design thinking could be an invaluable approach to fostering organisational and behaviour change. Other benefits of a design thinking approach may also include—developing a stronger and more robust customer orientation, better decision making and competitive advantage. Over the last ten years, design thinking has attracted the attention of senior management professionals, as indicated by the burgeoning amount of journal articles in management circles. Olson et al. (1998) argue that design can be translated into competitive advantage through the creation of customer value. Dunne (2011) lends further support to this sentiment by adding, "Designers seek to empathise with users and understand how the experience of use appears from their perspective". Kumar and Whitney (2007) concur by suggesting "in doing so, they hope to create innovations that appeal to unarticulated needs, and can become a source of competitive advantage". Design as a problem solving process could be introduced within the organisation, being deployed as an alternative means of competitive advantage where traditional methodologies and tools are insufficient in turbulent fast past markets. Furthermore, where existing data is either non-existent or insufficient, a design thinking approach to new market opportunities could yield significant results to the company. Management activities and routines in less turbulent markets are often, detailed, analytical and stable, characterised with predictable outcomes; outcomes that frequently cannot satisfy ever demanding market audiences. With strong emphasis on gleaning detailed user insights, design thinking for new business contexts could provide richer criteria for user-centred innovation. Firstly, the vast array of design's ethnographic tools could be applied to the ideation process, supported with input from other business functions, thus fostering a strong multi-disciplinary approach to innovation.

If unfamiliar with the use of an ethnographic approach to data collection, in essence it features observing end-users using products or services to gain a deeper understanding of their experiences, frustrations or modes of delight in their everyday practices. This approach can be focused solely on the individual or scaled wider to groups and communities. The use of tools to collect this information could be based on the complexity of the design project, as in, observing an individual using a particular product within the home right through to a community using public transportation. Due to the onset of Covid-19, the use of online digital tools has grown exponentially over the last 12 months, which has led to a series of innovations in the development of ethnographic studies. Subsequently, proactive, and entrepreneurial organisations have embraced these new approaches and methodologies, embedding them within their own design strategies and developmental systems. As such, these design orientated additions add an extra dimension of design 'capability' and 'Intensity' to organisational agility and resilience. By adopting a diverse range of data collection approaches (be it in person or online) organisations can redefine and/or augment their own existing resource base in the pursuit of innovation.

Often, such ethnographic data collection activities could lead to a 'shift' in perspectives from those taking part, moving from a place of 'judgement' to a place of endless 'possibilities.' This move towards 'reframing' the problem based on and around detailed user-insights limits the immediate need for 'quick' solutions. Design theorist Kees Dorst (2015) argues, "problem framing is one of the key design practices that make the method [problem re-framing] more likely to yield better solutions than conventional approaches to problem solving". To move the organisation to a more user-centred orientation, this philosophical shift could be strengthened by aligning departmental perspectives, thus allowing the prioritisation of information that decision-makers are working with. Heterogeneous teams (comprised of professionals drawn from the major functional disciplines) are commonly acknowledged to produce more creative and innovative solutions that afford real value to their customers. Liedtka (2018, p. 16) points out the merits of heterogeneous teams, arguing, "diversity brings new data and perspectives, whether from customers, internal colleagues or external networks, into the process that are capable of producing novel insights and solutions, often by inducing reformulation of the initial problem".

It is worthwhile to note, that with any change management process, fostering cultural change is a challenging task—even change driven by design. By embarking on a series of short design projects, confidence in the role of design as a driver for success will percolate throughout the organisation. This process is not without its risks, the often quoted mantra "fail faster, succeed sooner" by IDEO founder David Kelley holds true, that to be truly innovative, at some point there will inevitably be failures. In order to overcome this pitfall, a coherent and consistent communications strategy is vital to bolster the chances for successful change. To further support this sentiment, Thomas Jefferson, third US President, presciently adds, "if you want something you have never had, you must be willing to do something you have never done" which underpins the notion of design thinking as an organisational cultural mindset as opposed to a predefined process. The Design Management Institute identified that 'design-led' companies outperform other companies by 228% on the Standard and Poor's 500 index. (DMI, 2014) Through open collaboration between organisational functions, teams and individuals, behavioural attitudes will shift away from that of competition to one of collaboration. This in turn would foster the cultural conditions for the creation of meaningful value for the customer as opposed to extracting value from traditional management processes. One of the most authoritative voices advocating design for organisational change, Richard Buchanan (2015), succinctly articulates that:

> The principle of design that stands behind the organizational culture reform movement in which design thinking is central is grounded in the quality of experience for all of those served by the organization. This includes the individuals who directly use the products and services of the organization, but it also includes those who are affected by the internal and external operations of the organization and by those in society at large who are ultimately affected by the vision and strategies of the organization.

Buchanan (2001) proposed his '4 Orders of Design' model that positions product type and their area of influence and complexity. Traditional design disciplines are 'loosely' situated within each of the four orders, which demonstrates the increasing development of design as an emergent field of activity. The four orders include: (1) Communications, signs and symbols; (2) Objects and artefacts; (3) Interactions and experiences; (4) Environments and systems.

- *Communications, signs and symbols*: The first order is primarily information design, outlining the work of visual communication designers, mainly graphic and visual design (2D design). Specific themes of activity that sit within this include, typography, illustration, photography and print, which focus upon the nature, shape and meaning of symbols.
- *Objects and artefacts*: The second order embraces tangible, physical objects and artefacts, such as products, engineering and architecture (3D design). This type of design creates useful, usable and desirable products for people to use.
- *Interactions and experiences*: The third order includes the theme of design to create meaningful design interactions via services and experiences (4D design that is time and motion orientated).

- *Environments and systems*: The fourth order arguably is the most complex area of design activity within which the other three orders sit, covering architecture, urban planning, organisational design, systems architecture and so forth (Fig. 4.4).

Turning our attention towards the fourth order of design, this includes the discourse of design to effect change in cultures, systems and capabilities—with organisation/business design central to this process. We are now witnessing many leading multinational organisations (IBM being one notable example) radically implementing cultural change with design at the heart of this process. Strong leadership and support at the top of the organisation, is shifting organisational mindsets away from traditional command and control management approaches now introducing design capabilities into the wider organisational environment. This top-down approach (4th order design) would then permeate across business divisions, which would influence the other three orders that sit beneath it. Jenkins (2008) argues, "in effect, the design leader must be willing to take on the organization itself as the object of design, not just a particular product or process. This means both actively working to reshape the underlying cultural values on which the organization is based and being willing to challenge and rebuild some of the major organizational systems and corporate processes".

Jenkins (ibid.) based on his extensive industry consultancy experience, proposes a seven-point plan in implementing a designerly approach to fostering cultural change within the organisation. These can be summarised as:

- Be selective in choosing which organisations to work with: setting realistic expectations as to how design can accommodate and sit within the overall organisational culture. Identify with the senior management team where obstacles

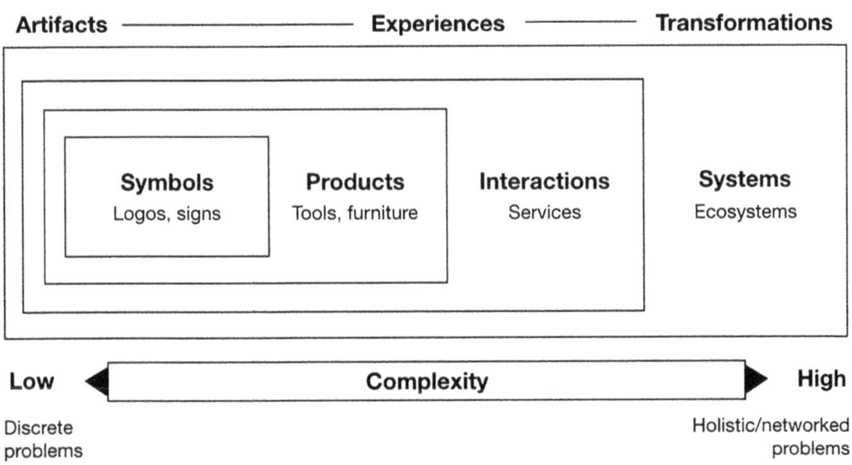

Fig. 4.4 Richard Buchanan 4 orders of design (adapted by authors)

could occur within their existing processes and systems, and identify on how design could change these parts of the wider eco-system. In essence, the challenge here is 'cultural alignment'.

- Work with senior leaders to build strong intent and an embedded culture of design: cultural transformation requires the firm commitment from the very top of the organisation in order to be truly effective. Jenkins adds, "for example, they should be able to demonstrate a strong awareness of where and how to use design, use a shared language about design processes, and ask good questions that reflect their familiarity with design thinking".
- Be a systems thinker: breaking down the organisation into a series of subsystems, then being to identify the most effective ways in changing those interrelated component parts. Each element could pose their own particular challenges, and as such, different strategies and methodologies may need to be drawn upon from the repertoire of design thinking tools.
- Focus on human interactions and social processes: to create a working environment that fosters and encourages meaningful human-to-human interactions in both formal and informal settings. Furthermore, with the removal of bureaucratic barriers, more time could be allocated to creative activities that could lead to innovative ideas for exploitation.
- Exercise well-directed discipline when implementing new processes: ensuring the commitment to change is maintained and that old processes and behaviours are discouraged. One such approach would be to implement an engagement strategy that extols the benefits of the change management process and where design is a fundamental part of its overall success.
- Kill some sacred cows: undertaking a fundamental review of key aspects of the company, be it established processes, systems and orthodoxies and question their relevance in the new organisational culture. This demonstrates commitment to change and would need authoritative support in order to demonstrate strategic intent.
- Help the organisation to learn more about itself from experience: finally, to encourage reflection and self-learning that reviews what worked and where pockets of resistance were encountered. This process of reflection should be considered as an ongoing process of continual learning and refinement that underpins the new organisational culture.

Chapter Summary With the rise of uncertainty and constant new challenges, organisations are beginning to realise that the old solutions put forward by management consultants are no longer enough sufficient in order to remain competitive. In the new market economy where consumers hold considerable purchasing power, the creation of meaningful value is at the forefront of business activities, and businesses are turning towards the design profession for their design thinking skills to foster transformative change. At the beginning of this chapter, it introduced the many differing forces that are impacting upon the organisation, in particular Covid-19 and the financial devastation that lies in its aftermath; not only to the organisation, but to the individual and society as a whole. Turbulent times and uncertainty are placing new challenging demands on how we act, think and organise our daily lives—this is no different from the organisation, regardless of size and areas of operation.

It then offered a series of insights into the diverse types of organisational structures that we see today. Each type of structure is informed by the industry in which the company operates, some are very unique to their particular industry, some very common, in a way, illustrating the rich and varied ways the business shapes itself in order to remain competitive. However, these structures have their own inherent and unique strengths and weaknesses that shape, form and influence their respective cultures and values.

In the quest for profitability and long-term survival, often it is necessary to embark upon transformational change. However, as this chapter discusses change and the complex issue of change management, it presents many challenges to the organisation in order to be successfully implemented. Three commonly known and widely used change management models were critically analysed as to their effectiveness and applicability; although the three discussed were one of the many models and frameworks currently being used by industry at present. Finally, we conclude this chapter by introducing design as a powerful tool to effect transformational change, or as Buchanan argues, the fourth order of design as a new and alternative means of fostering meaningful cultural change within the organisation. The following chapter will focus in more detail on how individual companies managed to achieve significant competitive advantage offered by design, and the many benefits that they secured to ensure continued survival and profitability.

Review Questions

1. Global disasters and environmental crises present many challenges to the organisation. Can you identify one notable example and describe how it affects the organisation?
2. Identify and critically debate an emergent theme that poses significant challenges to the long-term survival of large and complex organisations.
3. Select an organisational structure that you consider the most appropriate to its area of industrial operation; what are the elements that makes it unique to that particular industry setting.
4. What other change management models can you identify that would be specifically suitable for non-profit organisations as opposed to commercially driven businesses.

5. Julian Jenkins (2008) outlines a seven-point plan to drive change by design within the organisation; what other points would you consider to add to these that could further strengthen cultural change.

Project Questions

1. Global challenges encompass a vast array of themes, identify and critically analyse one such challenge where design could contribute a significant role.
2. List five leading organisations which failed to keep up with the changing consumer landscape. What are the factors that contributed to their inevitable demise?
3. With the rise of working from home, identify two significant challenges to the organisation in relation to team-based activities where creativity is fundamental.
4. Many organisations are hesitant to invest in design (in its broadest sense); create a hypothetical ten-point general plan outlining the benefits of design that would convince the CEO.
5. Identify one widely acclaimed example of a large organisation adopting a design thinking approach to foster transformational change; outline the key aspects of this approach that were fundamental to its success.

Chapter Tasks

1. The Aviation industry has been particularly affected by the global Covid-19 pandemic, identify 3 areas of operation that have been significantly disrupted; what recommendations would you provide that would minimise these risks in the future.
2. Within 60 minutes, list as many advantages that a digital start-up enterprise that could potentially challenge the dominance of a leading organisation within its established market sector.
3. You have the opportunity to pitch to your company CEO the benefits of design; provide a 5-minute speech articulating where design could specifically add value to the customer.
4. Identify a leading organisation and then create a simple SWOT analysis as to why they should undertake a change management project.
5. In a group setting, you have ten minutes to rank the most commonly used design thinking techniques in business; rank them in importance on an A4 piece of paper to be discussed amongst your group.

References

Anderson, J., Rainie, L., & Vogels, E. (2021). *Experts Say the 'New Normal' in 2025 Will Be Far More Tech-Driven, Presenting More Big Challenges*. [Online]. Pew Research Center. Retrieved March 05, 2021, from https://www.pewresearch.org/internet/2021/02/18/experts-say-the-new-normal-in-2025-will-be-far-more-tech-driven-presenting-more-big-challenges/

Aronowitz, S., Smet De, A., & McGinty, D. (2015, June). Getting Reorganisation Redesign Right. *McKinsey Quarterly*. McKinsey.com

Balogun, J., & Hope Hailey, V. (2004). *Exploring Strategic Change*. Prentice Hall.

Bolin, M., & Härenstam, A. (2008). An Empirical Study of Bureaucratic and Post-Bureaucratic Characteristics in 90 Workplaces. *Economic and Industrial Democracy*. Department of Economic History, Uppsala University, Sweden, *29*(4), 541–564.

Buchanan, R. (2001, Autumn). Design Research and the New Learning. *Design Issues, 17*(4), 3–23.

Buchanan, R. (2015, Autumn). Worlds in the Making: Design, Management, and the Reform of Organizational Culture. *She Ji: The Journal of Design, Economics, and Innovation, 1*(1), 5–21.

Burnes, B. (2004). *Managing Change: A Strategic Approach to Organisational Dynamics*. Prentice Hall.

Carrier, C. (1996). Intrapreneurship in Small Businesses: An Exploratory Study. *Entrepreneurship: Theory & Practice, 21*(1), 5–21.

Carrillo, J. D., & Gromb, D. (October 2007). Cultural Inertia and Uniformity in Organizations. *Journal of Law, Economics, & Organization, 23*(3), 743–771.

Cassidy, F. (2019). The Big Challenges Facing UK Retailers in 2019. [Online]. *Raconteur*. Retrieved March 4, 2021, from https://www.raconteur.net/retail/uk-retail-2019/

Churchill, N., & Lewis, V. (1983). The Five Stages of Small Business Growth. [Online]. *Harvard Business Review*. Retrieved March 4, 2021, from https://hbr.org/1983/05/the-five-stages-of-small-business-growth

DMI. (2014). Design-Driven Companies Outperform S&P By 228% Over Ten Years. [Online]. *The 'DMI Design Value Index'*. Retrieved March 23, 2021, from https://www.dmi.org/blogpost/1093220/182956/Design-Driven-Companies-Outperform-S-P-by-228-Over-Ten-Years%2D%2DThe-DMI-Design-Value-Index

Dorst, K. (2015). *Frame Innovation: Create New Thinking by Design*. MIT Press.

Dunne, D. (2011). User-Centred Design and Design-Centred Business Schools. In R. Cooper, S. Junginger, & T. Lockwood (Eds.), *The Handbook of Design Management*. Berg.

Ellen MacArthur Foundation. (2018). *Eleven Companies Take Major Step Towards a New Plastics Economy*. [Online]. Retrieved March 9, 2021, from https://www.ellenmacarthurfoundation.org/news/11-companies-take-major-step-towards-a-new-plastics-economy

European Union. (2019). *First Circular Economy Action Plan*. [Online]. Retrieved March 8, 2021, from https://ec.europa.eu/environment/circular-economy/first_circular_economy_action_plan.html

Ghobadian, A., & Gallear, D. (1997). TQM and Organisation Size. *International Journal of Operations and Production Management, 17*(2), 121–163.

IMF. (2020). A Long and Difficult Ascent. In *World Economic Outlook* (pp. 141–142). International Monetary Fund, October. Imf.org.

IoT Business News. (2020). Limitless Possibilities: Delivering Disruption with IoT. [Online]. Retrieved March 8, 2021, from https://iotbusinessnews.com/2020/09/25/98414-limitless-possibilities-delivering-disruption-with-iot/

Jenkins, J. (2008). Creating the Right Environment for Design. *Design Management Review, 19*(3), 16–22.

Kotter, J. (1996). *Leading Change*. Harvard Business School Press.

Kumar, V., & Whitney, P. (2007). Daily Life, Not Markets: Customer-Centred Design. *Journal of Business Strategy, 28*(4), 46–58.

Lewin, K. (1947). Frontiers in Group Dynamics: Concept, Method and Reality in Social Science. *Equilibrium and Social Change. Human Relations, 1*(1), 5–41.

Liedtka, J. (2018). *Exploring the Impact of Design Thinking in Action*. Darden Working Paper Series, University of Virginia.

McKinsey. (2016). *The Circular Economy: Moving from Theory to Practice*. McKinsey Center for Business and Environment—Special edition, October. [Online]. Retrieved March 8, 2021, from https://www.mckinsey.com/~/media/McKinsey/Business%20Functions/Sustainability/Our%20Insights/The%20circular%20economy%20Moving%20from%20theory%20to%20practice/The%20circular%20economy%20Moving%20from%20theory%20to%20practice.ashx

Morgan, G. (1988). *Images of Organisation*. Sage Publications.

Oertig, M., & Buergi, T. (2006). The Challenges of Managing Cross-cultural Virtual Project Teams. *Team Performance Management, 12*(1/2), 23–30.

Olson, E. M., Cooper, R., & Slater, S. F. (1998). Design Strategy and Competitive Advantage. *Business Horizons, 41*(2), 55–61.

Robbins, S. P., & Barnwell, N. (2002). *Organisation Theory: Concepts and Cases*. Pearson Education Australia.

Seetharaman, P. (2020). 'Business Models Shifts: Impact of Covid-19'. Opinion Paper. *International Journal of Information Management, 54*, 102173.

Stringer, R. (2000). How to Manage Radical Innovation. *California Management Review, 42*(4), 70–88.

5 Business Thinking Through Design

Learning Objectives

- To introduce the four main economic systems and debate their inherent strengths and weaknesses.
- To provide an understanding of the social economy and how design can support its continued growth as a means of widening social prosperity.
- To examine and debate three types of businesses and the basic forms of business organisation.
- To introduce the common types of business structures and liability implications for owners and shareholders:
- To provide a general overview of business formations and how design thinking can support the continual pursuit of innovation.

5.1 Introduction

The world is experiencing exceptional uncertainty, as humanity faces multiple crises ranging from health, economy and social to the natural environment. Nations confront specific tensions that demand individual (or regional) policy actions, financial conditions, socio-political responses and environmental changes. Even though these crises are systematic and global, they are also reflected in a diverse range of

Contribution by Dr Beatriz Itzel Cruz Megchun, Assistant Professor of Design & Innovation at Pamplin School of Business, University of Portland, USA.

Supplementary Information The online version contains supplementary material available at [https://doi.org/10.1007/978-3-030-94206-9_5].

Y. Huang, D. Hands, *Design Thinking for New Business Contexts*,
https://doi.org/10.1007/978-3-030-94206-9_5

business environments. Organisations face hypercompetitive environments, global economic failures, collapse of traditional business organisations, fast-pace management processes and crisis of trust and credibility in their branding activities. Their survival goes beyond planning new products, services, brand extensions or technological innovations. They need a refreshed, revitalised and rejuvenated approach to address complex, ambiguous, uncertain, volatile circumstances in their business operations while responding to continual global crises. Thus, governments must enable environments that facilitate systemic change. The education system should provide instruments that better prepare people for the economic, technological, environmental, social and political changes ahead.

Over the past three decades, prominent practitioners have called governments (and business managers) to adopt a 'design' perspective to consider these challenges from a system level. The business community have welcomed design thinking across all sectors of the economy (Beckman & Barry, 2007; Brown, 2009; Dunne, 2018; Kolko, 2015; Liedtka et al., 2017; Liedtka, 2018, 2020; Martin, 2009; Maeda, 2020). It is an approach to inquiry, cognitive processes and expression that complements and enhances existing skills, methods, techniques and attitudes. Its mode of analysis focuses on forms, relationships, behaviours and real human interactions and emotions, as its scholarly approach deals with social complex practice. Its impact is seen in organisational learning (Beckman & Barry, 2007; Smulders, 2004), decision making (Liedtka, 2015), customer orientation (Kumar & Whitney, 2007), innovation outcomes (Brown, 2009; Verganti, 2009), and competitive advantage (Martin, 2009; Verganti, 2016). Nonetheless, business people and the business press reduce it to an overly simplistic activity, process or toolkit that anyone can easily use, typically characterised as a step-by-step process with a human-centric approach that identifies problems followed by rapid prototyping that tests ideas to solve problems. It is assumed that it is an effective way to enable business people to think like designers, solve problems and drive profit.

Throughout the following subsections, the discussion will examine the application of design thinking within a business context. First, it will explore the different economic systems that might hinder or facilitate nations and/or businesses to thrive in the face of the twenty-first century challenges that lie ahead. It then discusses how mainstream economic systems and the new economic systems adopt design thinking to offer a more adaptive and resilient approach, in some cases approaches that support human and environmental well-being. Then, it focuses on the types of organisations and how they implement design thinking within their daily business activities. Finally, it will conclude with a discussion on the tensions and challenges experienced in implementing and adopting design thinking practices.

5.2 Economic Systems that Shape Business Environments

An economic system is a means by which governments or societies set a system of production to organise and distribute available resources, services and goods across a geographic area or country. These systems regulate the factors of production, including land,[1] capital,[2] labour[3] and physical resources. Most governments can shape their economic system using different mechanisms (institutions, agencies, entities, decision-making processes, and patterns of consumption) to allocate resources that ensure that producers and consumers obtain the goods and services they need. Therefore, governments need to study how various agencies and institutions connect, how information flows between them, and the social relations within the system (including intellectual property rights and structures of management). In addition, the government relies on economic theory to define the types of markets their economic system encourages and how much influence they exert over markets. This exercise helps answer questions about what to produce, how to produce it, from whom to produce it, and when to produce. Governments tend to select among four primary mainstream economic systems: traditional, command, market and mixed (Grossman, 1963; Mamedov et al., 2016; Reisman, 1995). Ergo, there are many types of economies around the world, and each has its own distinguishing characteristics. Moreover, each economy functions based on a unique set of conditions, static and dynamic components,[4] put in situ. In the following paragraphs, we will discuss the four mainstream economic systems.

1. *The traditional economic system*: is the oldest type of economy and still functions in rural nations closely tied to the land, based around agriculture, fishing, hunting or gathering. Their societies tend to be more close-knit and socially satisfied because their members play specific and distinct roles guided by customs, history and honour beliefs. It centres on family or tribe (traditions guide everyday life and economic decisions). It exists in a hunter-gathering and nomadic society that relies on barter to trade and produces only what they need. It might evolve to form some type of currency to trade. Examples of this type of economic system still exist in countries where nearly 70% of the population lives in rural areas and relies on subsistence farming, such as Yemen or Haiti. Similarly, it exists in countries with pockets of indigenous people who live in remote villages, such as those who live in the Amazon rainforest or the Arctic regions.

[1] Land, in economics, refers to the resource that encompasses the natural resources used in production. In modern economics, it includes all that nature provides, including minerals, forest products and water and land resources. Those organisations that use land have to pay a rent.

[2] Capital, in economics, describes anything that confers value or benefit, factory and its machinery, intellectual property, or financial assets, to its owner. It is a critical component of running a business day to day and financing its future growth. It may derive from the operations of the business or be raised from debt or equity financing.

[3] Labour, in economics, refers to the general body of wage earners. It includes any valuable service rendered by a human agent in the production of wealth. Labourers might have different amount and character of training, degree of skills, knowledge and capacity to direct their own work or the work of others.

[4] Static and dynamic components such as institutions, infrastructure, microeconomic environment, health and primary education, higher education and training, goods market efficiency, labour market efficiency, financial market development, technological readiness, market size, business sophistication and innovation.

2. *The command economic system*: has a centralised power (government) that plays a dominant role in the economy. The government focuses on the good for society to maximise social welfare rather than the individual or market. It creates a central economic plan that allocates all resources, sets priorities for producing goods and services, owns critical industries and creates laws, regulations and directives to enforce the plan. However, it discourages free market competition and innovation as it offers a healthy supply of resources, employment and affordable prices in goods and services for customers. Goods are not always based on consumer demands, the system does not allow taking risks required to create new solutions, and the inputs about consumers' needs lack measure and control. A command economy is a key feature of any communist society, such as the ones experienced in Cuba, North Korea and the former Soviet Union. China had a command economy for decades before transitioning to a mixed economy.
3. *The market economic system*: is where firms and households act in self-interest to determine how resources get allocated, what goods are produced and who purchases the goods. It has six characteristics that define them, private property, freedom of choice, motive of self-interest, competition, system of markets and prices, and limited government. The separation between the government and the market prevents the former from becoming too powerful. Its interest aligns with that of the markets. Governments may intervene by regulating or attempting to control fair trade, programmes, monopolies and so on. Consequently, people find many incentives for entrepreneurship, and businesses have reasons to innovate and be competitive. However, fierce competition may lead governments to provide support to vulnerable members of society, such as cover social welfare benefits and accessible healthcare. Currently, there are no purely free-market economies in the world, but some economies tend to be freer than others. The five countries with the most economic freedom are Hong Kong, Singapore, New Zealand, Switzerland and the United States (Fraser Institute, 2017).
4. *The mixed economy system*: is a combination of the free market economy and the command economy. Generally, the market is more or less free of government ownership except for few key sensitive industries. It incorporates policies that are social[5] and capitalist[6] in nature. As a result, private businesses can run more efficiently and reduce costs. At the same time, the government can correct market failures and use taxation policies to redistribute income in order to reduce inequality. Most developed nations in the world have elements of all three economies, making them mixed economies. For example, the United States

[5] Social (socialism) is a populist economic and political system based on public ownership of the means of production, machinery, tools and factories to produce goods. All legal production and distribution decisions are made by the government, and individuals rely on the state for everything from healthcare to energy, the government determines the output and pricing levels of these goods and services.

[6] Capitalist (capitalism) is an economic system in which private individuals or businesses own capital goods. The production of and services is based on supply and demand in the general market (market economy) rather than central planning (command economy).

leaves ownership of the means of production in most private hands. Still, it incorporates partial or total public ownership in some industries like defence and postal service.

These mainstream economic systems portray the whole economy with just one minimal image that reinforces a neoliberal[7] narrative of the state and the domesticity of the household. In recent years, public and private agencies have stimulated the market, and governments have promoted a range of design-led innovation process initiatives. They have established ambitious programmes towards the potential of design to stimulate innovation and accelerate economic growth across many industry sectors. Nations have seen a rise of open innovation labs to support design activities across sectors. Furthermore, they have established social impact investments to drive innovation for public good and to test public policy methods. For example, its application improves processes, develops new concepts and governance models and envisages new business strategies and services in the public sector. Designers have been drawing upon cultural learning theory, complex theory, institutional and behavioural theory to understand systematic conditions of the main problems or challenges, their value chain, the institutional or societal contexts in which they operate.

5.3 New Economic Systems Reshaping the Business Environment

The current mainstream economic systems work differently around the globe. Nations have distinct realities and societies that make it enormously complex to delimit their impact. However, there seems to be a growing consensus that these systems might not align with the scale of the challenges faced by humanity. There are clear symptoms of generalise failures, such as increasing social inequalities between rich and poor or raising numbers of people displaced due to global warming or conflicts. Therefore, societies need to collectively reimagine a world where they build the foundations of something new. Academics, researchers, advisors and non-governmental organisations, among others, are creating new narratives about the power of the market, the partnership with the state and the creativity of society. They have designed plausible ways to redistribute wealth, focusing on controlling land, enterprise, technology, knowledge, and the power to create value. These new economic systems tend to have a multilevel approach that addresses different levels of networks and complex interconnections. Their application can be seen from the individual, community, business and city levels to the regional level. They can co-exist inside the mainstream economic systems. Still, their origin is to become an

[7] Neoliberalism is a term used to describe the twentieth century ideas associated with economic liberalism and free-market capitalism. It is generally associated with policies of economic liberalisation, including privatisation, deregulation, globalisation, free trade, austerity, and reductions in government spending to increase the role of the private sector in the economy and society.

alternative to these existing economic systems. The most prominent emergent systems feature the sharing economy, circular economy, doughnut economy and social economy.

- *The sharing economy*: is a socio-economic system built around sharing (the excess capacity of) resources. The sharing economy is often used as a general umbrella term for new merging concepts such as collaborative consumption, collaborative economy, peer-to-peer economy or the gig economy (WEF, 2017). However, many of these terms simply refer to relatively new methods of interaction facilitated by centralised online platforms. This peer-to-peer (P2P) based activity uses information technology and platforms to enable individuals, corporations, non-profits and/or government in distributing, sharing and/or reusing goods and services. For example, its application at the community level focuses on initiatives that increase the sense of belonging, create social bonding, promote values or achieve a social mission through a collective project. Whereas, when we regard it as a business model, we regard it as an organised interaction. Individuals make money from underused or idle assets that can be rented or shared as a service when not in use. It differs from traditional businesses where employers hire employees to produce products to sell to consumers, as it has three distinguishing features. First, they use digital technologies to match buyers and sellers. Second, they capitalise on idle capacity and third, they rely on people building trust (trust verification). Recently, it has evolved to include business-to-business (B2B) interactions and co-working, peer-to-peer lending, fashion, and freelancing platforms. For instance, in China, companies like MoBike (bike-sharing) and Molisan (umbrella-sharing) supplement the supply of services in demand periods of peak demands. Criticisms often involve regulatory uncertainty, lack of government oversight, abuses of buyers and sellers, and fear of increased information that is widely shared.

- *The circular economy*: aims to redefine growth by building a sustainable society regarding economic, natural and social capital. It proposes a closed-loop system based on re-using, sharing, repairing, refurbishing, re-manufacturing and recycling that minimises resource inputs, the excess creation of waste, pollution, and carbon emissions. The objective is to gradually decouple economic activity from consuming finite resources and designing waste out of the system. This model enables a new form of society and an economy more autonomous, sustainable and mindful of environmental resources. Organisations rely on fundamental principles of sustainable procurement, eco-design, industrial and territorial ecology, economy of functionality, responsible consumption, waste prevention, management and recycling to conceive new processes and solutions for optimising resources and using and re-using waste. The Dutch government aims to implement the circular economy by 2050. They have implemented government-wide programme across several ministries to create a safe and healthy human environment. For example, some of these programmes handle raw materials more efficiently, such as the From Waste to Resource (VANG), Green Growth and Biobased economy.

- *The doughnut economy*: aims to meet the needs of all within the means of the planet (Raworth, 2017). It ensures that everyone has access to life's essentials such as water, food, housing, healthcare, education, income and work, peace and justice, political voice, social equity, gender equality, networks and energy. It also guarantees that collectively we do not exceed our pressure on Earth's life-supporting systems on which we fundamentally depend (stable climate, fertile soils, protective ozone layer, ocean care and biodiversity life). This system acts as a compass for human progress. It draws inspiration from complexity theory, ecological, feminist, institutional and behavioural economics. Amsterdam is the first city in the world to adopt the doughnut economy officially. The Amsterdam Donut Coalition involved different players in collecting data, analysing scenarios and drawing up proposals. They aim to achieve a zero-impact city by 2050.

- *The social economy*: encompasses various organisations, cooperatives, mutuals, associations, foundations and social enterprises that occupy the space between the state and the market. These organisations place priority on individuals and social objectives, voluntary and open membership, democratic governance, general interest, defence of solidarity, cross-collaboration, autonomous management, and reinvestment of most profits. The central premise is on satisfying needs or solving complex problems that have been ignored or inadequately fulfilled by the public or private sector. They pursue economic practices that are sustainable and inclusive: (1) by addressing societal needs; (2) by organising economic activities built on local roots; and (3) by working in close cooperation with other economic actors and relevant stakeholders (OECD, 2020). They support alternative ways of organising economic activities that might be adopted by the rest of the economy, such as fair trade, organic food movements or ethical and social investment.

The adoption of design thinking in mainstream and new economic systems has experienced a significant rise over the last decade. Organisations capitalise on it via equipping people with instruments to face contemporary challenges such as interconnected and diffused economic, social patterns, blurred governance boundaries and reduced trust in public actions (UNDP Global Centre for Public Service Excellence, 2014). It has two broad applications, either as policy formulation or as public service delivery. In the former, it facilitates an iterative process where multiple stakeholders engage progressively to refine feasible solutions. Team leaders use ethnography, behavioural science, communication, design and architecture, among other fields and skills to frame problems. They explore and consider multiple perspectives to give voice to everyone that will be affected by policy decisions. They experiment with potential ideas to reduce the risk of inconsistencies or duplication of actions and minimise unintended consequences. In the latter, design thinking helps develop, adopt, and implement policies while bolstering their legitimisation. It encourages small-scale and local initiatives that prove effectiveness, create momentum and possibly facilitate potential scaling of policies. It also simplifies the logistical arrangements required for the implementation of policies. Bason (2010, p. 139) argues, "design thinking represents a structured and systematic attitude or a way of reasoning that allows bridging and managing two opposing (yet complementary) cognitive styles, analysis and synthesis". The analytical attitude mindset encourages rational, logical and deductive processes that lead to thinking through solutions. Teams are cross-disciplinary, facilitating single disciplines proposals and effective outcomes. Conversely, the synthesis attitude fosters emotional, intuitive and inductive processes that promote thinking through doing and challenge existing paradigms. T-shape people work in multidisciplinary teams that co-create to deliver meaningful outcomes.

5.4 Types of Organisations

A nation's prosperity is created through the capacity of their industries to innovate. They rely on the composition of different types and forms of businesses to compete. Some nations succeed in particular industries because their contextual environment, national values, cultures, histories and institutions contribute to their success. As well as, they rely on economic systems that may support their competitive advantage. Each entity uses financial resources to provide goods and/or services to customers (consumers or businesses) in exchange for money or other goods and services. To be a viable business, they need to generate a financial return in exchange for work undertaken, time spent, and risk taken (satisfy the market and make a profit) to become a viable business. They adopt different forms of ownership that entail distinct cultures, beliefs, and assumptions about how they measure success and what their core values are. This section will introduce three main types of business and the basic forms of business organisation.

- *Service businesses*: focus on the exchange between providers and users. They are a people-centric entity that is related, social, temporal, and the interactions are unpredictable and uncertain. Service providers perform a particular activity that results in some benefits that include a specific output and/or involve a specific experience. In comparison, service users need to see value in the output, the experience or both as they are willing to pay for it or exchange for something else of equivalent value. They are organised under three broad categories: (1) typical service categories include transportation, restaurants, banks, phone and internet services, entertainment, healthcare and education institution. (2) Utility service categories concentrate on water, plumbing services and gas electricity. Finally, (3) digital service categories focus on social media platforms, communication and data sharing platforms facilitating exchanges. This industry represents 70% of the Gross Domestic Product (GDP) in a number of countries, such as the United States of America, the United Kingdom; Hong Kong, Luxembourg, Lebanon, France, Portugal, Denmark, among others (The World Bank, 2021).

- *Merchandising businesses*: buys products at wholesale price and sells the same products at retail price. They do not change the form of the merchandise, only stock inventory. The origin of their profits is by increasing the price of the selling products. Some categories include departmental stores, grocery, hardware, clothes and accessories shop, consumer electronics, home furniture, appliance store, drug stores and so on.

- *Manufacturing businesses*: buy raw materials to transform them into new products. They combine raw materials, labour, and overhead costs within their production processes. The nature of their offering is interchangeable, as the key attributes are natural, and the factors of demands depend on their characteristics. The buyer is the market and therefore the supply method is stored in bulk. Categories include food processing, textile production, metalwork, oil refineries, shipbuilders, and so forth.

The demand for design and its use can change across industries, types and size of organisations. Industries have organisational and structural differences, but they share a growing interest in customer experience and a progressive liberalisation with the entry of new players. The widespread application and use of radical new technologies have facilitated new types of businesses and organisational structures. Augmented reality, automation, artificial intelligence, blockchain, cryptocurrency, machine learning and the internet of things (IoT) have become the dominant mode where we experience everyday interactions. As a result, organisations, especially digitally based services are investing in a human centred design approaches to create products and services that humans can adapt and accept. According to *Design Thinking for Business* (2020, p. 4), design thinking is booming in industries where digital transformation requires new competencies and capabilities for developing meaningful customer experiences. This approach looks at value and exchange from user's perspective and what is meaningful for them. It combines three factors:

- Technology (feasibility) concentrate on how things are made and how their process performance improves;
- People (desirability) focuses on how things are valuable for customers (brand);
- Business (viability) emphasises how organisations can profit from offering them.

Design thinking adopts different forms and interpretations according to the companies' nature, the specific challenges and project objectives. For example, some organisations can use new technologies as enablers of more fluid and less bounded entrepreneurial processes and outcomes. Similarly, they can have a continuous evolution of the offering's scope, features and value. *Design Thinking for Business* (2020) suggests four generic implementations of design thinking.

1. *Creative problem solving*: concentrates on solving wicked problems adopting both analytical and intuitive thinking. This design thinking approach is one of the most widely known and used among organisations. Teams undergo an iterative process to understand user needs and latent desires to unveil and create ideas to solve wicked problems. The process starts outside, as researchers need to observe users interacting with products and services to understand user behaviours' complexity and dynamism (desirability). They employ a cross-disciplinary team that interprets these observations, shares insights, makes sense of the vast amount of data and identifies opportunities for new solutions. Here, designers facilitate combining the conscious and unconscious mind, rational thought and

imagination, to inspire original solutions. They transform innovative ideas into tangible prototypes to interact and test with users, obtain feedback, and learn from failures. They learn to frame and reframe the problem throughout the process while experimentation becomes fundamental to validate or confirm previous reflections and hypotheses at different stages of development. The solutions may provide incremental or even radical improvements to the products or services offered by the organisation.

The National Australia Bank (NAB) is one of the four largest financial institutions in Australia. It ranked the 21st largest bank in the world measuring market capitalisation and 52nd largest bank in the world measuring total assets in 2019. It serves around 12.7 million customers across Australia, New Zealand and Asia. It partnered with Oliver Wyman, an American management consulting firm specialising in financial institutions, to improve its financial results and financial products. They developed a new solution, called the NAB Quickbiz Loan, for their small and medium-sized enterprises (SMEs) clients. They applied design thinking through five distinct steps (empathise, define, ideate, prototype and test), where they worked backwards from the client's needs to create a truly compelling product. They identified four main issues: (1) the loan process was too complex, SMEs predominantly prefer unsecured product options, online/mobile services, which make the largest difference in the credit experience, and the process was time-consuming (Oliver Wyman & IESE, 2017). In the ideation stage, the team agreed that the product should be radically simple (access anytime, anywhere), out of friction (data available) and rapid decision making (automated data). The final output consisted of a three-step online application linked to a dynamic cash-flow credit model that provides unsecured business loans up to $50,000 to SMEs.

2. *Sprint execution*: aims at accelerating the development process between the generation and execution of ideas while reducing risk and uncertainty in launching new solutions to the market. It emerges from the hybridization of creative problem solving and the lean-agile[8] movement. Businesses that rely on digital technologies have increased their possibility of accessing many ideas and opportunities and speeding up the development process. Furthermore, they challenge setting time constraints and iterations on the effectiveness of the process and of executing subsequent ideas. The process starts with teams conceiving new ideas brought into a product or service and tested with users to obtain feedback (inside-out approach). Teams are composed of experts (usually internal stakeholders) who can deal with different categories of constraints and opportunities from other business units within the firm. Their objective is to design a product

[8] Lean and Agile movement is a new management approach and an enhanced company culture that enables business agility. Their methodologies took root in IT organisations. These methodologies help businesses to move faster and produce higher-quality offerings. Their principles promote focusing on work and the processes through which workflows, rather than the people responsible for the work.

concept or an innovative idea and make products ready to be launched on the market in line with users' needs. The product is the principal vehicle to capture the value and learn from the reactions of the marketplace. The experimentation in the sprint execution significantly leverages the contributions of minimum viable products[9] (MVP) to obtain feedback for future developments. MVPs allow the team to gain insights from early adopters of a product and to explore market viability. They are not the final product but the means to learn the reaction of potential users earlier within the development process. Teams learn by doing, as they accrue knowledge through the development and interaction with products and services.

Spotify is a Swedish audio streaming and media services provider. It is one of the world's largest music streaming providers, with over 356 million active users and 158 million paying subscribers. It uses a people-driven model, an autonomous approach for scaling agile and increasing innovation and productivity. This model champions team autonomy, communication, accountability and quality so that each team (or squad) selects their framework (e.g., Scrum, Kanban, etc.). Squads (cross-functional autonomous teams) are organised into tribes (feature area) and guilds (passion about a topic) to help keep people aligned and cross-pollinates knowledge. Designers join these teams to facilitate the improvements of features, the creation of experiences or the design of new services and systems innovations (Spotify, 2019). Each new project aims to keep humans-in-the-loop to create frictionless process and enhanced human experiences. The design team developed a website, Spotify Design, where they share tools and stories that they use in their design process.

3. *Creative confidence*: focuses on promoting an innovation mindset to engage employees with a new set of approaches, practices and methodologies to foster innovation and change. Design thinking is a medium to reshape the organisational culture and enable transformations through people. This approach uses human-centeredness and deep empathy-based methods to co-design a shared sense of purpose that inspires employees. This approach enables employees to feel confident in facing organisational changes and innovation challenges, allowing them to propose (design) and realise (develop) the change according to their beliefs and attitudes. Engaging key stakeholders to feel confident with new perspectives and horizons stimulates proactive behaviours and creates the appropriate premises to deal with innovation challenges. It also engages and keeps its employees motivated. Furthermore, these improvements can be incremental or even radical organisational innovations.

   Ericsson is a Swedish multinational leading provider of telecommunications, networking, and Information and Communication Technology (ICT) to service

[9] A minimum viable product (MVP) is a version of a product with just enough features to be usable by early customers who can then provide feedback for future product development. Developers typically deploy the product to a subset of feasible customers, as they are more likely to provide feedback and able to grasp a product vision from an early prototype or marketing information.

providers. It aims to create technology and services that are easy to use, adopt, and scale, making customers communicate successful in a globally connected world. Ericsson's CEO Hans Vestberg introduced in 2010 a companywide transformational initiative called Innova (design thinking approach). It was an internal programme that functions as a systematic approach to innovation. It intensifies already existing ideas so that employees can convert them into marketable concepts. The Innova system consists of several elements, which included VC funding model; the Innova squad (a team of internal innovation consultancies); an incubation process to advance ideas into products; an innovation ecosystem to collaborate with partners and universities; and Innova method (based on design thinking). Since its three years of operation, the platform holds 6000 users, and more than 4000 ideas were submitted, with more than 450 ideas receiving first-round funding. Innova's incubation process aims to take further and realise what employees have formulated thus far.

4. *Innovation of meaning*: concentrates on creating an innovative vision that supports new strategic directions. It allows identifying a novel purpose (a new 'how' and 'why'), redefining the problems worth addressing and providing a new interpretation of what is meaningful to customers/users. Teams use a human-centred design approach to observe users and become inspired for new solutions, as they need to interpret what is good or bad and define new meanings. They utilise curious criticism to unveil what lies beneath the surface to develop richer and more robust interpretations. Selecting few interpretations and going deeper with fewer perspectives, contrasting them, and fusing them can help create a powerful, robust and meaningful vision. It is vital to debate and criticise to stimulate progress, which requires comparing different perspectives and leveraging curiosity. Subsequently, the organisation selects experts who address the same strategic context but from different perspectives to reflect deeper on the implications of the emerging vision. Continuous debates with interpreters allow companies to exchange information and then test the robustness of their assumptions. Organisations use metaphors to represent concepts and emotions that are new and abstract, such as new meanings.

   IKEA is a Swedish founded, multinational conglomerate that designs and sells ready-to-assemble furniture, kitchen appliances and home accessories, services and home appliances. It integrates democratic design into its business policy and designs the principles that everyone has the right to purchase high quality, sustainable and well-designed products at an affordable price. This vision aligns with Ikea's sustainability strategy to make everyone's home environmentally friendly by saving energy, reducing excess waste, and depend on recycled and renewable materials. Design thinking helped identify novel purposes that align with their higher values, such as supporting UN sustainable development goals. In addition, they facilitated re-thinking the inner workings to ensure that shareholders inside and outside of the company implemented the new vision. They worked directly with suppliers to ensure the IKEA code of conduct, IWAY (IKEA for suppliers, 2021), the quality of production and working conditions. They also selected sustainable raw material as part of their design process, thus ensuring that their products are renewable, recyclable and recycled.

5.5 Business Structures

Business managers leading any organisation need to understand the challenges and opportunities inherent to their industries competition. They need to be aware of standard business and management processes, practices and the dependent ways in which different enterprises relate and operate. Businesses have an organising framework legally recognised in a particular jurisdiction for conducting commercial activities, such as sole-proprietorship, partnership, limited liability company, corporation (certified B and corporation S (S Corp), close, non-profit) and cooperative. This framework facilitates an organisational system that supports distinct cultures, beliefs and values. This culture can lead to a meaningful and powerful advantage when investing time and resources in promoting the value inside and outside of their organisations about their mission and new products or services design (process).

- *A sole proprietorship*, also known as a sole trader, is owned by one person solely liable for it and any profits made or debts incurred. The business assets and liabilities are not separate from the owners' personal assets and liabilities. They may work alone or hire employees or enlist the services of independent consultants. These low-risk businesses and owners who want to test their business idea before formalising a more formal business entity tend to choose sole proprietorship. One disadvantage is that it can be difficult to raise money because they cannot sell stocks, and banks are hesitant to lend money.
- *Partnerships* are businesses owned by two or more people. They can be either limited partnership (LP) or limited liability partnership (LLP). The former has only one general partner with unlimited liability, and the rest of the partners have limited liability defined by a partnership agreement. Profits are passed through to personal tax returns and the general partner, the partner without limited liability must also pay employment taxes. The latter protects each partner from debts against the partnership. Partners will not be responsible for the actions of other partners. Its advantage is that partners contribute with money, property, labour or skills to become a viable business.
- *Limited liability Company (private or public)* is a business structure allowed by state statute. It takes advantage of the benefits of both corporation and partnerships business structures. It protects members from personal liability in most instances. Their personal assets (cars, house and saving accounts) will not be at risk if their LCC faces bankruptcy or a lawsuit. LCCs can be an ideal choice for medium or higher-risk businesses, owners with significant personal assets they want protected.

- *A Corporation* is a legally separate business from its owners. It is overseen by a board of directors, who hires managerial staff to run the corporation. Assets and liabilities belong to the corporation, not the owners. In configuring a corporation, prospective shareholders exchange money, property, or both for capital stock. A corporation generally takes the same deductions as a sole proprietorship to define its taxable income, and it can also take special deductions. It conducts business, realises net income or loss, pays taxes and distributes subsequent profits to shareholders. In contrast, the Non-Profit Organisation (NOP) is a business that has been granted tax-exempt status because it furthers a social cause and provides public benefit. They are called NOPs, and the donations received are typically tax-deductible to individuals and businesses. These are earned through fundraising activities. It is important to emphasise that this term is not interchangeable with a Non-Governmental Organisation (NGOs). Its generic definition is a voluntary group or institution with a social mission, which operates independently from the government. NGOs can vary from country to country in their legal definitions, permitted activities, monitoring and oversight.
- *Certified B corporations* are new forms of organisations that blur the boundaries between the for-profit and non-profit sector by adopting social and environmentally driven missions while generating profit to sustainably accomplish those missions (Haigh & Hoffman, 2012). They are legally required to consider the impact of their decisions on their workers, customers, suppliers, community and the wider environment. These type of organisations demonstrates viable new business models that generate mutually enriching correlations among economics, social and environmental value creation. Shareholders hold the company accountable to produce a certain degree of public benefit in addition to financial profits. The overarching goal is to create a positive triple impact towards the economy, society and environment by using the forces of a for-profit business.
- *A cooperative* is an organisation owned and operated for the benefits of those using its service. Its members share decision making authority, profits and earnings generated by the cooperative. Members can become part of the cooperative by purchasing a share, although their shares do not affect the weight of their vote. The cooperative model is increasingly becoming very popular across many industry sectors.

Design thinking implementation is versatile across industries like agriculture; arts entertainment and recreation; automotive; consulting; education; energy; engineering; finance and insurance; food and beverage forestry and fishing; healthcare; hospitality; information and communication; manufacturing; mining; public administration; real estate; retail; transportation and logistics. Its application and impact on the organisation can differ upon whom or which business unit is sponsoring its implementation, the board, business development, design, human resources, information technology, marketing, operations, research and development, and sales. Its outcomes can have different internal and external impacts such as market innovation, organisational innovation, process innovation, technological innovation, product/service innovation and business-mission innovation. It also supports businesses established in different organisational frameworks.

5.6 Business Composition

The different historical conditions, economic developments and industrial structures shape each nations' business and industry. Organisations face pressures regarding the changes in the dynamic of the business environments and customer preferences. They make internal and external decisions to survive. Some organisations prioritize introducing a market orientation strategy to acquire, disseminate and respond to feedback obtained from customers, associates and competitors. Those firms concentrating on market orientation (Narver & Slater, 1990) and learning orientation (Sinkula, 1994) influence the firm's overall innovativeness and competitiveness. However, these circumstances do not apply to all sizes and types of businesses established in emerging, developing, and developed nations.

Defining the size of businesses may vary by industry and country. Table 5.1 exhibits diverse definitions from Australia, the People's Republic of China, the European Union, the United Kingdom and the United States. It uses generic information addressing different business dimensions through formulated variables as the number of employees, an annual turnover (the amount of money taken in a particular period) or a balance sheet (a statement of a company's assets and liabilities). As seen from the statistics within the table, there is a disparity in the headcount, turnover and/or balance sheet between China and the other nations. Chinese businesses that are small, medium and large-sized businesses almost double the headcount of employees. The rest of the definitions show similar parameters on the headcount of people. The European Union and the UK are the only nations with standardised financial turnover and balance sheets.

- *Microbusinesses*: have fewer than ten employees and an annual turnover or a balance sheet below €2 million. These businesses are of paramount importance in Latin America, and African nations as they drive economic development (and innovation), employment, and poverty alleviation. Many people inhabiting these regions live in rural or poor urban areas, where they produce and/or distribute goods and services in unregulated but competitive markets. These businesses are generally independent, largely family-oriented, and/or employ low levels of skills. They tend to account for more than 60% of all regional enterprises and up to 50% of paid employment. They face a lack of access to adequate financing, a high failure rate and a low level of internationalisation. According to Snodgrass and Biggs (1996), most of these corporations in low-income countries are small-sized. Indeed, there is a scarcity of research exploring the impact of design under the conditions of micro-enterprises.

- *Small-sized businesses*: have fewer than 50 employees and annual turnover or balance sheet below €10 million. In the U.S., this generic size standard varies on an industry-by-industry basis. Still, its limitations generally specify having fewer than 250 employees for manufacturing businesses and less than $7.5 million in annual receipts for most non-manufacturing businesses. They are eligible if, after counting its receipts or employees plus the receipts or employees of all its domestic and

Table 5.1 Size of businesses definition

Size	OZ	US	EU	UK	China
Micro	1–4 people (a)	1–6 people (a)	<10 people (a) ≤ €2 million (b) ≤ €2 million (c)	<10 people (a) £ 1.7 million (b) £ 1.7 million (c)	<10 people (a) < 1 million ¥ (c)
Small	<19 (a)	<250 (a)	<50 (a) ≤€10 million (b) ≤€10 million (c)	<50 (a) £8.2 million (b) £8.2 million (c)	<100 (a) <5 million ¥ (c)
Medium	<199 (a)	<500 (a)	<250 (a) ≤€50 million (b) ≤€43 million (c)	<250 (a) £41 million (b) £35.2 million (c)	100–400 (a) <10 million ¥ (c)
Large	>200 (a)	<1000 (a)	>250 (a) ≥€50 million (b) >€45 million (c)	>250 (a) >£41 million (b) >35.2 million (c)	>400 (a) >10 million (c)

(a) head count; (b) turnover; (c) balance sheet Source: UCL, 2021; Australian Securities and Investments commissions Act, 2001.; Australian Bureau of Statistics; U.S. Small Business Administration; Company Act 2006, Section 382 and 465, UK; Ministry of Industry and Information Technology, the Ministry of Finance, the National Development and Reform Commission, and the National Bureau of Statistics (NBS)

foreign affiliates, regardless of whether the affiliates are organised for profit, meets the limits. In the UK, sections 382 and 465 of the Companies Act (2006) define SME for accounting requirements. While, the U.S. Small Business Administration (SBA) size regulations determine whether an entity qualifies as a small business for all SBA and Federal business development programmes, such as small business innovation research (SBIR) programme; small business technology transfer (STTR) programme; historically underutilised business zone (HUBZone) programme; women-owned Small Business (WOSB) and Economically Disadvantaged Women-Owned Small Business (EDWOSB) programmes; and Service-Disabled Veteran-Owned Small Business (SDVOSB) programme.

- *Medium-sized businesses* are required to meet two out of three characteristics, either less than £41 million turnover, less than 250 employees, or less than £35.2 million gross assets. The majority of production and employment belongs to this size of business in medium-income countries.

The application of design thinking has been studied primarily in developed western countries, where national bodies, programmes and academic institutions support these interventions (Design Council; Design Thinking for Businesses; Danish Design Centre). It is mainly embedded in enterprises from or associated with creative industries (Larsen & Lewis, 2007) and manufacturing industries (Christensen & Nielsen, 2019). Its role is to support businesses in engraining design and innovation capabilities under five headings: vision and strategy; brand and identity; product and service; user experience, and innovative culture (Ward et al., 2009). Some studies have concentrated specifically on building innovation and entrepreneurship capabilities in SMEs (Lawlor et al., 2015; Christensen & Nielsen, 2019). Design thinking supports them in developing an innovation capacity that results in new desirable, feasible and viable business opportunities. It also offers a more adaptive, explorative and inclusive approach to business strategy and management (Golsby-Smith, 2007; Holloway, 2009). It functions as an integrator of diverse knowledge, as it offers a holistic view, inclusive, adaptive and multi-functional approach (Owen, 2007), and opportunity creation process. Nonetheless, the constraints on its implementation are on the behest of the individual managers during the main level of analysis of their development process. SME managers' embed their cognitive structure and biases on their decision making, thinking and actions across the organisation. Another constraint is the contextual setting of the SMEs, where employees read the signals of context and act at times with immediacy. Cognitive structure influences the way managers and employees react, perceive opportunities, and threats. The implementation of design thinking is key to developing the ability to reduce the cognitive tensions while building capabilities that minimise bias and cognitive structures that fosters the creation of new opportunities.

- *Large sized businesses*: employ more than 250 employees, have an annual turnover greater than €50 million and a balance sheet total of more than €45 million. Generally, countries with high income per-capita have a larger number of businesses. They are more innovative in capital-intensive low-technology industries such as chemistry and food industry (Biggs, 2002). There are also corporations, which are a large company or group of companies authorised to act as single entity and recognised as such in law.

The application of design thinking in large leading western organisations is commonplace. Proponents argue that it is a key capability for innovators and a source of sustainable competitive advantage for organisations. Liedtka (2014), points out, "businesses using design thinking not only produce organic growth in business organization, but also facilitate dealing with internal organizational, management and cultural challenges, building individual skills and regarding management development. Organizations can embed it as a problem-solving process and an innovation process". Design thinking can be applied in different areas such as marketing, new product development, business planning, research and development, externally facing functions and internally facing function. According to the Design Council (2017), business in the UK identifies that design contributes to either greater market share, increased turnover, development of new markets, increased profit, competitiveness, new product/service, and increased employment.

5.7 Design Thinking: Tensions and Challenges

Management has evolved through time as external and internal factors change. It has affected the way managers lead people, the way they solve problems and innovate. Management science emerged in the early twentieth century. The publication of Taylor's 1911 treatise, *The principles of scientific management* set directions to focus on increasing productivity and efficiency through standardisation, division of labour, centralisation and hierarchy. The development of business models like the Ford assembly line spurred the discipline of speeding up productivity, controlling quality, and minimising costs. The next development was the functional organisation during the 1950s and 1960s, where it saw the emergence of the human resources movement. Managers began to understand the human factors in production and productivity and tools such as goal setting, performance reviews and job descriptions. The third change concentrated on understanding and measuring functions to resource allocation and tools, models and diagrams to formalise the strategic planning process as in strategic planning, growth-share matrix and SWOT analysis. In the 1980s, the business environment grew increasingly competitive and connected with a blooming management consultancy sector. Competitive advantage became a priority, and with it, the tools to measure processes and improve productivity such as Total Quality Management (TQM), Six Sigma and Lean. Managers still took decisions while employees collected data, and goals served to manage people and maintain control. The next series of developments concentrated more on process optimisation. In the 1990s, benchmarking and business processes re-engineering drove an organisation-wide approach and strategy implementation of multiple Fortune 500 companies. Tools such as strategy maps and balance scorecards gained prominence in the C-suite.[10]

The last management development turned its attention to big data, where they concentrated on using technology for growth and value creation. The over-saturation of competition led to concepts such as Blue Ocean Strategy[11] and Value Innovation.[12] However, many managers still see organisations like machines, valuing profit, maintaining authority and relying on six sigma to improve quality. They focus on defining potential problems or markets opportunities through continual market

[10] C-Suite, also known as C-level, refers commonly to a cluster of the corporation's most important senior executives. It gets the name from the titles of top senior executives that start with the letter C, like Chief Executive Officer (CEO), Chief Financial Officer (CFO), Chief Operating Officer and Chief Information Officer (CIO).

[11] The blue ocean strategy concerns with creating and capturing uncontested market spaces, thereby making the competition irrelevant. In this proposition, market boundaries and industry structure are not given and can be restructured by the actions and beliefs of industry players. The concept is developed by Professor Chan Kim and Professor Renée Mauborgne from INSEAD.

[12] Value Innovation strategy focus on creating a leap in value for both buyers and the company. The value to buyers comes from the offering's utility minus its price because the value to the company is generated from the offering's price minus its costs. It is achieved only when the whole system of utility, price and cost aligned. The concept is developed by Professor Chan Kim and Professor Renée Mauborgne from INSEAD.

analysis. They use primary and secondary market research and testing in order to move on to more concrete phases of developing business plans based on estimates of market penetrations, pricing and distribution strategies. The problem with modern management is its quest to ensure consistency and predictability, attempting to eliminate variation. However, they keep confronting common issues such as the best ways to deal with complexity and uncertainty, how to lead people or how to innovate. Two constant aspects of management are the management approach and the approach of innovation. The former focus on whether the style of top management controls, sets goals or inspires employees. The latter concentrates on how leaders solve strategic problems and develop new products and services, whether it is from the top-down, or top-down with bottom-up data, or participatory actions.

Design thinking in management is not without its vocal critics. Modern management aims to ensure consistency and predictability. Organisations function like machines, value profits and authority model, as they are built for efficiency and quality. They are confronted with new challenges that have no previous history or points of reference. Currently, strategic initiatives depend on big data, the volume of information, the variety of information and the velocity of information and business capacity to draw meaningful analysis. The excess of data and the lack of analysis can lead organisations to suffer data paralysis. The advent of new technologies has also brought relevance to the engineering approach, which is more technical, rooted in analysing the problem and deconstructing its component elements. They develop a systematic process to identify and assess potential solutions for each component and then create a systematic response to solve them. The consideration of design thinking focuses on its holistic and iterative process with a distinct mindset and set of attitudes that offers unlimited possibilities. It enables people to collaborate, communicate, empathise, anticipate, understand and exchange ideas facilitating intimate relationships inside and outside of the organisation. It allows organisations to create economic value for all shareholders instead of value capture. Designerly and multidisciplinary approaches can complement and enhance traditional business management towards solving business problems, filling critical gaps and deficiencies, and establishing more comprehensive bodies of knowledge. As a relatively new concept to the business world, design thinking needs to be mindfully adopted and integrated into current (and traditional) management practices. Managers and designers need to be analytical and critical towards adopting and applying design thinking whilst avoiding using it as a PR exercise or a panacea for organisational deficiencies.

Chapter Summary This chapter introduced the main economic systems that feature across the globe; each one featuring their relative strengths and weaknesses and how they either support or hinder the organisation to develop innovative products and services. Design has had to adapt and is continually adapting to the fluid nature of these systems; as such, design profession needs to become more cognizant of these changes and proactively plan ahead in order to remain relevant. With different business emerging on a daily basis, new organisational forms arise, each one presenting their own challenges as to where and how design sits within and operates across traditional organisational boundaries. The business sector is widely recognising the value of design and in particular design thinking as a strategic tool to maintain commercial competitiveness. If understood and implemented effectively, design can be a powerful transformative force of both commercial and societal good; however, design thinking is fundamentally more than just a set of basic 'thinking' tools. Adopting a designerly approach needs to respect and be fully mindful of the context in which it is being used; otherwise, the potential gains that it has to offer will never be fully utilised and recognised—More so today than ever before, in global and hyper competitive marketplaces.

Review Questions

1. How can government ensure and legislate for fairness in a mixed economy system whilst also driving wider prosperity to its citizens?
2. Peer-to-Peer (P2P) platforms are gaining prominence as a popular means of sharing excess or idle assets; what other benefits do they offer to the user?
3. With the rise of IoT businesses, new business models are created based around satisfying user needs, how and where could design contribute to this challenge?
4. SME's are notoriously difficult to define, often leading to inconsistencies across the globe, which SME definition do you consider the most comprehensive?
5. Big Data has many potential advantages to the organisation, however, it also has many pitfalls that could hinder commercial success if not properly addressed; how could an organisation overcome data 'paralysis' which is one common problem?

Project Questions

1. A traditional economic system may seem irrelevant in developed countries, however many elements of it could contribute to sustainable development. Identify and formulate a ten-point framework where these key elements could support sustainable design and community development.
2. P2P is incredibly popular in relation to re-purposing unwanted clothing ('Rent the Runway' is a successful e-commerce platform as an example); develop a short business proposition where other household items could be shared amongst peers.
3. IoT is an exponential growth industry; however, developing IoT products/services is fundamentally different to that of developing traditional products. Identify and critique IoT design development process models to identify what these differences are.

4. Developing innovative products and services within SMEs is often considered high risk; list 5 main risks that are common to many SMEs and strategies to mitigate these risks.
5. Businesses are interested in three types of big data: (1) customer, (2) financial, and (3) operational. Create a marketing plan as to where and how big data could lead to the development of innovative new products or services (or both).

Chapter Tasks

1. Form a small group of no more than 4 people; then you have >60 minutes to identify the relative strengths and weaknesses of the four main economic systems.
2. Using flip-chart sheets and marker pens, provide a user-journey map of a conceptual e-commerce platform that is based around clothes sharing aimed at Generation Z female users.
3. Identify two leading IoT product/service systems and identify 5 key points of where meaningful value is offered to the end-users.
4. Embedding design thinking practices and principles within SMEs is a challenging task, outline 3 main routes to design enhancement an SME could adopt and implement.
5. Develop a propositional design process map identifying where and how big data could feed into and inform subsequent design activities.

References

Bason, C. (2010). *Leading Public Sector Innovation: Co-creating for a Better Society*. Policy Press.

Beckman, S. L., & Barry, M. (2007). Innovation as a Learning Process. *California Management Review, 50*, 25–56.

Biggs, T. (2002). *Is Small Beautiful and Worthy of Subsidy? Literature Review*. IFC.

Brown, T. (2009). *Change by Design: How Design Thinking Transforms Organizations and Inspires Innovation*. Harper Collins.

Christensen, P., & Nielsen, S. (2019). The Beauty of Design Thinking—Is There a Small Beast in the Box. *The Design Journal, 22*(1), 147–161.

Design Council. (2017). The Value of Design Factfinder Report. Retrieved April 20, 2021, from https://www.designcouncil.org.uk/sites/default/files/asset/document/TheValueOfDesignFactfinder_Design_Council.pdf

Design Thinking for Business. (2020). Humanizing Digital Technologies Through Design Thinking: The Role of Design Thinking in Digital Transformation Report.

Dunne, D. (2018). Implementing Design Thinking in Organizations: An Exploratory Study. *Journal of Organization Design, 7*(16), 1–16.

Fraser Institute. (2017). Economic Freedom of the World. Retrieved May 25, 2021, from https://www.fraserinstitute.org/economic-freedom/map?geozone=world&page=map&year=2017

Golsby-Smith, T. (2007). The Second Road of Thought: How Design Offers Strategy a New Toolkit. *The Journal of Business Strategy, 28*(4), 22–29.

Grossman, G. (1963). Notes for a Theory of the Command Economy. *Soviet Studies, 15*(2), 101–123.

Haigh, N., & Hoffman, A. J. (2012). Hybrid Organizations: The Next Chapter of Sustainable Business. *Organizational Dynamics, 41*(2), 126–134.

Holloway, M. (2009). How Tangible Is Your Strategy? How Design Thinking Can Turn Your Strategy into Reality. *Journal of Business Strategy, 30*(2/3), 50–56.
IKEA. (2021). IWAY: The IKEA Code of Conduct. [Online]. Retrieved May 31, 2021, from https://about.ikea.com/en/work-with-us/for-suppliers/iway-our-supplier-code%2D%2Dof-conduct
Kolko, J. (2015). Design Thinking Comes of Age. *Harvard Business Reviews, 93*(9), 66–69.
Kumar, V., & Whitney, P. (2007). Daily Life, Not Markets: Customer-Centered Design. *Journal of Business Strategy, 28*(4), 46–58.
Larsen, P., & Lewis, A. (2007). How Award-Winning SMEs Manage the Barriers of Innovation. *Creativity and Innovation Management, 16*(2), 142–151.
Lawlor, P., O'Donoghue, A., Wafer, B., & Commins, E. (2015). *Design-Driven Innovation in Your Organization*. Wiley.
Liedtka, J. (2014). Innovative Ways Companies are Using Design Thinking. *Strategy & Leadership, 42*(2), 40–45.
Liedtka, J. (2015). Perspective: Linking Design Thinking with Innovation Outcomes Through Cognitive Bias Reduction. *Journal of Product Innovation Management, 32*(6), 925–938.
Liedtka, J. (2018). Innovation, Strategy, and Design: Design Thinking as a Dynamic Capability. *Academy of Management Proceedings, 1*, 13004.
Liedtka, J. (2020). Putting Technology in Its Place: Design Thinking's Social Technology at Work. *California Management Review, 62*(2), 53–83.
Liedtka, J., Azer, D., & Salzman, R. (2017). *Design Thinking for the Greater Good*. Columbia University Press.
Maeda, J. (2020). The CX Report. Retrieved May 31, 2021, from https://designintech.report/
Mamedov, O., Movchan, I., Ishchenko-Padukova, O., & Grabowska, M. (2016). Traditional Economy: Innovation, Efficiency and Globalization. *Economics and Sociology, 9*(2), 61–72.
Martin, R. L. (2009). *The Design of Business: Why Design Thinking Tool Kit for Managers*. Columbia University Press.
Narver, J. C., & Slater, S. F. (1990). The Effect of a Market Orientation on Business Profitability. *Journal of Marketing, 54*(4), 20. https://doi.org/10.2307/1251757
OECD. (2020). Social Economy and the COVID-19 Crisis: Current and Future Roles. Retrieved May 30, 2021, from https://www.oecd.org/coronavirus/policy-responses/social-economy-and-the-covid-19-crisis-current-and-future-roles-f904b89f/
Oliver Wyman & IESE. (2017). Design Thinking the New DNA of the Financial Sector: How Banks can Boost Their Growth Through Design Thinking in an Era of De-Banking. Retrieved May 31, 2021, from https://www.oliverwyman.com/content/dam/oliver-wyman/v2/publications/2017/apr/Design_Thinking.pdf
Owen, C. (2007). Design Thinking: Notes on Its Nature and Use. *Design Research Quarterly, 2*(1), 16–27.
Raworth, K. (2017). *Doughnut Economics: Seven Ways to Think Like a 21st Century Economist*. Random House Business Books.
Reisman, D. (Ed.). (1995). *Theories of the Mixed Economy Selected Texts 1931–1968*. Routledge.
Sinkula, J. M. (1994). Market Information Processing and Organizational Learning. *Journal of Marketing, 58*(1), 35. https://doi.org/10.2307/1252249
Smulders, F. E. (2004). Co-operation in NPD: Coping with Different Learning Styles. *Creativity and Innovation Management, 13*(4), 263–273.
Snodgrass, D., & Biggs, T. (1996). *Industrialization and the Small Firm: Patterns and Policies*. International Center for Economic Growth.
Spotify. (2019). How can Design Thinking Build Trust in the Age of Machine Learning. Retrieved May 31, 2021, from https://spotify.design/article/how-can-design-thinking-build-trust-in-the-age-of-machine-learning
The World Bank. (2021). Service Exports. Retrieved May 31, 2021, from https://data.worldbank.org/indicator/BX.GSR.NFSV.CD?end=2019&start=2019&view=map

UNDP Global Centre for Public Service Excellence. (2014). Design Thinking for Public Service Excellence. Retrieved May 31, 2021, from http://www.undp.org/content/dam/undp/library/capacity-development/English/Singapore%20Centre/GCPSE%20Design%20Thinking%20Summary.pdf

Verganti, R. (2009). *Design-Driven Innovation: Changing the Rules of Competition by Radically Innovating What Things Mean*. Harvard Business Press.

Verganti, R. (2016). *Overcrowded: Designing Meaningful Products in a World Awash with Ideas*. The MIT Press.

Ward, A., Runcie, E., & Morris, L. (2009). Embedding Innovation: Design Thinking for Small Enterprises. *The Journal of Business Strategy, 30*(2/3), 78–84.

World Economic Forum. (2017). Collaboration in Cities: From Sharing to 'Sharing Economy'. White Paper.

Design Thinking for Sustainable Futures

6

Learning Objectives

- To introduce and critically examine the value of the Mission Statement as a vision document that drives strategic ambition.
- To explore the wide range of themes associated with sustainable development and introduce the Triple Bottom Line (TBL) framework that focuses on profit, people and planet.
- To examine the rise of Corporate Social Responsibility (CSR) and articulate its critical role to foster ethical business practices in industry.
- To development an understanding of new business models that characterise Social Enterprises when addressing distinct social problems for the common good.
- To gain a deeper understanding of business development growth strategies within the creative industries.

6.1 Introduction

Chapter 6 takes an exploratory approach to a wide variety of interrelated themes that encompass the communication of organisational values and how these can be used as an effective means of competitive differentiation. Firstly, the primary starting point of business vision is encapsulated in the Mission Statement, which is a fluid document that elegantly captures and communicates the main purpose of the

Supplementary Information The online version contains supplementary material available at [https://doi.org/10.1007/978-3-030-94206-9_6].

Y. Huang, D. Hands, *Design Thinking for New Business Contexts*,
https://doi.org/10.1007/978-3-030-94206-9_6

business to its relative stakeholders. Here, values, purpose and ambition are defined and used as a guiding force to direct overall strategic vision; be it to deliver the best IT business solutions; the most affordable and durable products within its market sector and so forth. In addition, to many companies, it is a statement of intent towards their commitment to the ongoing climate debate and towards the sustainable development agenda. Sustainability is taking prominence in policy development activities, company strategy formulation and consumers purchasing decisions; as such, organisations of varying size, regardless of business activity, are now meaningfully engaging with this ongoing and timely critical agenda.

Alongside sustainability, its natural companion Corporate Social Responsibility is becoming more widespread and readily adopted, demonstrating the organisations commitment to ethical practice and transparency in how they achieve these goals. There are many actors and beneficiaries involved in CSR practice, and this chapter touches upon where and how they play a vital role in its effective operation. Through this multi-agency approach to responsible practice, opportunities for product/service innovation present themselves, which could lead to the development of new product and market opportunities. At the heart of this is design, where design links creativity and innovation, especially during the initial stages of the new product development process. In terms of innovation, new business models can be established based on addressing broader societal problems, such as access to affordable healthcare, assistance into meaningful employment by marginalised communities and poverty reduction.

The rise of social enterprises demonstrates the strong egalitarian values by entrepreneurs, and how they take these socially orientated principles into the commercial marketplace with common good as its primary purpose. The chapter concludes that by focusing upon an ongoing research project conducted by the University of Dundee, UK, investigating how small high growth potential businesses involved in the gaming industry can achieve long-term commercial survival and success.

6.2 Mission Impossible?

'Values made visible' is a perquisite for success, and design plays a fundamental role in that process. Design gives meaning and presence to the strategic ambitions of the company; for instance, BMW automotive are committed to the manufacture of high precision-engineered motor vehicles, where quality is embedded within every aspect of their vehicles development; design ensures this integrity is maintained and carefully communicated to their customers. In terms of service provision, The AirlineRatings.com Airline Excellence Awards (2020) rated Air New Zealand, the Kiwi flag carrier the top spot due to inflight innovations, environmental leadership and staff motivation. Air New Zealand Acting Chief Executive Officer Jeff McDowall points out "winning the award for a record sixth time was a testament to the efforts of the airline's 12,500 staff who were focused on delivering an excellent uniquely Kiwi experience to its customers every day". (ibid.) This commitment to outstanding service delivery and celebrating New Zealand as a leading destination is at the heart of the company's mission statement—"Enrich our country by connecting New Zealanders to each other and New Zealand to the world". (Air New Zealand, 2021) This introduces us to the value and role of the company mission statement as a powerful tool to communicate strategic intent to all its stakeholders.

A concise mission statement can foster employee satisfaction and productivity in equal measure, as provides a strong sense of purpose, where they can focus of daily activities that will enable them to realise company related goals. During the 1990s, more than half of US businesses had some kind of mission or vision statement; this number doubled from ten years earlier. (Levering, 2000). Table 6.1 outlines a brief series of mission statements from some of the world's leading brands.

Falsey (1989) argues "a mission statement tells two things about a company: who it is and what it does". Furthermore, it extols the primary purpose of the business, the reason as to why the business exists. It should articulate its priorities, values and core beliefs. Williams (2008) raises an interesting point regarding the benefits of a mission statement, suggesting, "In addition to specific benefits that are said to accrue from having such a statement, successfully completing the mission statement process demonstrates that a firm can think reflectively, plan carefully, work collaboratively and make informed decisions".

It is worthwhile to note, that mission statements are different to vision statements, which are often used interchangeably—but are two different entities. Even though strategic management distinguishes between vision and mission statement, many organizations confuse them and put them together in the same statement (Sufi & Lyons, 2003). A vision statement is where the company or organisation wishes to go to in the future; it sets the scene for long-term ambitions and goals. Unlike a Mission statement, the Vision statement is solely for internal purposes, outlining long-term aspirations for the future, serving as a touchstone for strategic planning purposes within the organisation (or divisions within a larger organisation).

Table 6.1 Mission statements from leading brands

Company	Mission statement
LinkedIn	"To connect the world's professionals to make them more productive and successful."
Alibaba	"To make it easy to do business anywhere."
BBC	"To enrich people's lives with programmes and services that inform, educate and entertain."
Asana	"To help humanity thrive by enabling all teams to work together effortlessly."
Google	"To organize the world's information and make it universally accessible and useful."
3M	"To Improve Every Life through Innovative Giving in Education, Community and the Environment."
Patagonia	"Build the best product, cause no unnecessary harm, use business to inspire and implement solutions to the environmental crisis."

A mission statement is a short term (usually between three and five years) describing the organisations 'current' state and their core values. This should be continually up-dated to remain relevant and timely. One survey of 220 small businesses found that: 64% did not have a written mission statement; 7% had mission statements that were only accessible to senior managers; 29% had a written mission statement accessible to all employees. (Toftoy & Chatterjee, 2004) There is considerable debate as to what to include in an overarching mission statement, but it is commonly agreed that a focus should be on the employees, a clear understanding as to who your customers are, and then an element looking to future growth and profitability. As such, a carefully crafted statement should link the employees, the business and the customer. Uniting these elements should be defining the company and importantly, what does the company stand for in terms of purpose.

David (2007) argues, "effective mission statement must be broad in scope, generate strategic alternatives, not overly specific, reconcile diverse interest of different stakeholders, arouse positive feelings and emotions among stakeholders, motivate readers to action and must generate favourable impression of the organization". Interestingly, David includes the term 'favourable impression' regarding how its many stakeholders perceives company image; this can be achieved in a variety of ways, one notable way could be how the company demonstrates its commitment to ethical practices, towards the environment or places sustainability centre to its operations; or all three combined. This raises the issue of corporate 'reputation' as a huge asset to the organisation, contributing to its overall performance and financial value, especially to leading international brands. Kim Harrison (2020) Founder and Principal of Cutting Edge PR, argues, "Sometimes reputation is the biggest single organizational asset, especially with big brands. For instance, the reputation capital of some top companies is more than half of their market value, including Apple, Disney, Alphabet (parent company of Google), ExxonMobil, Unilever and Shell" We are now witnessing a growing number of businesses integrating sustainability and ethical practices into their company strategies, demonstrating that they can do well by doing good. As such, they can enhance reputation, whilst exceeding customer expectations in the development of new growth opportunities. These new values could then be incorporated into the development of the company's overall mission statement (see Patagonia in Table 6.1).

6.3 Sustainable Futures

Over the last few decades, we have been witnessing the rise of sustainability and a conscious move towards adopting eco-friendly principles and practices into every aspect of our lives; none more so than organisations, embracing the sustainable development agenda. This shift has come from the heightened environmentally orientated approach to our culture, economic, and communications infrastructure. There is a reason the term 'eco-friendly' edged its way into the modern spotlight and has been dominating the conversation ever since the late 1970's. One defining moment in its development was the Brundtland Report (Sustainable Development, 1987) named after the chairperson of the World Commission on Environment and Development (WCED), Gro Harlem Brundtland. In essence, this comprehensive report highlighted that global environmental challenges were centred on the massive poverty and inequalities of the global south and the unsustainable levels of consumption and production in the North. Recommendations arising from the report, called for a cohesive strategy that unified both development and the environment—now commonly described as 'Sustainable Development.' The report defined the term as the "development that meets the needs of the present generations without compromising the ability of the future generations to meet their own needs". A useful way of examining the vast terrain of literature surrounding sustainability is to see it through the lens of the 'Triple Bottom Line' (TBL) framework as an interrelated set of overarching themes that are inextricably intertwined. In the framework developed by Elkington (1997), the equally weighted economic, social and environmental lines could also be referred to as 'profit, people, and planet' respectively (Fig. 6.1).

- *Economic (Profit)*: Focuses heavily on how businesses can be economically sustainable in the long term. Essentially, it depicts a revolution in values within the organisation. Elkington (1997) argues that the traditional belief in business, that is, 'the business of business is about the creation of economic value.' Broadly speaking, the main goal of economic sustainability is to develop an inclusive, innovative economy for the benefit of wider society; to shape the future of a community by creating the right kinds of jobs; and to improve the skills of people (Edwards, 2005). This emerged from traditional environmentalism. It is a recognition of the importance of secure, long-term employment in ensuring the health of the ecosystem, as poverty has been a critical contributor to environmental degradation.

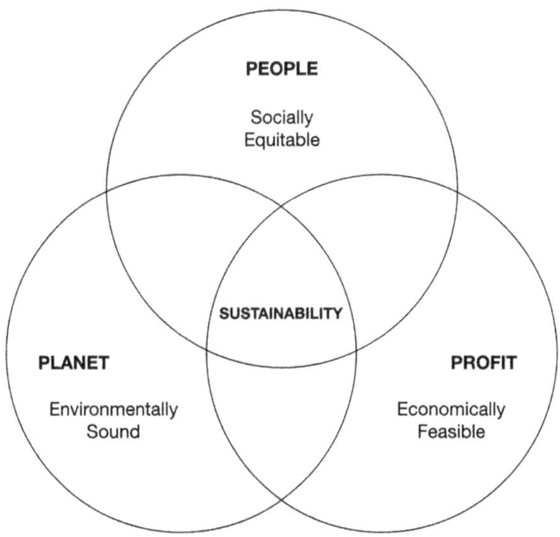

Fig. 6.1 The Triple Bottom Line (TBL) (adapted by authors)

- *Social (People)*: The social bottom line is predominantly a business term in the field of 'sustainable business' which defines the way in which an organisation should operate in a society while considering the social, ethical and political context of that community (Jeurissen, 2000). However, in a broader context, social issues of sustainability are about the ways in which we interact with the economy, environment and each other. One main obstacle to achieving social sustainability is the growth of poverty and rising inequality, which is at the heart of the 17 sustainable development goals featured within 'The 2030 Agenda for Sustainable Development', (sdgs, 2015) set out by the United Nations in 2015.
- *Environmental (Planet)*: Arguably, this bottom line could be considered the most worthy for particular attention when discussing sustainability. Elkington (1997) attempts to raise organisational awareness of environmental issues as their operations impact the environment through consumption of renewable and non-renewable resources. Moreover, their impacts also degrade the ecosystem as the result of water, land and air pollution. Bhamra and Lofthouse (2007) regard this principle of sustainability as 'environmental justice.' This gives equal access to a clean environment and equal protection from possible environmental harm. (Cutter, 1995) This in essence, argues that human activities should use natural resources at levels at which they can be replenished naturally. The principle of environmental sustainability can alter current forms of human interactions with the environment in ways that keep the environment as pristine as possible; otherwise, the resulting degradation could lead to the inability of the planet to sustain life.

The TBL contains three equal areas of consideration, and when combined, provide a clear focus for action in terms of meaningful engagement when addressing sustainability issues. However, these do present further and quite significant challenges to the organisation—measuring impact and defining the metrics for success. For instance, turnover and profit can be measured in Pounds, Dollars, Euros and so forth; however, how does the organisation measure environmental health and enhanced social capital? There has been considerable debate regarding establishing common units of measurement that could be applied to the three pillars of the TBL. Referring back to the earlier discussion on company mission, Jackson et al. (2011) make an interesting observation regarding the inclusion of sustainable business practices, arguing, "to create a company whose mission is true sustainability, all engaged individuals need to have a better understanding of what sustainability entails. The spotlight needs to move from the financial bottom line to a more encompassing viewpoint of the company's impact on the world. Once this information is shared, it is then necessary to begin looking at the community to realize what environmental concerns are being voiced by the public". In terms of TBL reporting, there are some distinct concerns surrounding that company activities and actions do not support their strategic intentions. For instance, in a drive to become more environmentally responsible, they may only produce limited evidence of limited financial achievements regarding this commitment. As such, adhering to sustainability principles aligned to TBL can be both difficult to maintain and importantly, communicate to a wide set of stakeholder audiences. Consequently, organisations could be reticent to embracing a sustainability ethos during the shift to TBL reporting.

With a desire to adopt sustainable principles, there are also a number of other benefits that can be enjoyed by the organisation—one involves becoming truly more innovative. In a few different studies by the Harvard Business Review (2009) and by Deloitte (2012), researchers found that organisations that were leaders in sustainability were also leaders in innovation (and specifically with sustainability leading the way for innovation). Significantly, what we are currently witnessing are organisations and businesses worldwide, reappraising their core product/service offerings set against the backdrop of the Covid-19 pandemic. This can be said of the ongoing climate crisis, whereby companies being seen as a good steward and averting disaster of their own making, enables them to reflect and look for alternative environmentally solutions. Kerrigan and Kulasooriya (2020) point out, "Yet crises can also be profound catalysts for change, creating opportunities to gain new perspectives. Businesses that see climate change—and sustainability—not only as a threat but also as an opportunity might be best placed to unlock new innovations and ignite unexpected collaborations. Businesses may need to transform themselves to thrive in an era where tackling sustainability is becoming an imperative". In the marketplace, we are reaching a tipping point whereby ethically minded consumers are fast becoming the norm for their desire to purchase and consume sustainable products and services, especially older Millennials and Generation Zs (defined as those being aged 9–24 in 2021). One of the defining features of this demographic group is that "To win the hearts of Gen Z, companies and employers will need to highlight their efforts to be good global citizens. While focusing on the quality of the goods/services you provide is still important, a company's ethics are more important than ever. Moreover, actions speak more loudly than words: 'Companies must demonstrate their commitment to a broader set of societal challenges, such as sustainability, climate change and hunger". (Gomez et al., 2021). With this increasing demand for sustainable alternatives, new market demands are opening up that offer strong potential for long-term growth.

To exploit these emergent growing opportunities, three potential design/business strategies could be adopted: (1) Future Forecasting (2) Internal Design-Driven Innovation (3) Design Alliances.

1. *Future Forecasting*: Benjamin Franklin's often quoted maxim "If You Fail to Plan, You Are Planning to Fail" is more pertinent now in these times of uncertainty. By developing a long-term future facing strategy, it will prepare the organisation for resilience and potential growth through the creation of lasting value in mid to long-term planning activities. One invaluable design approach that could aid these activities or inspire radical new ideas for latent market opportunities is design 'fiction'. It is commonly acknowledged that design is used to solve current actual problems, making things better or modifying an existing product currently in use. However, design fiction is fundamentally more different, is it part of a group of design practice, which we would refer to as

'speculative design.' Leading design theorists Dunne and Raby (2009) argue, "rather than solving existing problems, these approaches use design to ask questions". They do this by creating prototypes, but instead of being actually created, these prototypes are used to encourage people to think critically about issues where design can make a meaningful contribution. A speculative design approach, asks how things might be in the future, why things might be that particular way, with a view to identifying potential problems and their subsequent solutions.

2. *Internal Design-Driven Innovation*: In terms of adopting a future focused philosophy, organisations can plan for the long-term by critically reappraising the skills-sets, knowledge and competencies that they currently have and leverage them within new business strategies. Referring back to Chap. 2, we tentatively introduced a series of design process frameworks and models that could be drawn upon to drive innovation. In addition to these, digitally orientated and novel ethnographic design approaches (as discussed in Chap 4) could be enhanced and tailored to a wide range of user centred contexts to drive new design inspired opportunities for business development. However, these new approaches are not solely for identifying new business avenues, they can be equally as invaluable for identifying new sustainable interventions into product development. At the time of writing this textbook, both authors have been inspired by discussion and debates being shared at the 2021 COP26 Climate Change Summit in Glasgow, UK. Throughout the week, numerous discussions were focused on ways of protecting and restoring forests and critical ecosystems, and on how individuals, organisations and governments can transition towards sustainable, resilient and natural positive futures. Design can be placed central to this ambition in the way it could be innovatively used to change current attitudes towards the creation and development of energy, environmental and sustainable products and services. Here, design can be viewed as an organisation resource to change established orthodoxies and dated practices.

   In essence, raising the sustainability agenda within the organisation, can spur the creation of new business models supported by innovative new products that satisfy consumer trends for ethically orientated goods and services. An integral part of this approach would be to formalise the visibility and role of design as a driver for innovation. Central to successfully managing design is an understanding within the organisation of how it can use design as a key part of any new business strategy; raising its value as a strategic 'visionary' asset is one way to ensure this. Von Stamm (2004) argues, "it is essential to understand that the key to success is to make design and innovation the core of the company's strategy. It is not about bringing in a designer for a new product once every few years; it is about making design and innovation a way of life—about questioning and challenging what and how things are done, and asking where there might be an opportunity to add value".

3. *Design Alliances*: Demand driven innovation is a highly responsive and flexible type of innovation that not only satisfies customer's wants and needs, but also more often exceeds them. In order to achieve this, the organisation needs to

anticipate shifting consumer trends and build them into any forward thinking strategy. There are many different and often complex variables that need to be considered and accommodated in order to remain flexible in the face of shifting market demands. The first variable is the relationship between the marketing and design functions, market-led information can be translated into design requirements. Critically, the second factor is forging closer, more collaborative relationships between all the differing partners within the company's eco-system, where they can consult and seek specialist knowledge when developing initial conceptual ideas for either new or modified product families and services that lean towards sustainable values and principles. This in turn, shifts the power from the organisation to the consumer; organisations that fail to do this will be the ones that see falling sales and diminished reputation in ethically orientated markets calling for greater sustainability.

6.4 Corporate Social Responsibility

A companion theme in addition to sustainable development is that of Corporate Social Responsibility (CSR) which places ethical accountability and responsible organisational practice. In essence, CSR is a philosophy adopted by the organisation that illustrates its commitment to fostering social change for the benefit of all of its stakeholders and the wider community. CSR can take many different forms that range from corporate philanthropy and employee volunteering through to ethical labour practices, environmental efforts and community development. The main stakeholders who benefit from CSR activities include:

- *Increased employee satisfaction*: which leads to the retention of a highly satisfied workforce, which takes pride in their work through the opportunity to develop their skills and career aspirations.
- *Consumers*: through transparent and honest business practices, customers are becoming more aware of ethical considerations and expect the same from the brands that they are loyal to. Forbes (2017) has identified that Millennials prefer to do business with corporations and brands with pro-social messages, sustainable manufacturing methods and ethical business standards. An earlier research study undertaken by Nielsen (2015) indicated that, globally, 66% of consumers are willing to spend more on a product if it comes from a sustainable brand. Millennials gave an even more impressive showing, with 73% of surveyed millennials indicating a similar preference.
- *Suppliers*: organisations often select suppliers who equally demonstrate their commitment to CSR practices, as this can also reflect on their own reputation. An increasing amount of customers is demanding transparency in both supply chain and production systems that responsible practices are being respected. Furthermore, with growing demand for the protection of human rights, employee welfare further back in the supply chain is also under increased scrutiny.

Questions such as—is child labour used? Are fair wages being paid? What are the working conditions like and so forth?

- *Communities*: community engagement is one of the core principles of CSR. Working with the local community can reap a wide range of benefits for both parties. For example, many businesses, local customers are an important revenue for sales; as such, demonstrating a strong community focus builds reputational value, which in turn could make it easier to recruit and retain local employees. Community based activities could include supporting local charity initiatives, working with schools and colleges on a long-term basis and supporting local good causes via financial or voluntary support offered by their employees.

In addition to the above beneficiaries, CSR practices could also lead to increased creativity within the company. CSR initiatives encourage employees to continually identify new ways and means of ethical behaviour and practices. As such, existing products and services offered by the company could be viewed from an alternative position, where they are scrutinised and reappraised in order to reduce environmental impact, for instance, developing new products. This often involves working with several internal business functions within the company, and with external suppliers and ideally, customers. Therefore, new product development (NPD) is an effective means from which to analyse product characteristics and features that could generate innovative solutions for future product specifications. This in turn could lead to the opportunity to differentiate products from competing rivals whilst also communicating CSR and environmentally friendly credentials. Over time, these egalitarian values would influence the mindset of the stakeholders, employees and end-users towards adopting CSR principles that would not only benefit the company, but also the wider community as well. Yang et al. (2016) point out "input of CSR requirements during the initial stage of product design can minimize the need for frequent design changes. Consideration of CSR in product design thus not only reduces waste but also enhances company image". Furthermore, when discussing environmental impact, CSR can contribute via a wide number of ways. Firstly, reducing energy consumption, as it often affects the customer's lives immediately and directly, which is the same for organisations, which could translate into lower or higher energy bills. Energy efficiency management is a growing industry that provides companies of all sizes, strategies and frameworks to reduce their use of energy, which often results in increased performance and lower manufacturing costs.

Effective CSR practices adopted by the company can offer a significant advantage in terms of raising company profile and corporate reputation in highly competitive markets. Therefore, CSR reporting and communication activities are important to any forward thinking branding and business strategy. Effective PR can provide a basis for a CSR orientated company to differentiate itself from their rivals. According to the 2015, Global CSR study (Cone Communications, 2015) key findings identified that:

- 91% of global consumers expect companies to do more than make a profit, but also operate responsibly to address social and environmental issues;
- 84% say they seek out responsible products whenever possible;
- 90% would boycott a company if they learned of irresponsible or deceptive business practices.

Identifying that 84% of customers would seek out CSR led companies in terms of product purchasing intentions, an integrated CSR communications strategy would enable the company to stand out in highly competitive markets. Therefore, a strong and authentic communications strategy is crucial in publicising CSR practices; however, the key term here is 'authenticity' as consumers are increasingly becoming aware of companies using CSR as a superficial marketing strategy without meaningfully practising it. Otherwise, the discrepancy between what they say and what they actually do, can lead to serious reputational damage that could significantly harm the company. Therefore, companies need to clearly demonstrate and articulate as to how they support CSR activities through their daily activities. Marketing agency, Lewis Marketing (2020) points out that "At the end of the day, organizations should prioritize CSR activity because they genuinely care about those causes. That doesn't have to mean, however, that they can't also benefit from the initiatives. From the lens of a public relations professional, CSR campaigns can provide a valuable boost to a company's reputation, especially when those efforts attract attention from news and media for their impact".

6.5 Social Enterprises—A Hybrid Business Model

Referring back to our earlier discussion regarding company mission (as in "what is the purpose of our business?"), we turn our attention to social enterprises that place greater emphasis on 'purpose' as opposed to pure profit. In essence, they provide business solutions to social problems, whereby all profit is re-invested for the pursuit of greater social impact. A succinct definition of a social enterprise defines its purpose, as "a cause-driven business whose primary reason for being is to improve social objectives and serve the common good" (Thegoodtrade, 2021). What makes a social enterprise different to an ethical business is that it uses its mission as a vehicle to provide a business solution to a social problem. An ethical business primarily is for shareholder profit, but adopts an ethically orientated approach to business activities. Depending on its core mission, a social enterprise will adapt its business model according to the problem that it is aiming to address; hence, the wide variety of business models that feature in social enterprises. Here are six common examples of social enterprise business models:

1. *The Business Support model*: offers business support solutions to the social entrepreneur who wishes to start a business. Business support could be offered in the form of marketing, financial and training support activities in order to grow the nascent business.

2. *The Sales Intermediary model*: this type of SE business acts on behalf of their client(s); often this could take the form of selling produce and goods grown by a farmer (i.e., cocoa beans, bananas etc.,) to the wider general public. In a way, they would be providing access to market in order to generate sales and income.
3. *The Employment model*: whereby the SE would provide employment / training opportunities for disadvantaged people/communities who would otherwise struggle to find meaningful employment with a fair wage.
4. *The Service / Fee model*: the SE would directly charge the customer for socially beneficial services offered. Commercial settings for this model would be varied across many customer facing service industries.
5. *The Cooperative model*: is a fee-based membership organisation, that would provide member services to a group or community that shares a common social need. Common examples of this cooperative structure would include employee owned businesses and credit unions. A credit union is a financial co-operative, which provides savings, loans and a range of services to its members.
6. *The Subsidised Service model*: would fund social programmes by selling products or offering services in the commercial marketplace. For example, a dentistry practice could provide dental services to those most in need who otherwise would find it difficult to access affordable health treatment.

A major survey of social enterprises undertaken by Social Enterprise UK in 2019 identified a series of key findings regarding the contribution of social enterprises to the UK economy (Table 6.2)

The report goes on to say, "we believe social enterprises are leading the way for business in many areas, and this report makes that clear. The start-up wave of social enterprises continues to surge, with 42% under 5 years old. This movement is being driven by women and BAME-led start-ups, demonstrating the vibrancy and diversity of the sector. Social enterprises create vital opportunities in uncertain times, employing those who are disadvantaged, and reinvesting over 75% of their profits into delivering their mission". (ibid., p. 4.)

Table 6.2 Key findings from the Social Enterprise UK, 2019 survey

Themes	Key findings
1: Growing in Size	52% of social enterprises grew their turnover in the last 12 months. This is higher than in 2017 and much higher than the 34% of SMEs who have seen an increase.
2: Independent Businesses	Social enterprises are businesses that earn their income through trading, competing in the marketplace—77% of social enterprises earn more than 75% of their income from trading, up on our previous survey.
3: More Innovative	The proportion of social enterprises introducing a new product or service was 56% in 2019, higher again than previous years and far outstripping SMEs, at 36%.
4: Commercially Successful	48% of social enterprises made a profit in the past year, with 27% breaking even and a lower percentage losing money than in previous research. The longer a social enterprise has been around, the more likely it is to make a profit.

Finding three, regarding innovation is worthy of further discussion as to where design can make a meaningful contribution to and by the social enterprise. Firstly, adopting a design thinking approach can allow the social entrepreneur to identify latent customer needs (often through design thinking tools and techniques). This could yield new opportunities where gaps in the marketplace, and importantly, avenues for social good, could be embraced. Rather than creating and offering products for high volume sales, new product introductions could be centred upon individual needs where profit is not the sole purpose. Secondly, with financial resources being a significant limitation to the social enterprise, design thinking through making could be an efficient and viable alternative to the purchasing of expensive manufacturing equipment. Low fidelity prototyping, can allow the company to explore and test initial ideas relatively quickly and inexpensively. This could then lead onto the subsequent benefit of design and production via additive manufacturing (otherwise commonly known as 3D printing). Based on the principle of reducing excess wastage, this approach could benefit individuals and communities around the world that have limited access to materials and financial assistance. For instance, the New Story and ICON partnership in Mexico 2020 aims to 'provide 3D printed homes that are intended to offer low-cost housing for low-income communities in Latin America that adapt to their day-to-day lives. The new homes that have been successfully 3D printed will be granted to local families in Mexico currently living in extreme poverty and makeshift, unsafe shelter. This project is to tackle the global housing crisis, which has identified 3D printing as a viable solution. 3D printing allows New Story to reach more families faster, while simultaneously improving quality and design flexibility.' (3d printing industry, 2020)

In an 'opinion', piece for the Design Council (2015) Mat Hunter, Chief Design Officer, eloquently points out, "What fascinated me most about this act of reflection was to see that while we still believe design is of great benefit to the world of social enterprises, it is also true to say that the world of social enterprise is good for design".

CASE STUDY: Creating Design Tools to Enable Games Studios to Address Long-term Business Sustainability Challenges

The following case study offered by Dr Xinya You, R&D fellow in sustainable creative business, InGAME: Innovation for Games and Media Enterprise at the University of Dundee, UK, provides a set of tools to enable young start-up companies within the Gaming industry, to develop and grow their fledgling businesses. It provides a systematic account of how these tools can be easily used within business planning activities.

Introduction

Dundee is a small Scotland city in Scotland with a population of about 150,000. In 2014, it was recognised by the United Nations as the first UNESCO City of Design in the UK for its outstanding contributions in the fields of video games, comics and medical research. Since the Game Boy era, Dundee has been an important contributor to the video game industry. The famous video games IP Lemmings and Grant Theft Auto were created in the city. A game studio in Dundee also produced the console version of Minecraft. In addition, Abertay University in Dundee is the first university in the world launched a video games degree and the prestigious Princeton Review has ranked the quality of its video games education number one in Europe for seven years. More importantly, in the past 20 years, a video game cluster has gradually formed in Dundee and its surrounding areas. Today, there are more than 80 video game companies operating in the cluster, many of which are small and medium enterprises formed by graduates of Abertay University.

In 2018, a new multimillion-pound Innovation for Games and Media Enterprise (InGAME) project established a dedicated research and development (R&D) centre in Dundee to increase the value and scale of the cluster (The project is part of the AHRC Creative Industries Clusters Programme: https://creativeindustriesclusters.com/clusters/ingame/. Grant Reference: AH/S002871/1). Led by Abertay University, in partnership with the University of Dundee and the University of St Andrews, InGAME establishes a collaborative network of academic researchers, students, industry experts and business leaders–it enables the project to benefit from the expertise and experience held in the Dundee games cluster and the HEI partnership. Moreover, InGAME engages the wider creative district and sector support agencies such as TIGA, Ukie and UK Games Fund, to promote economic growth, sector diversification and cultural engagement in the UK.

Sustainability challenges facing Dundee games cluster:

In order to increase the value and scale of the Dundee video games cluster, InGAME prioritises three high-level challenges that the cluster needs to solve.

1. *Creativity Risk*: The financial risk that comes with developing speculative original IP for the games market is often fatal for start-up and micro-SMEs.
2. *Technology Innovation Risk*: Technology innovations within the cluster, though often iterative, inventive and ingenious, are not systematically captured or tested for generalisation or re-use value. This leads to missed commercial opportunities.
3. *Commercialisation Risk*: Although the cluster is comprised primarily of mid-sized SMEs and an even larger number of start-ups and micro-SMEs, these smaller organisations often lack the commercial expertise to innovate new business models and recognise new market opportunities.

Understanding Sustainability Challenges from a Game Studios' Perspective

To better understand the sustainability challenge from the perspective of a game studio, InGAME interviewed the founders of three Dundee game companies. All three game companies are committed to creative experimentation and are keen to explore innovation opportunities. InGAME wanted to gain some insights from the interviewees on how their company maintains business sustainability in a challenging market environment. Some interesting findings from the interview data are shown below.

Finding 1: There are several popular business models in the gaming industry. In the video game industry, there are three popular types of business models: third party publishing, self-publishing and work-for-hire business models.

Finding 2: The sustainability risk of self-published business models is relatively high. For many game studios, the self-publishing model is relatively risky because they lack the ability to successfully connect their games to the target market, and they do not have sufficient capital reserves to support the development of original IPs in the long term. However, for game studios, self-publishing is also the most desirable type of business model because it provides the highest degree of creative freedom. In the best-case scenario, a successful original game IP will make a game studio successful both commercially and creatively.

Finding 3: The sustainability risk of third-party publishing models is medium. Compared with self-publishing, the third-party publishing model is relatively less risky. When applying this type of models, the game studio is usually paid by a publisher to make an original IP within a period of time and the publisher is responsible for the formulation and implementation of product marketing strategies. The commercial success of the game in the market largely depends on the capability of the publisher and the collaboration does not guarantee good sales. For game studios, third-party publishing models usually provide a certain degree of creative freedom and moderate game development revenue.

Finding 4: The sustainability risk of work-for-hire models is relatively low. The work-for-hire model is an ideal choice for game studios to develop industry networks, enhance game development capabilities and create predictable income. When applying this type of model, game studios generate revenue by developing games for clients, and usually do not participate in the formulation and implementation of product-market strategies, nor are they responsible for sales performance. The work-for-hire model usually means limited creative freedom and relatively low service revenue.

Finding 5: Hybrid business model designs can help game studios achieve sustainable growth. Game studios sometimes apply more than one business model at the same period of time. For example, two interviewees stated that their companies use both a work-for-hire and third-party publishing models. As they said, the former is used to maintain and strengthen their business, while the latter is a model that is expected to create a stable higher income in the near future.

Finding 6: Game studios may change their business model in response to the needs of business growth and their long-term goals. For instance, the two interviewees mentioned above regarded their work-for-hire models as transitional models to ensure business sustainability in a short period. Both companies plan to switch to third-party publishing and self-publishing models in the next few years, so that they can create their own games and obtain higher market returns.

Finding 7: The co-evolution of organisation design, business model and product-market strategy is important for business sustainability. A few years ago, one of interviewees wanted to add a new console game development service to his company's work-for-hire model. What he did was to use the company's own funds to develop a multi-platform console game. The whole process involves the evolution of product-market strategy (i.e., entering a new market), business model (i.e., using a new third-party publishing model) and organisational design (e.g., scaling up the team and learning new skills). The successful release of the new game proved its ability to provide a new console game development service and made its work-for-hire business model more competitive, thereby enhancing its business sustainability.

InGAME's Business Sustainability Triangle Model

Based on the above findings, InGAME proposed a business sustainability triangle model consisting of product-market strategy, business model and organisational design (see Fig. 6.2).

As Zott and Amit (2013, p. 409) pointed out, "Examining the dynamics of business model evolution (how they emerge and how they are shaped and adapted by entrepreneurial actors over time)—as well as how business models co-evolve with product market strategy and organization design—reflects an important cross-disciplinary research program that will substantially solidify the business model as a pivotal level and unit of analysis in our understanding of value creation and capture." InGAME's business sustainability triangle model provides a research direction for helping video game studios achieve sustainable success.

Creating Design Tools That Can Help Game Studios Achieve Sustainable Success

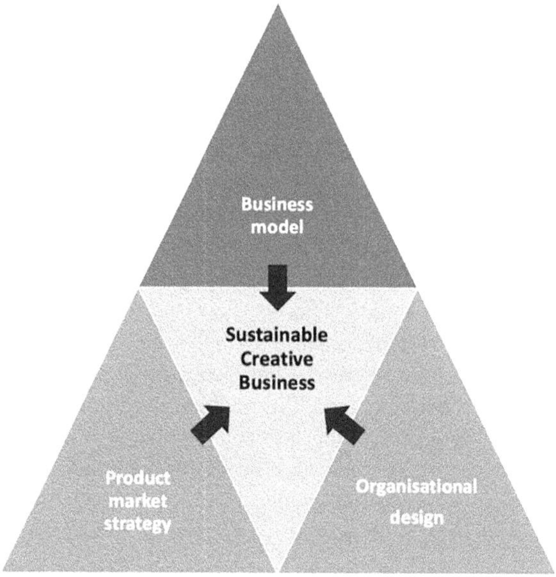

Fig. 6.2 InGAME's business sustainability triangle model (developed by author)

Guided by the business sustainability triangle model, InGAME conducted an in-depth case study of another Dundee game studio. Founded in 2000, the company has developed over 150 casual video games, covering a range of platforms such as Game Boy Advance, HTML5 Browser, Xbox, iOS & Android devices and Microsoft Windows. It not only has extensive experience in using work-for-hire, self-publishing and third party publishing business models, but also has undergone six business model transitions. It provides a suitable case to illustrate how a game studio's product-market strategy, business model and organisational design can co-evolve to support its long-term sustainable development. Two design tools were created and validated as the outputs of the case study.

Design Tool 1: Business Modelling Blueprint

The Business Modelling Blueprint (BMB) is an integrated tool that can help companies understand the relationship among business models, product-market strategies and organisational design (see Fig. 6.3). The purpose of creating this tool is to facilitate the data collection and analysis of the case study. The BMB tool will be provided to Dundee game studios to help them analyse, develop established businesses and create new businesses.

The creation of the tool is inspired by Osterwalder and Pigneur's (2010) "Business Model Canvas" (BMC), highlighting the construction of value chains (i.e., value co-creators, value propositions, value co-creation, value delivery and value capture) and value co-creation process. The BMC has nine building blocks: Key Partners, Key Activities, Key Resources, Value Propositions, Customer Relationships, Channels, Customer segments, Cost structure and Revenue Streams. All of these building blocks are embedded in the InGAME BMB tool in the form of retained building blocks, new building blocks and questions.

The BMB tool has two dimensions:

Horizontal dimension: It describes the value co-creation process. For example, users need to identify customer segments, create value propositions, develop products and services, design customer journeys and ultimately provide customer experience.

Vertical dimension: The vertical dimension indicates how value co-creators need to be considered and can be engaged in the value creation process. For example, when creating a value proposition, users should consider customer needs, organisational capabilities and resources, and which key capabilities and resources should be outsourced to key partners.

How to use the BMB tool it shown below:

Step 1: Answer all the questions in each component of the blueprint.

Step 2: If you find some questions are difficult to answer, you need to do some research to obtain the necessary data to help you answer the questions.

Step 3: If you are unsure of some answers, treat the answers as assumptions. Go collect data, test your assumptions and use your findings to modify your original answers.

Some of InGAME's findings from using the BMB tool to analyse the case study data are as follows:

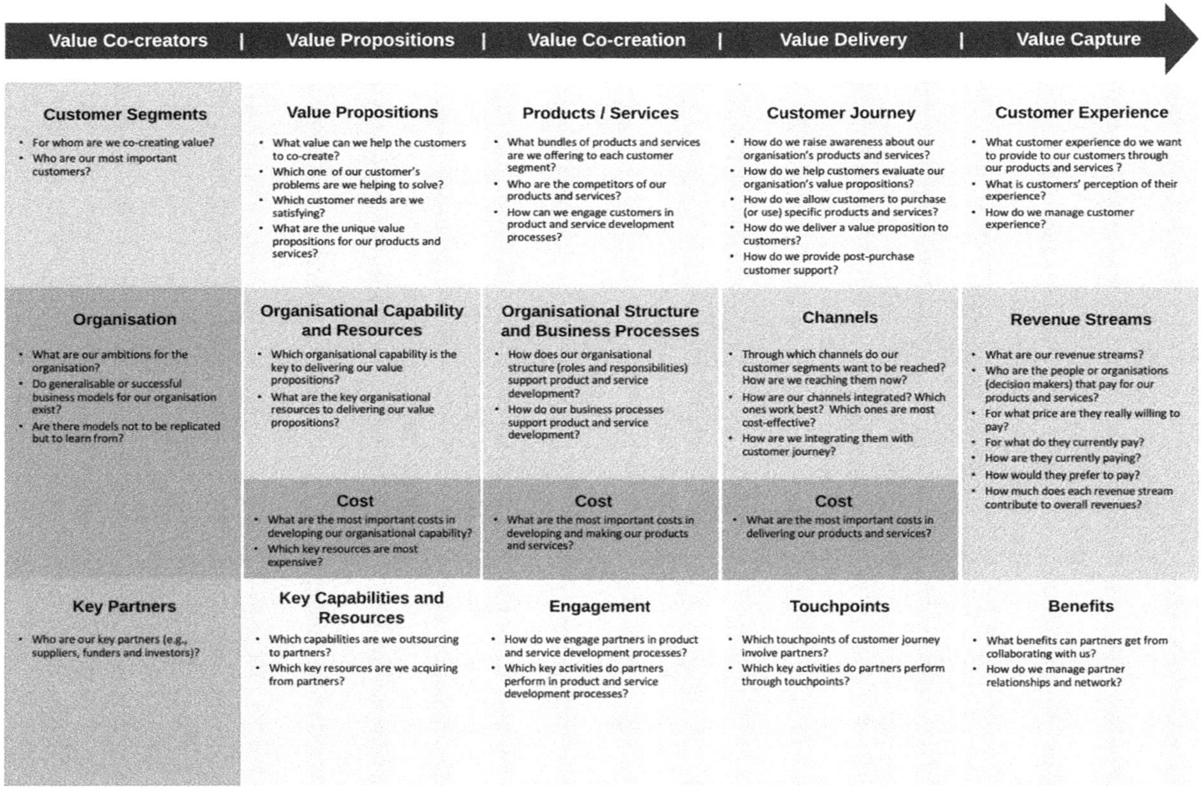

Fig. 6.3 Business-Modelling Blueprint (developed by author)

Analytical framework. The BMB tool offers a useful analytical framework for business modelling. It can help companies explore their strengths and weaknesses of using different business models from a comprehensive perspective and provide information for key strategic decisions related to organisational design, business models and product-market strategy. For example, the case study found that the company's organisational structure and business process allow its employees work efficiently and effective for clients when using the work-for-hire model. However, when there are few constraints, they cannot support employees to strike a balance between creativity and productivity, which in turn leads to higher product development costs and lower commercial viability. This problem surfaced when the company applied the self-publishing and third-publishing business models to develop its own product. In order to improve the business sustainability of these two models, the company needs to redesign its organisational structure and business processes for them.

Units of analysis. Each block of the BMB can represent a unit of analysis. InGAME have found many related examples from the case study. Taking the "organisational capability and resources" as an example, the case study shows that when using a work-for-hire model, the company often competes with many other game studios on price and there is a limited scope for what the company can upsell in terms of its creative team's skill. In order to enhance the sustainability of the business, the company needs to further develop its organisational capabilities.

Building block stability. Some building blocks related to organisational design are relatively stable, directing the direction of co-evolution of business models, organisational design and product-market strategy. For example, the company's ambition to succeed both creatively and commercially (i.e., the "organisation" block) is such a stable building block. In terms of commercialisation, the company wants to achieve significant success in the market. In terms of creativity, the company is not only committed to making creative games, but also constantly trying to create games in better ways. These thoughts have profoundly affected the company's organisational design and development and have not changed when the business model changed.

Design Tool 2: Business Model Evolution Journey Canvas

The Business Model Evolution Journey Canvas (BMEJC) is a reflective tool that can help game studios evolve their business models and successfully transition from one business model to another (Fig. 6.4). The reason for creating it is to facilitate data collection and analysis of the case study as well. This tool will be provided to game studios to help them understand when, why and how to successful transform and evolve their business models.

The BMEJC tool is created on the basis of the BMB tool: the building blocks of the BMB can be used to identify decision-making factors for business model transformation in the BMEJC. These blocks can be labelled as organisation factors, key partner factors and market factors. How to use the tool is shown below.

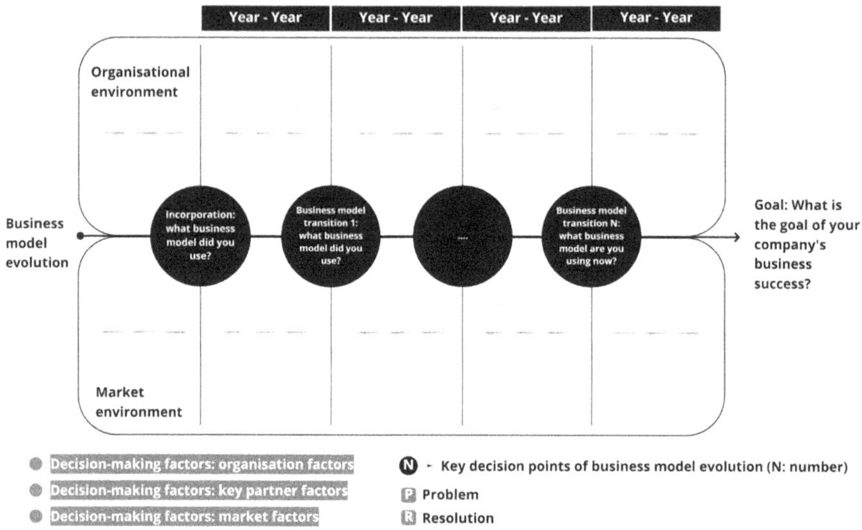

Fig. 6.4 Business Model Evolution Journey Canvas (developed by author)

Step 1: Business models. Fill in all the business models that your company has used and are going to use in the blocks in round shape in the middle of the canvas in chronological order (the canvas is extendable).

Step 2: Business model evolution timeline. Fill in the years of use of each business model in the black boxes at the top of the canvas.

Step 3: Business goal. Fill in your business goal next to the arrow on the right side of the canvas. Your business model(s) should help you to achieve the goal.

Step 4: Organisational and market environments. Use sticky notes to describe the organisational and market environments before and after the transition period of using new or different business models.

Step 5: Key decision-making factors. Use the building blocks of the BMB tool to identify key decision-making factors (organisation, key partner and market factors) related to the applying new or different business models. Place the labels in the corresponding organisational and market environment zones on the canvas: put organisation factors in organisational environment zones, put market factors in market environment zones, put key partners on the line between organisational and market environment zones.

Step 6: Key decision points of business model evolution: Put the key decision points of business model evolution icons on the canvas and number them in chronological order. The numbered key decision points show how the organisation, key partner and market factors affect the evolution of a company's business model over time.

Step 7: Problems and resolutions. If your company encountered a problem when using a certain business model or has difficulty applying a new business model, mark the problem area with the problem icon—this can help you find the relevance of the problem to your organisation, market, or key partners. Then, use the resolution icon to mark the resolution area(s)—how did and/or will you resolve the problem? A solution may involve new product-market strategy, organisational design and business model transformation.

Figure 6.5 is an example of how InGAME used the tool to analyse case study data. Some findings from using the BMEJC tool to analyse the case study data are as follows:

Analytical framework. The BMEJC tool provides users with a useful analytical framework that can help them understand how to evolve business models and how to transition from one business model to another. As shown in Fig. 6.5, it enables users to map out the evolution history of their company's business model, reflect on the organisational and market environments of the business model transition period, and identify the market, organisation and key partner factors involved in key decision-making.

Business model evolution and business sustainability. The BMEJC tool can help users better understand when, why and how to successful transform and evolve their business models, thereby enhancing the business sustainability of their companies. For example, Fig. 6.5 shows that the company encountered a problem when it applied a third-party publishing model between 2000 and 2002: the publisher failed to connect the company's games with the market–despite the good feedback from players on the game experience. To solve this problem, in 2002, the company decided to enter a new market by adopting a work-for-hire model and make innovative games for a client who owned the sales channel of that market. This decision was made based on the company's game development capability. In order to meet the client's needs, the company revised its business processes, relocated its resource and reduced the cost of game development. As a result, the new business model significantly increased the company's revenue and enhanced its business sustainability.

Conclusions

The case of InGAME shows that it is feasible to create design tools to help game studios solve long-term business sustainability challenges. Applying a challenge-driven approach and collaborating with industry experts and business leaders are critical to solving such challenges. For InGAME, the collaboration with four Dundee game studios helped it understand the existence of three popular industry business models, the different sustainability risk levels of these business models, and some organisational design and product-market strategy challenges that game companies may encounter when using these models. The two design tools created base on their experience will be used to create an InGAME Business Model Design Booklet. InGAME will share the booklet with

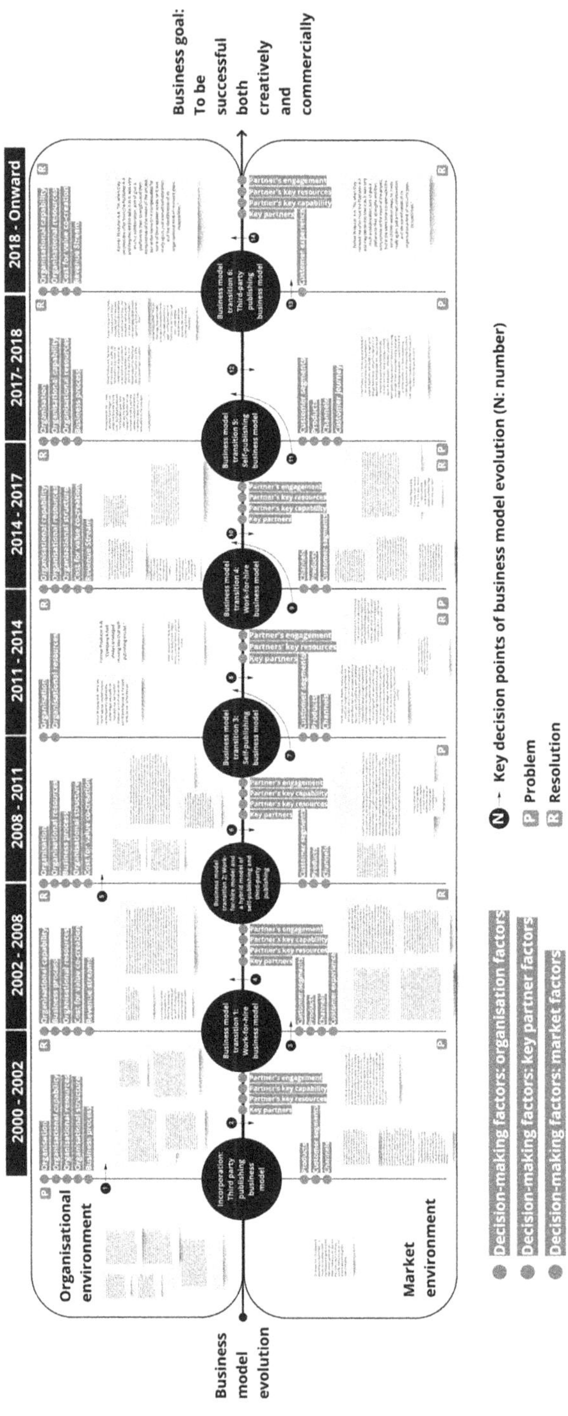

Fig. 6.5 Business Model Evolution Journey Canvas–application example (developed by author)

Dundee's video game studios to help them enhance the sustainability of their business, thereby increasing the value and scale of the Dundee games cluster. ◀

Chapter Summary It is commonly agreed that the world's leading brands enjoy strong customer loyalty, which in turn reflects their longevity and commercial success. One factor that contributes to this is their clear commitment to providing meaningful experiences to their customers, be it through online / offline activities or a combination of both. These experiences could be considered 'values made visible' reflecting the values of the brand and the purpose of these values to their stakeholders. A powerful mission statement encapsulates these values and the reason why the company is in business. Defining corporate values is linked to the new perspective of sustainability and Corporate Social Responsibility in which ethical values shape and direct organisational decision-making and strategic vision. The Climate Change agenda is gaining prominence, affecting our lives in the here and now, and future generations to come, as such, sustainable business practices are now becoming imperative to organisations, regardless of size and location. Not only is there a need to radically re-think common business models and established orthodoxies, but also mission in terms of social impact and societal 'good.' Across the commercial landscape, we are witnessing the rise of dynamic social enterprises that are actively engaging with complex social problems that affect individuals and communities and across the globe. They may sound like charitable enterprises, of which they are not; they are businesses with a purpose to make meaningful change to their customers. Innovative in nature, they are value generators across diverse sectors that genuinely place people before profit. In terms of contribution and impact to the local economy, Dr Xinya You provided a succinct account of her current research activities, based around the gaming industry in Dundee, Scotland. SMEs often encounter significant challenges to their growth and long-term commercial development; here, she outlined key approaches and strategies to enable their sustainable growth. Through the development and support of the flourishing gaming industry, its contribution to the local and regional economy is significant in the creation of employment opportunities and wider social prosperity. Chapter 7 now turns its attention towards design thinking for branding activities by Dr Sotiris Lalaounis, based in the Department of Management, University of Exeter Business School, UK.

Review Questions

1. What is the primary aim of a Mission Statement and who would be responsible for its development and wider dissemination?
2. What are the three interrelated elements of the Triple Bottom Line framework and how would these inform any sustainable development strategy?
3. Corporate Social Responsibility is a holistic organisational philosophy, as such, who would be the main stakeholders in its effective operation?
4. What makes Social Enterprise business models uniquely distinct from established commercial rivals?
5. Fledgling gaming companies encounter significant challenges to business survival, what are the main challenges that they face on a day-to-day basis?

Project Questions

1. Devise a succinct Mission Statement for a business proposition that could be adopted by a Social Enterprise.
2. What other metrics of success could be used to quantify impact within the Triple Bottom Line framework?
3. CSR has many benefits to the organisation and its stakeholders; however, what are the disadvantages of CSR to company reputation if not fully practiced?
4. Within your regional setting, identify one Social Enterprise and explore how its business model addressed a particular social need.
5. Referring to the Business Modelling Blueprint, develop a new product introduction strategy for an environmentally friendly consumer durable product.

Chapter Tasks

1. Take a Mission Statement from a leading international brand and provide your own interpretation as to how it could embrace their core organisational values.
2. Identify one Sustainable Development Goal defined by the UN, (2015) and list key 5 points as to how design can make a meaningful contribution to its achievement.
3. Within 60 minutes, list as many challenges as you can, outlining the introduction of CSR to an international courier company.
4. Form a small group of no more than 4 people and then devise a new business model for a social enterprise that seeks to provide accessible financial support/loans to marginalised communities.
5. Identify how a small gaming company could diversify its existing products to a completely new market audience.

References

3d printing industry. (2020). *The First Homes Have Been Built in New Story's 3d Printed Community for Low-Income Families in Mexico*. Retrieved April 16, 2021, from https://3dprintingindustry.com/news/the-first-homes-have-been-built-in-new-storys-3d-printed-community-for-low-income-families-in-mexico-166830/

Air New Zealand. (2021). Company Profile. Retrieved April 1, 2021, from https://www.airnewzealand.co.uk/corporate-profile

Airline Ratings. (2020). Best Airlines 2020: Airline Ratings Names Air New Zealand Top Carrier. Retrieved April 1, 2021, from https://www.airlineratings.com/news/airline-ratings-names-best-airlines-2020/

Bhamra, T., & Lofthouse, V. (2007). *Design or Sustainability. A Practical Approach*. Gower Publishing Ltd.

Cone Communications. (2015). *2015 Cone Communications/Ebiquity Global CSR Study*. Retrieved April 15, 2021, from https://www.conecomm.com/research-blog/2015-cone-communications-ebiquity-global-csr-study

Cutter, S. (1995). Race, Class and Environmental Justice. *Progress in Human Geography, 19*(1), 111–122.

David, F. R. (2007). *Strategic Management: Cases and Practices*. McGraw Hill Co Inc.

Deloitte. (2012). *Sustainability 2.0—Using Sustainability to Drive Business Innovation and Growth*. Retrieved April 9, 2021, from https://www2.deloitte.com/us/en/insights/deloitte-review/issue-10/sustainability-2-0-innovation-and-growth-through-sustainability.html

Design Council. (2015). *Social Enterprise Is Good for Design*. Retrieved April 16, 2021, from https://www.designcouncil.org.uk/news-opinion/social-enterprise-good-design

Dunne, A., & Raby, F. (2009). *Dunne and Raby—Projects*. Retrieved April 12, 2021, from http://dunneandraby.co.uk/content/projects

Edwards, A. R. (2005). *The Sustainability Revolution: Portrait of a Paradigm Shift*. New Society Publishers.

Elkington, J. (1997). *Cannibals with Forks: The Triple Bottom Line of 21st Century Business*. Capstone.

Falsey, T. A. (1989). *Corporate Philosophies and Mission Statements: A Survey and Guide for Corporate Communicators and Management*. Greenwood.

Forbes. (2017). *Millennials Driving Brands to Practice Socially Responsible Marketing*. Retrieved April 13, 2021, from https://www.forbes.com/sites/sarahlandrum/2017/03/17/millennials-driving-brands-to-practice-socially-responsible-marketing/?sh=3d5c4a254990

Gomez, K., Mawhinney, T., & Betts, K. (2021). *Welcome to Generation Z*. Network of Executive Women / Deloitte. Retrieved April 12, 2021, from https://www2.deloitte.com/us/en/pages/consumer-business/articles/understanding-generation-z-in-the-workplace.html

Harrison, K. (2020). *How Your Corporate Reputation May Be Your Biggest Financial Asset*. Cutting Edge PR. Retrieved April 8, 2021, from https://cuttingedgepr.com/corporate-reputation-may-biggest-financial-asset/

HBR. (2009). *Why Sustainability Is Now the Key Driver of Innovation*. Retrieved April 9, 2021, from https://hbr.org/2009/09/why-sustainability-is-now-the-key-driver-of-innovation

Jackson, A., Boswell, K., & Davis, D. (2011, November). Sustainability and Triple Bottom Line Reporting—What Is It All About? *International Journal of Business, Humanities and Technology, 1*(3), 55–59.

Jeurissen, R. (2000). The Social Function of Business Ethics. *Business Ethics Quarterly, 10*(4), 821–843.

Kerrigan, S., & Kulasooriya, D. (2020). The Sustainability Transformation: Look Ahead, Look Inside, and Look Around. *Deloitte Review, 27*. July 31, 2020. Retrieved April 10, 2021, from https://www2.deloitte.com/us/en/insights/topics/strategy/sustainable-transformation-in-business.html

Levering, R. (2000). *The 100 Best Companies to Work for in America*. Institute Inc.

Lewis Marketing. (2020, August 19). *Understanding Corporate Social Responsibility in PR*. Retrieved April 15, 2021, from https://www.teamlewis.com/magazine/understanding-corporate-social-responsibility-in-public-relations/

Nielsen. (2015). *The Sustainability Imperative*. Retrieved April 13, 2021, from https://nielseniq.com/global/en/insights/analysis/2015/the-sustainability-imperative-2/

Osterwalder, A., & Pigneur, Y. (2010). *Business Model Generation: A Handbook for Visionaries, Game Changers, and Challengers*. John Wiley & Sons, Inc.

SDGS. (2015). *Transforming Our World: The 2030 Agenda for Sustainable Development*. United Nations, Department of Economic and Social Affairs Sustainable Development. Retrieved April 9, 2021, from https://sdgs.un.org/2030agenda

Social Enterprise UK. (2019). Survey *Capitalism in Crisis—Transforming Our Economy for People and Planet*. Retrieved April 16, 2021, from https://www.socialenterprise.org.uk/state-of-social-enterprise-reports/capitalism-in-crisis-transforming-our-economy-for-people-and-planet/

Sufi, T., & Lyons, H. (2003). Mission Statement Exposed. *International Journal of Contemporary Hospitality Management, 15*(5), 255–262.

Sustainable Development. (1987). *Report of the World Commission on Environment and Development: Our Common Future*. World Commission on Environment and Development (WCED). Retrieved April 9, 2021, from https://sustainabledevelopment.un.org/content/documents/5987our-common-future.pdf

Thegoodtrade. (2021). *What Is a Social Enterprise? A Simple Definition & 3 Examples*. Retrieved April 15, 2021, from https://www.thegoodtrade.com/features/what-is-a-social-enterprise

Toftoy, C. N., & Chatterjee, J. (2004). Mission Statements and the Small Business. *Business Strategy Review, 15*(3), 41–44. Print.

Von Stamm, B. (2004). Innovation—What's Design Got to Do with It? *Design Management Review, 15*(1), 10–19.

Williams, L. S. (2008, April). The Mission Statement: A Corporate Reporting Tool with a Past, Present, and Future. *Journal of Business Communication, 45*(2), 94–119.

Yang, C.-L., Huang, K.-P., Huang, C.-L., & Huang, R.-H. (2016). Integration of Corporate Social Responsibility into New Product Development, March 15, 2016. *International Journal of Management, Economics and Social Sciences, 5*(1), 14–34.

Zott, C., & Amit, R. (2013). The Business Model: A Theoretically Anchored Robust Construct for Strategic Analysis. *Strategic Organization, 11*(4), 403–411.

Design Thinking for Branding 7

Learning Objectives

- Explain the two components of the brand audit: brand inventory and brand exploratory and discuss how brand exploratory contributes to brand equity development.
- Explore how design thinking (inspiration stage) can facilitate a thorough brand exploratory by pursuing consumer ethnography to achieve the required levels of empathy.
- Discuss how the findings of the brand audit can help brand marketers identify branding problems and/or opportunities.
- Discuss how design thinking (ideation and implementation stages) can provide solutions to branding problems and/or strategies to harness branding opportunities.
- Explore how design thinking can help brand managers and designers develop branding strategies which balance the need for brand consistency and brand relevance (through the concept of brand ambidexterity).

7.1 Introduction

Bringing together concepts and frameworks from extant academic literature in marketing, brand management, consumer culture theory and design management, the overall purpose of this chapter is to provide an understanding of how design

Contribution by Dr Sotiris T. Lalaounis, Senior Lecturer in Marketing and Design Management, University of Exeter Business School, UK.

Supplementary Information The online version contains supplementary material available at [https://doi.org/10.1007/978-3-030-94206-9_7].

Y. Huang, D. Hands, *Design Thinking for New Business Contexts*,
https://doi.org/10.1007/978-3-030-94206-9_7

thinking can contribute to brand management. Nowadays, organisations recognise that brands are (their most) valuable intangible assets and there is "a shift in emphasis from a notion of brands as logos to a more integrated view as the matching of a firm's functional and emotional values with the performance and psychosocial values sought by consumers" (de Chernatony & Dall'Olmo Riley, 1998, p. 418). Brands reside in consumers' minds and require significant and continuous organisational investment because they provide firms the ability to develop and maintain unique propositions in consumers' hearts and minds. Organisations need to develop and maintain a holistic perspective in order to bring together brand identity and brand image to define their brands and their meaning (Dall'Olmo Riley, 2016). Inspired by the service-dominant logic in marketing (Vargo & Lusch, 2004, 2008) which advocates that consumers co-create value with organisations by taking part in value-creation networks (Baron & Harris, 2008; Tynan & McKechnie, 2009), brand managers and designers recognise that meaning itself is dialogic and socially constructed (Morris, 2003) and that, similarly, brand meaning is co-created by consumers (as the main external stakeholder) with organisations. Organisations create the brand identity, that is, the brand expressions and messages (input) (Aaker, 2010; Schmitt & Simonson, 1997) communicated to consumers in the market. The consumers' unique interpretations of these brand expressions and messages (output) (Margulies, 1977) lead to brand image which is all about consumer impressions (Schmitt & Simonson, 1997). Hence, organisations communicate their brand messages (output) which are perceived and are uniquely interpreted by the target audience who then add their own experiences to generate an ever-evolving brand narrative. This notion of a co-created brand meaning is reflected in the following definition of brand.

> A brand is a customer experience represented by a collection of images and ideas; often it refers to a symbol such as a name, logo, slogan, and design scheme. Brand recognition and other reactions are created by the accumulation of experiences with the specific product or service, both directly relating to its use, and through the influence of advertising, design, and media commentary. (American Marketing Association, 2015, cited in Dall'Olmo Riley, 2016, p. 4)

The main objectives of branding, as an essential part of business strategy, are creating identification, differentiation and value for consumers, organisations and society. From a consumers' perspective, a brand is important because it provides consumers the ability to identify the organisation producing the product or delivering the service, and in consequence, assign responsibility to this organisation. If consumers are happy with product performance or the quality of the service, they can purchase the brand again, if not, it is very likely they will avoid the brand in the future (Keller & Swaminathan, 2020). Over time, consumers who purchase a brand develop their own brand knowledge, that is, their own brand meaning stored in their memory (Keller & Lehmann, 2003), leading to trust towards the brand. This trust reduces any risks associated with purchasing and consuming a product; buying from a brand which consumers know and trust, means that consumers feel safe that the product will perform or the service will deliver what was expected

(Delgado-Ballester & Munuera-Alemán, 2001). This also means that brands can reduce the cost for searching for new products or services because consumers return to the brands they trust. Finally, and most importantly, brands are symbolic devices, they help consumers satisfy their emotional needs because they empower consumers to construct and communicate their own self-identities. As consumers, we buy brands whose personality and values correspond to our own; brands speak to us and speak for us. "Brands create the construct that empowers people to be, experience, and become whatever they desire" (Jacobs & Wintrob, 2016, p. 55). Consumers gather together a constellation of brands and possessions (Chaplin & Lowrey, 2009; Solomon, 1988) which over time become part of their extended self as explained by Belk (1988) with the following:

> we learn, define, and remind ourselves of who we are by our possessions…we seek to express ourselves through possessions, and use material possessions to seek happiness, remind ourselves of experiences, accomplishments, and other people in our lives, and even create a sense of immortality after death. Our accumulation of possessions provides a sense of past and tells us who we are, where we have come from, and perhaps where we are going. (Belk, 1988, p. 160)

From a societal perspective, brands are important because they generate and own a significant part of global wealth and provide employment (with associated social benefits) (Hales, 2011). Society demands from brands to operate with social and environmental responsibility. In fact, brands can reflect many societal values, dominant ideologies, the aspects that people like about their society and its representations (Holt, 2004, 2006; McCracken, 1986; Shepherd et al., 2015). Over time, many brands have become expressions of political ideologies, especially nowadays where political and societal discourse has become explosive and rather divisive. Nevertheless, many brands could also "pre-empt cultural spheres of religion, politics, and myth, as they generally promote an ideology linked to political and theological models that equate consumption with happiness" (Schroeder, 2009, p. 124).

Finally, brands are important to organisations because they create identification and differentiation, act as guarantee of quality to consumers leading to brand trust and generate added value. This "added value with which a given brand endows a product [or service]" (Farquhar, 1989, p. 24) is what we call brand equity. The implication of brand equity is that consumers are willing to accept a higher price for a comparable product because of the brand, while suppliers (to the organisation) are willing to charge the organisation lower costs due to the popularity of the brand. Putting these two together means that the organisation's profit margins improve (lower costs to the organisation and higher price to the consumers). As Keller (1993) explains:

> Customer-based brand equity involves consumers' reactions to an element of the marketing mix [product, price, place, and promotion] for the brand in comparison with their reactions to the same marketing mix element attributed to [an]…unnamed version of the product or service. (Keller, 1993, p. 2)

Brand managers ought to maintain a good understanding of brand performance to determine brand value and how this manifests in financial contributions to the organisation. To assess brand performance, brand managers need to regularly conduct a brand audit, a consumer-focused task which evaluates the health of the brand and identifies ways to improve brand equity (Keller & Swaminathan, 2020). Indeed, once brand equity is developed, the onus is on brand managers to maintain, defend and enhance the brand's equity in a dynamic market environment (Van Rekom et al., 2006). Design thinking, and in particular, engaging in the inspiration stage (of the design thinking process), can help brand managers successfully conduct the brand audit. Consumer ethnography allows brand mangers understand consumers' thoughts, feelings and behaviour towards the brand (purchase and consumption) to achieve the required level of empathy. This can lead to identifying branding problems and/or opportunities for the brand which organisations must address. The ideation and implementation stages of the design thinking process can then enable brand managers brainstorm ideas and determine the most optimum strategies to solve these branding problems and/or to harness these branding opportunities. Ultimately, this allows organisations sustain and enhance brand equity further. Figure 7.1 diagrammatically presents the connections between the stages of the design thinking process, brand audit and brand equity management, and provides the structure based on which we frame how design thinking can contribute to brand management. We will be referring to this conceptual model at every stage of our discussion in this chapter.

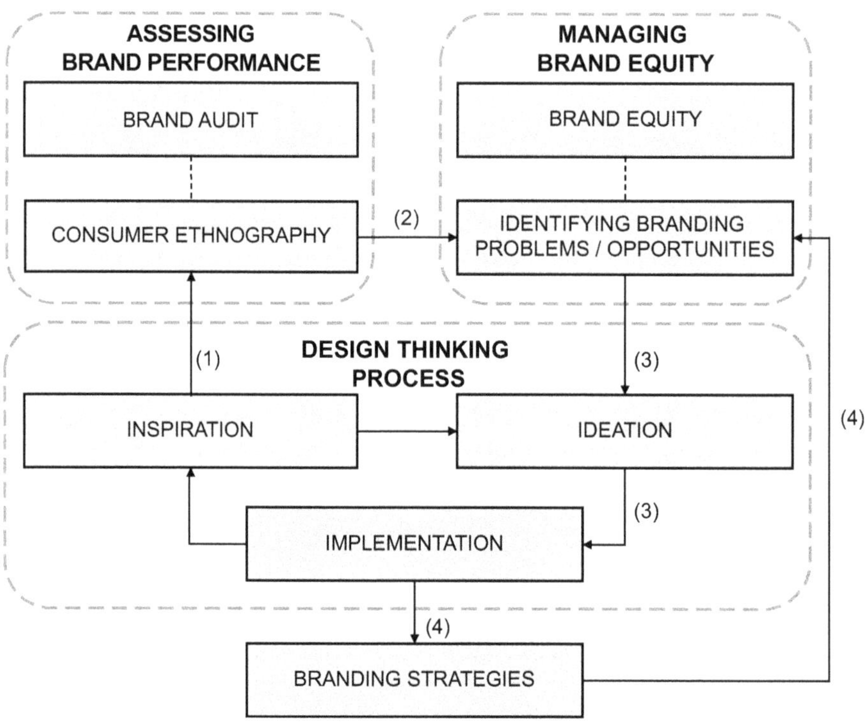

Fig. 7.1 Design thinking and brand management (adapted by author)

7.2 Brand Audit, Consumer Ethnography, and Design Thinking

The brand audit allows brand managers to assess the performance of the brand from both organisation and consumer perspectives. Keller and Swaminathan define brand audit as a "consumer-focused exercise…to assess the health of the brand, uncover its sources of brand equity and suggest ways to improve and leverage its equity" (2020, p. 329). The brand audit has two constituent components: the brand inventory and the brand exploratory which examine the brand from organisation and consumer perspectives, respectively.

Brand inventory involves "carrying out a detailed profiling of the organisation's products and/or services to determine how these are marketed and branded. This requires a thorough examination of brand elements and supporting marketing campaign materials" (Lalaounis, 2020, p. 257). Brand elements include brand names, logos, and symbols used by the organisation while marketing campaign elements include the organisation's marketing strategies (in relation product, pricing, promotion, and distribution decisions) (Keller & Swaminathan, 2020). The second component of the brand audit, the brand exploratory examines the performance of the brand from the consumer perspective. It is defined as "research directed to understanding what consumers think and feel about the brand and act toward it in order to better understand sources of brand equity, as well as any possible barriers" (Keller & Swaminathan, 2020, p. 332). This will help brand managers understand the true meaning of the brand to its target group of consumers.

Brand exploratory can be conducted by pursuing quantitative and qualitative techniques. Quantitative techniques can include methods to measure levels of awareness, the strength, favourability, and uniqueness of brand associations (brand meaning), consumers' purchase intentions, their brand loyalty, and brand substitutability, that is, the consumers' willingness to substitute the brand with another (when the brand is not available). Qualitative techniques involve open-ended interpretivist methods to uncover consumers' deeply held perceptions and feelings, such as free associations exercises, completion and interpretation tasks, and comparison tasks (for more on quantitative and qualitative methodologies for brand exploratory, see Chap. 8 in Lalaounis, 2020).

In addition to these qualitative techniques, organisations have also harnessed the power of ethnography in order to mitigate the say/do gap bias (Liedtka, 2015) whereby consumers do not always behave in the way they say or think they do (Fellman, 1999), as well as to overcome situations where consumers cannot convey the reasons behind their brand choices or are merely disinclined to do so. Users can have needs and desires they are not aware of, or cannot articulate (Chen & Venkatesh, 2013). They often lack the ability to identify problems with existing products and services, and are unable to envisage future product and service use and what they will want or will consume in the future (Cooper & Evans, 2006). Ethnography, a research method traditionally used in anthropology, "produces a detailed, in depth observation of people's behaviour, beliefs, and preferences by observing and interacting with them in a natural environment" (Ireland, 2003, p. 26). Traditionally, ethnography requires substantial time so that the researcher 'goes native' and is accepted as a member of the social group under study, minimising any influence on individual or group behaviour, while uncovering patterns of behaviour which original members of the social group have not been able to identify or explain themselves (Malinowski, 1922; Plowman, 2003).

Unlike in anthropology where an ethnographic study takes place over a long period of time, consumer or design ethnography is much more applied to suit the demands of organisations and suit the work of brand managers and designers. "[In] common with other kinds of applied anthropology, [design ethnography] is usually done more quickly and given less theoretical contextualisation…In addition….the data collection methods and ways ethnographic materials are analysed are shaped by the particular needs of industrial designers" (Wasson, 2000, p. 382). Ireland (2003) explains that there are six types of ethnography for design research:

1. Field ethnography, the most traditional approach where the researcher observes individuals' behaviour in a natural setting (e.g. at their home or in stores) (participant observation),
2. Digital ethnography where researchers use digital cameras to record people's behaviour and observe and analyse it later,
3. Photo ethnography where members of the social group under study are asked to take photos or videos of their daily lives and reflect on these with diary notes,
4. 'Real world' ethnographic enactments, pioneered by the MTV in its Real World Series, where a certain environment was custom-built in order to monitor people's behaviour,
5. Personas which are visual or textual scenarios or profiles generated to inspire and direct design based on studies of real people,
6. Ethno-futurism, which "combines digital tools capturing day-to-day activities and small details of cultural significance with future perspectives, which…explore major trends that can influence and change culture as a whole. Such approach is ideal for technology products that require understanding an individual's perspective and the broader picture, as well as for products whose success relies on trends, at least to a certain extent". (Lalaounis, 2017, p. 45)

With consumer ethnography, the researcher can gather consumer market insight by participating in consumers' daily life in particular settings (people's homes or in retail environments), collecting data using primarily participant observation, and personal, in-context interviews, and then reporting on the findings of this process (Moisander & Valtonen, 2012). Indeed, in a seminal ethnographic study, Peñaloza (1998) combined field and digital ethnography, that is, participant observation and photography, with interviews to explore the consumption of spectacle (a mix of a museum-like experience with commercial characteristics) at the Nike Town store in Chicago, USA.

Due to the ubiquity of the Internet and social media in daily life, purchasing, and consumption, consumers' online behaviour is as important as their physical behaviour. Humans have evolved to homo connectus (Llamas & Belk, 2013), who are wired or wirelessly connected so that they can be constantly logged on due to their fear of missing out (FOMO). On that basis, Belk (2013) argues that in the digital world, "there are many new possessions and technologies through which we present and extend our self, and they operate quite differently than in predigital days. They also create different ways through which we can meet, interact with, and extend our aggregate selves through other people while experiencing a transcendent sense that we are part of something bigger than us alone" (Belk, 2013, p. 494).

In response to these changes in consumer culture, Kozinets (2002) developed a special type of ethnography which seeks to observe and understand people's online behaviour. Netnography "adapts ethnographic research techniques to study the cultures and communities that are emerging through computer-mediated communications. [It] uses the information that is publicly available in online forums to identify and understand the needs and decision influences of relevant online consumer groups" (Kozinets, 2002, p. 62). In comparison with the aforementioned types of ethnography, netnography can be unobtrusive if the researcher decides to monitor and observe behaviour without participating (non-participant observation) which can be beneficial as there is minimum influence on online consumers' behaviour by the researcher. Netnography can also be less time-consuming than other types of ethnography yet it allows continuous access to the (online) social group under study which provides advantages to researchers (Kozinets, 2002). However, it is important to point out that netnography, similar to other qualitative methodologies, requires strong interpreting skills by the researcher, careful evaluations of emerging behavioural patterns, and the engagement of several methods for triangulation. These enable researchers to make shrewd data interpretations necessary to generate knowledge and insights so that brand managers and designers develop and manage successful brands (Moisander & Valtonen, 2012).

Ethnography is strongly connected with the process of design thinking. Liedtka contends that the design thinking process involves "iterative cycles of exploration using deep user research to develop insights and design criteria, followed by the generation of multiple ideas and concepts and the prototyping and experimentation to select the best ones—usually performed by functionally diverse groups working closely with users" (2015, p. 927). Hence, there are three stages: (1) inspiration which involves data gathering to achieve empathy, (2) ideation which is all about brainstorming and ideas development, and (3) implementation, which involves prototyping and testing to determine the most optimum solution and refine it further. This process is iterative rather than linear which is why Brown (2009) describes these stages as spheres of innovation (rather than stages). The inspiration stage of the design thinking process involves the use of applied ethnography to achieve the required level of empathy. Hence design thinking contributes to brand audit (and in particular, brand exploratory) through their common use of applied consumer ethnography (Fig. 7.1—arrow 1). In the inspiration stage of the design thinking process, brand managers and designers must go out in the real world to observe target users' behaviour and understand the socio-cultural context within which this behaviour takes place. Brown (2008) argues that design thinking follows a human-centred approach to understand people's behaviour and their explicit and latent needs and deliver solutions which satisfy these needs. Actually, "design thinking is not only human-centred; it is deeply human in and of itself" (Brown, 2009, p. 4).

Observing, living through and understanding users' behaviour allows brand managers and designers to achieve three levels of empathy:

1. Physical empathy, which requires physically living through, first hand, the user experience,
2. Cognitive empathy, which involves translating these physical experiences into opportunities to improve these experiences by asking questions which uncover users' latent needs,
3. Emotional empathy, which requires emotional understanding to work with ideas and concepts that matter to the target users at an emotional level.

This transforms target users from adversaries to advocates of these ideas and concepts (Brown, 2009). Ultimately achieving empathy enables brand managers and designers to understand users and their behaviour well; empathy enables them to see the world through the users' eyes, feel the world through the users' emotions, understand the world though the users' experiences and using the users' meanings of these experiences and the world in general (Brown, 2009; Elliott & Jankel-Elliott, 2003). From a branding perspective, the brand exploratory, based on inspiration through ethnography and empathy, allows brand managers and designers to understand the brand ecology (Percy et al., 2001) which involves "studying the lived experience of the consumer as a social being, and which considers not just the attitudinal, emotional, and behavioural aspects of brand consumption, but explores how this brand-related behaviour integrates with wider social and cultural experience in the life-world of the active consumer". (Elliott & Jankel-Elliott, 2003, p. 215).

7.3 Identifying Branding Problems and/or Opportunities

Assessing the performance of the brand based on the brand audit, and in particular, the brand exploratory, enables organisations to maintain and enhance the equity of the brand. As mentioned earlier, brand equity is all about the extra value the brand gives to a product or service beyond the objective quality of this product or service (Farquhar, 1989). Carrying out the brand audit, and in particular the brand exploratory based on consumer ethnography, enables brand managers and designers to identify any potential branding problems and/or opportunities for the brand, in relation to the four layers of the Customer-Based Brand Equity (CBBE) pyramid model (see Figs. 7.2 and 7.3) which is a seminal framework in brand management and development. For example the results of the brand exploratory could determine whether the levels of consumer awareness need to improve, identify any negative consumer associations which must be eliminated, understand what consumers think (is it a credible part of the consumers' consideration set?) and feel towards the brand (emotions towards the brand, and those generated by the brand) to address any

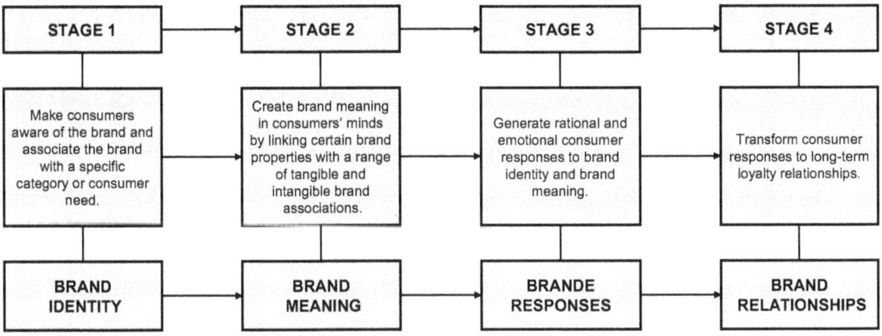

Fig. 7.2 Stages of brand development (based on Keller 2001, adapted by author)

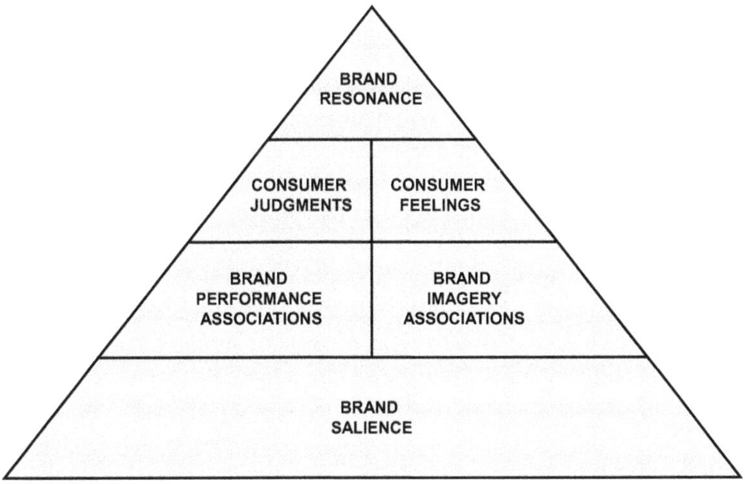

Fig. 7.3 Customer-based brand equity pyramid model (Keller, 2001, adapted by author)

negative cognitive and emotional elements, or assess the levels and the extent of the consumers' loyalty towards the brand.

According to the CBBE pyramid model, in order for organisations to develop high levels of brand equity, the first stage is to ensure that consumers are aware of the brand and that the brand is related to a specific product or service category or to a particular consumer need (first layer of the CBBE pyramid model). This therefore involves developing a brand identity to achieve brand awareness (brand salience). As previously explained the brand identity includes the brand's expressions and messages communicated to its target audiences (Aaker, 2010; Schmitt & Simonson, 1997). The brand identity integrates different design elements and combines product, graphic, and environmental design. Design management enables brand managers and designers to communicate consistent and coherent messages to target consumers (Johansson & Svengren Holm, 2006). Brand identity includes four elements: properties (buildings, offices, retail places, and company vehicles), products (the products' or services' sensory characteristics), presentations, that is, the elements surrounding the product (its packaging, labelling, and tags), or the elements surrounding the service (shopping bags, retail place settings, and employee uniforms), and publications (promotional materials, advertising, and stationery) (Schmitt & Simonson, 1997; Schmitt et al., 1995).

These brand identity elements can generate brand awareness which is all about consumers' ability to recall and recognise the brand. Brand recall "relates to consumers' ability to retrieve the brand when given the product category, the needs fulfilled by the category, or some other type of probe as a cue… [it] requires that consumers correctly generate the brand from memory" (Keller, 1993, p. 3). With brand recognition, consumers confirm they recognise the brand when exposed to a visual stimulus (a brand element e.g. brand logo or symbol), and are able to correctly determine that they have seen or heard of the brand before (Keller, 1993). Brand managers and designers must also work to achieve depth and breadth of brand awareness. A salient brand enjoys depth of brand awareness which is all about the ease of brand recall and recognition as well as how likely the brand will come in consumers' minds, and breadth of brand awareness which is all about the range of consumption situations in which the brand will come to consumers' minds. The greater the range of circumstances the brand will come to consumers' minds, the broader the consumers' awareness of the brand (Keller, 1993; Keller & Swaminathan, 2020).

The second stage involves linking the brand with a range of strong, favourable and unique associations in consumers' minds to develop brand meaning (second layer of the CBBE pyramid model). These associations can be performance associations related to the intrinsic properties of the brand, its inherent characteristics, that is, how the brand satisfies the consumers' functional needs, for example the product's characteristics, reliability, service effectiveness, and price, and imagery associations related to the extrinsic properties of the brand, that is, how the brand satisfies the consumers' emotional or symbolic needs, for example, associations related to who the user of the brand is, in which situations the brand can be used, or associations about the personality of the brand (Keller, 2001). Brand managers and designers can continuously assess and understand the consumers' brand associations by asking a sample of the target audience the following simple question: 'what comes to your mind when you think of [Brand X]? (free associations exercise) (Keller, 1993). Consumers' responses to this question include their thoughts, feelings and perceptions of the brand (their own image of brand); any negative associations uncover problems with the brand image which brand managers and designers must address with a branding strategy (discussed further below). Understanding consumers associations which constitute the brand meaning is essential because as mentioned before brand meaning is dialogic and socially constructed.

> Instead of constructing brands for consumers, [brand managers and designers] must coevolve brands with people and further embed the ability for meaning-making into [the] brand building process…[They] must acknowledge that the act of meaning-making occurs

> within the individual and is not something [they] can control. At best [they] can use design to create the opportunity, context, and tools for meaning-making and put them into the hands of people. (Jacobs & Wintrob, 2016, pp. 54–55)

In the third stage, the organisation must generate positive rational and emotional consumer reactions (consumer judgments and feelings) (third layer of the CBBE pyramid model) to the brand identity and brand meaning (stages 1 and 2). Consumer judgements rely on consumers' cognitive responses and involve (1) consumers' perceptions of brand quality which (similar to beauty) is a subjective construct, (2) brand credibility which is about the brand's expertise (competence and innovativeness), trustworthiness, and likeability, (3) brand consideration (its relevance and meaningfulness to target consumers), and (4) brand superiority, that is, whether or not it is unique and better than the competitors' brands in the product or service category. Consumer feelings are concerned with consumers' emotional responses to the brand identity and brand meaning. "Brand feelings relate to the social currency evoked by the brand" (Keller, 2001, p. 14). Richins (1997) determined the consumption emotions set, a list of positive and negative emotions occurring during the act of purchasing and during consumption (using the product or service) including emotions such as love, contentment, excitement, and joy (positive), and sadness, fear, shame, and anger (negative). Of course, brand managers and designers must ensure that brand purchase and consumption generates positive emotions with the target audience. They should try to render the brand with positive emotions which can be an effective branding strategy because consumers are not only rational but also emotional decision-makers and "we all respond emotionally to our life experiences and we naturally project emotional values onto the objects around us" (Gobé, 2009, p. xxix).

Finally, these responses must be transformed to long-lasting loyalty relationships between consumers and the brand (brand relationships to achieve brand resonance) (fourth layer of the CBBE pyramid model). "Brand resonance refers to the nature of the relationship that customers have with the brand and the extent to which they feel that they are 'in sync' with the brand. Brand resonance is characterised in terms of intensity or the depth of the psychological bond that customers have with the brand as well as the level of activity engendered by this loyalty". (Keller, 2001, p. 15)

High levels of brand equity are manifested by high levels of consumer loyalty towards the brand (Keller, 2001). There are four categories of brand resonance:

1. Behavioural loyalty which is about the number of consumers who buy the brand, how much they buy from it, and how often,
2. Attitudinal attachment which signifies that consumers have a strong emotional connection with the brand, they are in sync with the brand,
3. A sense of community where the brand becomes the centre of a social group (brand community) formed on the basis of social relationships among brand admirers (Muñiz Jr. & O'Guinn, 2001), and
4. Active engagement which involves loyal consumers evangelising about the brand, praising it to fellow consumers and urging them to try it. Active engage-

ment is "the strongest affirmation of brand loyalty [where] customers are willing to invest time, energy, money, or other resources into the brand beyond those expended during purchase or consumption of the brand" (Keller, 2001, p. 15) (for a further analysis of CBBE pyramid model, see Chap. 2 in Lalaounis, 2020).

7.4 Design Thinking and the Development of Branding Strategies

Once brand managers and designers have identified branding problems and/or opportunities, they can pursue the second and the third stages of the design thinking process, that is, the ideation and implementation stages (Fig. 7.1—arrows 3), in order to develop branding strategies which solve the branding problems and/or harness the branding opportunities identified (in the brand audit) (Fig. 7.1—arrows 4). This provides the organisation the capability to manage and harness its brand's equity further. The ideation stage requires from brand managers and designers interpreting the data gathered through consumer ethnography, to determine patterns of behaviour. At this stage, the team also needs to engage in brainstorming in order to come up with ideas which could potentially solve the problem at hand or help the organisation capitalise on the identified opportunity. Once different choices have been developed, brand managers and designers prototype and test these ideas to determine the best concept. The most optimum design concept will have to satisfy three overlapping criteria: feasibility, visibility and desirability. "Feasibility relates to what is functionally possible within the foreseeable future, viability is about what is likely to become part of a sustainable business model, and desirability is what makes sense to people and for people" (Lalaounis, 2017, p. 55). Brand managers and designers need to achieve a harmonious balance of these three criteria (Brown, 2009).

Brand Consistency Versus Brand Relevance

Beverland et al. (2015) argue that in order to preserve and enhance brand equity, brand managers "must maintain [brand] consistency (in both image and marketing support), take a long-term view, and carefully leverage existing brand equity. Yet at the same time, managers must also maintain brand relevance, which require change and importantly, innovation" (Beverland et al., 2015, p. 589). In a study of innovation cases in organisations across a range of sectors, they explored how design thinking enables brand managers to develop successful branding strategies by reconciling this tension between brand consistency and brand relevance. Extant literature has highlighted the importance of achieving both, in order to maintain or revive brand equity (Brown et al., 2003; Giesler, 2012; Thompson et al., 2006).

Brand consistency is concerned with the standardisation and maintenance of a well-defined brand image and meaning through consistent brand identity elements: properties, products (or services), presentations, and publications (Schmitt &

Simonson, 1997). This is essential for the preservation of strength and favourability of consumers' brand associations (Keller, 1999). "A commitment to consistency and stability is…revealed in the brand audit process, whereby managers are encouraged to focus on customer touch-points and journeys in order to close identity-image gaps" (Beverland et al., 2015, p. 590). However focusing too much on brand consistency can prove problematic because the brand needs to be adapted to market and consumer changes if it is to stay relevant. Hence, brand relevance is also required. A brand needs to be relevant, meaningful and appropriate to the target consumers so that it is part of their consideration set (Aaker, 2012; Rosenbaum-Elliott et al., 2011).

Drawing from management and organisation studies literature, Beverland et al. (2015) connect brand consistency with the concept of exploitation whose "essence is the refinement and extension of existing competencies, technologies, and paradigms" (March, 1991, p.85), and brand relevance with the concept of exploration which is all about pursuing new opportunities, developing new knowledge and capabilities, and achieving radical innovation with products and services (Tushman & O'Reilly, 1996). Design thinking can empower brand managers to achieve both exploitation and exploration, brand consistency and brand relevance, through the concept of brand ambidexterity which Beverland et al. "define as a marketing capability whereby a brand is strategically managed to create value through the pursuit of both consistency and relevance" (2015, p. 592).

Etymologically, the word ambidexterity includes the Latin 'ambi' which means both, and 'dexter' which means right or favourable (Maier, 2015). Tushman and O'Reilly define ambidextrous organisations as those which have the "ability to simultaneously pursue both incremental and discontinuous (radical) innovation and change results from hosting multiple contradictory structures, processes, and cultures within the same firm" (1996, p. 23). Such organisations are able to both exploit their existing resources, products and knowledge, and explore the new, the radical, the unconventional, which could be products, technologies or markets. Building and maintaining ambidexterity can be extremely difficult because it requires a combination of the contradictory demands of exploiting and exploring (Smith & Tushman, 2005). Ambidexterity requires a balance between exploitation and exploration and can lead to tensions because of their different knowledge management processes (March, 1991).

Design-Driven Brand Ambidexterity

Beverland et al. (2015) argue that the dominant logic in contemporary brand management has privileged brand consistency over relevance. A study by Högström et al. (2015) identified that certain mental schemas can define a brand manager's time horizon and his/her enacted environment width which includes the elements seen as important for brand performance. The authors found two mental schemes: calculative and heuristic, which both emphasise consistency at the expense of relevance, undermining the power and potential to (radically) innovate (Beverland et al., 2015; Högström et al., 2015). Design thinking can challenge this dominant logic in contemporary brand management through design-driven brand ambidexterity, avoiding stagnating practices caused by an over-emphasis on exploitation and brand consistency. Design thinking is based on abductive reasoning and can encourage brand managers and designers to consider the possibility of what 'might be' (Martin, 2009) and ask the question of 'what if' (Liedtka, 2015) leading to the generation of new insights and the creation of new knowledge. As Liedtka (2015) contends, design thinking "relies on abduction and experimentation involving multiple alternative solutions that actively mediate a variety of tensions between possibilities and constraints, and is best suited to decision contexts in which uncertainty and ambiguity are high. Iteration, based on learning through experimentation, is seen as a central task". (Liedtka, 2015, p. 927).

The human-centeredness of design thinking goes beyond customer orientation advocated in marketing and brand management literature because it enables brand managers and designers to identify unarticulated human needs and desires and reframe or develop new markets, products, services, and experiences (Beverland et al., 2015; Michlewski, 2008). In other words, design thinking cannot only help brand managers and designers solve branding problems, but also create new possibilities and harness these opportunities (Beverland et al., 2015; Liedtka, 2004). Design thinking can help them manage the tensions inherent in the dualism of brand consistency versus brand relevance, propelling brand growth in mature [product or service] categories, enhancing present associations in consumers' minds or generating new ones, and revitalising brands facing a decline (Beverland et al., 2015). These underlying tensions include brand position versus market, brand position versus effectiveness, and brand position versus emerging future (Beverland et al., 2015). In marketing, a product's position is the "the place the product occupies relative to competitors in consumers' minds" (Kotler et al., 2008, p. 157); it is the mental place the product occupies in consumers' minds on the basis of perceptions about the product's quality, price, and status. Brand positioning is all about building or adjusting consumers' brand perceptions (Fuchs & Diamantopoulos, 2010) and "involves establishing key brand associations in the minds of customers and other important constituents [internal and external stakeholders] to differentiate the brand and establish (to the extent possible) competitive superiority" (Keller & Lehmann, 2006, p. 740).

Process for Triggering Brand Ambidexterity Through Design Thinking

On the basis of their empirical study, Beverland et al. (2015) contend that design thinking's contribution to managing the tension of brand consistency versus brand relevance can be understood as a three-stage process: (1) destabilisation, (2) define and develop, and (3) transformation (see Fig. 7.4), with each stage involving a number of sub-practices which designers follow.

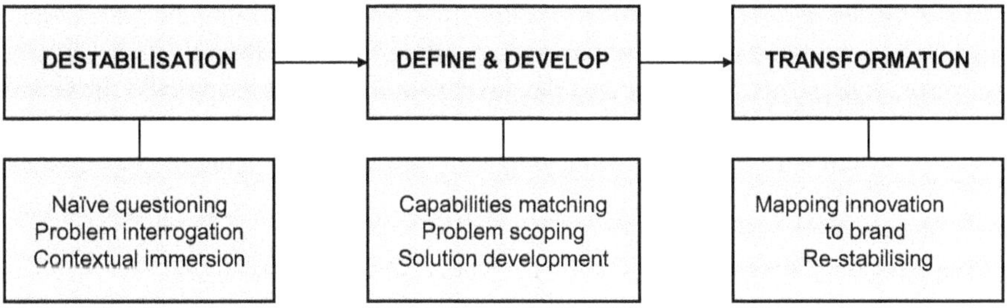

Fig. 7.4 Achieving brand ambidexterity through design thinking (based on Beverland et al. 2015, adapted by author)

- *The first stage, destabilisation*, involves designers challenging, or "destabilising the categories used by brand managers to frame their options for innovation" (Beverland et al., 2015, p. 599). This can be achieved by carrying out three sub-practices: naïve questioning, problem interrogation, and contextual immersion. Naïve questioning is all about asking 'what if' questions which on face of it might seem simplistic. Yet these questions are extremely useful because they can challenge the status quo and current norms to achieve problem interrogation which allows brand managers and designers to consider the wider socio-cultural and historical contexts where the brand consistency versus brand relevance tension develops (Beverland et al., 2015). Contextual immersion is about brand managers and designers immersing in the target consumers' world (this directly connects with consumer ethnography previously discussed) to foster a discussion about current assumptions in regards with consumers' thoughts, feelings, and behaviour towards the brand.
- *The second stage, define and develop*, involves designers interacting with brand managers to "leverage specific brand-related inputs such as customer research [e.g. results from ethnographic studies as explained above], and to ensure that the resulting innovation could be integrated within an expanded brand narrative" (Beverland et al., 2015, p. 602). In this stage designers and brand managers need to work together to define and develop possible solutions; this can be achieved by three inter-related sub-practices: capability matching, problem scoping and solution development. Capability matching allows brand managers and designers to work together to identify tangible and intangible inputs to a planned design, that is, functional and symbolic assets, respectively, making sure that any innovative offerings which are developed do not only go in line with the brand's position but also expand the brand identity "by adding associations that do not clash with existing ones, reinterpreting existing categories, or highlighting aspects of the firm's operation that had previously been downplayed or ignored" (Beverland et al., 2015, p. 602). Problem scoping seeks to understand the nature of the problem which needs solving by analysing the wider context any brand innovation has to address. These two sub-practices lead to the final sub-practice of this stage, solution development, allowing brand managers and designers to develop a solution which provides brand relevance without sacrificing brand consistency (Beverland et al., 2015).

- *The third and final stage, transformation*, involves transforming the brand, and it can be achieved by two sub-practices: mapping the innovation to the brand, and restabilising. It is important that the developed solution is mapped to the brand, that is, it is "formally located within the brand's narrative…tweaking the brand story by emphasising or revealing associations that the brand has [so far] ignored, but could credibly claim, as well as rebuilding the complete brand system (i.e., reworking all brand-supportive marketing materials)" (Beverland et al., 2015, p. 604). This means that the developed solution extends the brand narrative and the brand identity is refreshed. With the final sub-practice, restabilising, brand managers and designers use the outcomes and insights of the previous stages and sub-practices as the basis for determining brand consistency in the future.

The process explained above supports our main argument that design thinking can successfully contribute to the branding strategies through its main premise of human-centeredness and empathy (based on consumer ethnography), and the practices of brainstorming, and concept experimentation and testing. Unboundedly, Beverland et al.'s (2015) process embraces the essence of the inspiration, ideation and implementation stages of the design thinking process (Brown, 2009; Liedtka, 2015). Their recommended process enables brand managers and designers to closely and continuously collaborate in order to develop branding innovations and solutions which integrate brand consistency and brand relevance, "maintaining market relevance through innovation without unintentionally corrupting or distorting carefully cultivated brand equity" (Beverland et al., 2015, p. 606). Such innovations and solutions can take the form of, for example, new or improved products or services, brand communications campaigns, new or updated brand aesthetics, practices for fostering a brand community, emotional branding campaigns, as well as corporate and social responsibility activities, using product, service, graphic, and communications design practices.

In relation to new product development (NPD) in particular, Nagaraj, Berente, Lyytinen, and Gaskin argue that "design thinking can be framed as a dynamic capability that addresses routine and cognition-based inertia by expanding the organization's knowledge resource base, particularly in familiar contexts [contexts where there NPD team is familiar with the problem]" (2020, p. 297). In addition, an experimental comparison study conducted by Meinel et al. (2020) involving 53 NPD teams, sought to compare the application of design thinking (as a user experience-driven approach) with the user preference-driven approach, a more traditional innovation approach which focuses on translating user needs, desires, and aspirations into solutions which match the pre-determined problem. This translation process is conducted by "aggregating data and making trade-off decisions between user preferences traceable" (Meinel et al., 2020, p. 662). The purpose of this comparison was to investigate whether design thinking leads to the generation of "more superior new product (or service) concepts in terms of creativity" (Meinel et al., 2020, p. 662). Their research findings confirmed that pursuing design thinking enables brand managers and designers to develop more creative product or service concepts than the more traditional innovation approach, echoing Wattanasupachoke (2012) whose empirical study argued that applying design thinking in business management can enhance creativity leading to innovations for consumers. In particular, Meinel et al. (2020) determined that

> design thinking positively affects the feasibility, relevance, and specificity of the generated concepts. [The exception was] concept novelty [for which their] findings did not reveal a statistically significant effect of design thinking when compared to [the traditional] method. This could be due to the fact that whereas [the traditional method] is rather intuitive and leads to concepts of passable levels of novelty, applying design thinking has the potential to lead to concepts of greater novelty, but is more unusual and challenging and thus requires stronger guidance and support [which were beyond the scope of the time frame of their experimental study]. (Meinel et al., 2020, p. 668)

Chapter Summary The main purpose of this chapter was to discuss the contributions of design thinking to brand management. The chapter presented a conceptual framework which explains the connections of the design thinking process with brand equity and its management, through the power and scope of consumer ethnography and empathy. In a contemporary post-modern world, brand managers and designers must continuously assess the brand performance by conducting the brand audit. Organisations must maintain, protect and harness further the brand equity in a continuously evolving market environment. Design thinking, and in particular, the inspiration stage (of the design thinking process), can help brand managers successfully conduct the brand audit. The inspiration stage involves consumer ethnography which enables brand managers and designers to uncover consumers' thoughts, feelings and behaviour towards the brand (purchase and consumption) to achieve consumer empathy. Based on the findings of consumer ethnographic studies, they can identify branding problems and/or opportunities which require attention. The ideation and implementation stages of the design thinking process give brand managers and designers the necessary tools to brainstorm ideas and develop the most optimum strategies to solve these problems and/or to capitalise on these opportunities. Ultimately, design thinking provides the organisation immense power to balance brand consistency and brand relevance, and continuously manage and enhance brand equity. Most importantly, this is done with a human-centred approach, putting the target consumers at the heart of the process to deliver products, services, experiences which they embrace and develop a loving loyalty relationship with.

Review Questions

1. Explain the two parts of the brand audit and their contribution to the assessment of brand performance.
2. Discuss how brand managers and designers can apply consumer ethnography in order to successfully pursue the brand audit?

3. Which are the three levels of empathy brand managers and designers should seek to achieve?
4. Discuss the four layers of the Customer-Based Brand Equity (CBBE) pyramid model.
5. What are the potential problems and/or opportunities (in relation to the CBBE pyramid model) that brand managers and designers might identify by pursuing consumer ethnography?
6. How can the ideation and implementation stages of the design thinking process help brand managers and designers to develop branding strategies?
7. Why are brand consistency and brand relevance, both important for branding strategies?
8. How can design thinking help brand managers and designers balance brand consistency and brand relevance through brand ambidexterity?

Main Project Task

Choose a brand and critically evaluate its current branding strategies. Applying appropriate brand concepts and theories, discuss its future development.

Project steps:

To carry out the main project task, you should achieve the following steps:

1. Briefly introduce the brand and its market context (product or service category, target audience(s), and competitors).
2. Critically evaluate the brand and its current branding strategies by conducting both parts of brand audit: brand inventory and a brand exploratory. With regards to brand inventory, you should—textually and visually—profile the product(s) and/or service(s) of your chosen organisation explaining how they are marketed and branded. With regards to the brand exploratory, your evaluation should be based on secondary research data gathered from publicly available sources and primary research data gathered by pursuing an ethnographic study (participant observations of the target users and interviews with a small sample). This stage connects with the inspiration stage of the design thinking process (to achieve the necessary level of empathy).
3. Clearly determine what is the problem that the brand faces, and/or the opportunity that the brand should capitalise on (based on the brand exploratory carried out in step 2). It is important to 'place' this problem and/or opportunity on the CBBE pyramid model in order to provide solid foundation for the next step.
4. Develop a strategy to solve the identified problem and/or harness the identified opportunity (using the ideation and implementation stages). The strategy can include a new product or service, a new communications campaign, the design of an updated brand identity and so on.
5. Identify metrics that should be used to evaluate the effectiveness of your proposed brand development strategy in the future, that is, determine how you plan to evaluate, in the future, whether or not your strategy has achieved your brand development objectives.

Chapter Tasks

Carry out the following tasks to assess a brand's equity and its performance in its product or service category:

1. Name five brands from a specific product or service category (e.g. five cosmetics brands or five airline brands) (make a list of these brands).
2. Select one of the brands that you have included in the above list.
3. What comes to your mind when you think of this brand? (Make a list of your own brand associations).
4. What do you like or dislike about this brand?
5. In your opinion, how credible is this brand (in relation to its expertise, trustworthiness and likeability)?
6. Is the brand one you would consider buying in the future? Why/why not?
7. How is this brand similar and how is it different to other brands in the same category?
8. How does this brand make you feel? Does it generate any feelings about yourself or about your relationships with others?
9. Have you bought the brand before? If yes, how often? If no, (move to Q11).
10. If the brand is not available the next time you attempt to purchase it, what would you do?
    a. Wait until it becomes available.
    b. Visit another store or website to find and purchase it.
    c. Replace the brand with another brand.
11. Would you recommend the brand to others? Why/why not?

References

Aaker, D. A. (2010). *Building Strong Brands*. Simon and Schuster.

Aaker, D. A. (2012). Win the Brand Relevance Battle and Then Build Competitor Barriers. *California Management Review, 54*(2), 43–57.

American Marketing Association. (2015), cited in Dall'Olmo Riley, F. (2016). Brand Definitions and Conceptualizations. In F. Dall'Olmo Riley, J. Singh, & C. Blankson (Eds.), *The Routledge Companion to Contemporary Brand Management* (pp. 3–12). Routledge.

Baron, S., & Harris, K. (2008). Consumers as Resource Integrators. *Journal of Marketing Management, 24*(1–2), 113–130.

Belk, R. W. (1988). Possessions and the Extended Self. *Journal of Consumer Research, 15*(2), 139–168.

Belk, R. W. (2013). Extended Self in a Digital World. *Journal of Consumer Research, 40*(3), 477–500.

Beverland, M. B., Wilner, S. J., & Micheli, P. (2015). Reconciling the Tension Between Consistency and Relevance: Design Thinking as a Mechanism for Brand Ambidexterity. *Journal of the Academy of Marketing Science, 43*(5), 589–609.

Brown, S., Kozinets, R. V., & Sherry, J. F., Jr. (2003). Teaching Old Brands New Tricks: Retro Branding and the Revival of Brand Meaning. *Journal of Marketing, 67*(3), 19–33.

Brown, T. (2008). Design Thinking. *Harvard Business Review, 86*(6), 84.

Brown, T. (2009). *Change by Design: How Design Thinking Transforms Organisations and Inspires Innovation*. HarperCollins.

Chaplin, L. N., & Lowrey, T. M. (2009). The Development of Consumer-Based Consumption Constellations in Children. *Journal of Consumer Research, 36*(5), 757–777.

Chen, S., & Venkatesh, A. (2013). An Investigation of How Design-Oriented Organisations Implement Design Thinking. *Journal of Marketing Management, 29*(15–16), 1680–1700.

Cooper, R., & Evans, M. (2006). Breaking from Tradition: Market Research, Consumer Needs, and Design Futures. *Design Management Review, 17*(1), 68–74.

Dall'Olmo Riley, F. (2016). Brand Definitions and Conceptualizations. In F. Dall'Olmo Riley, J. Singh, & C. Blankson (Eds.), *The Routledge Companion to Contemporary Brand Management* (pp. 3–12). Routledge.

de Chernatony, L., & Dall'Olmo Riley, F. (1998). Defining a "Brand": Beyond the Literature with Experts' Interpretations. *Journal of Marketing Management, 14*(5), 417–443.

Delgado-Ballester, E., & Munuera-Alemán, J. L. (2001). Brand Trust in the Context of Consumer Loyalty. *European Journal of Marketing, 35*(11/12), 1238–1258.

Elliott, R., & Jankel-Elliott, N. (2003). Using Ethnography in Strategic Consumer Research. *Qualitative Market Research: An International Journal, 6*(4), 215–223.

Farquhar, P. H. (1989). Managing Brand Equity. *Marketing Research, 1*(3), 24–33.

Fellman, M. (1999). Breaking Tradition. *Marketing Research, 11*(3), 20–25.

Fuchs, C., & Diamantopoulos, A. (2010). Evaluating the Effectiveness of Brand-Positioning Strategies from a Consumer Perspective. *European Journal of Marketing, 44*(11/12), 1763–1786.

Giesler, M. (2012). How Doppelgänger Brand Images Influence the Market Creation Process: Longitudinal Insights from the Rise of Botox Cosmetic. *Journal of Marketing, 76*(6), 55–68.

Gobé, M. (2009). *Emotional Branding: The New Paradigm for Connecting Brands to People*. Allworth Press.

Hales, G. (2011). Branding. In J. J. Kourdi (Ed.), *The Marketing Century: How Marketing Drives Business and Shapes Society* (pp. 139–167). John Wiley & Sons.

Högström, C., Gustafsson, A., & Tronvoll, B. (2015). Strategic Brand Management: Archetypes for Managing Brands Through Paradoxes. *Journal of Business Research, 68*(2), 391–404.

Holt, D. B. (2004). *How Brands Become Icons: The Principles of Cultural Branding*. Harvard Business Press.

Holt, D. B. (2006). Jack Daniel's America: Iconic Brands as Ideological Parasites and Proselytizers. *Journal of Consumer Culture, 6*(3), 355–377.

Ireland, C. (2003). Qualitative Methods: From Boring to Brilliant. In B. Laurel (Ed.), *Design Research: Methods and Perspectives*. MIT Press.

Jacobs, V., & Wintrob, M. (2016). Manifestations of Design: Brand, Rhetoric, and Trends. In N. W. Nixon (Ed.), *Strategic Design Thinking: Innovation in Products, Services, Experiences, and Beyond* (pp. 43–61). Fairchild Books.

Johansson, U., & Svengren Holm, L. (2006). Brand Management and Design Management: A Nice Couple or False Friends? In J. E. Schroeder & M. Salzer-Mörling (Eds.), *Brand Culture* (pp. 136–152). Routledge.

Keller, K. L. (1993). Conceptualizing, Measuring, and Managing Customer-Based Brand Equity. *Journal of Marketing, 57*(1), 1–22.

Keller, K. L. (1999). Managing Brands for the Long Run: Brand Reinforcement and Revitalization Strategies. *California Management Review, 41*(3), 102–124.

Keller, K. L. (2001). *Building Customer-Based Brand Equity: A Blueprint for Creating Strong Brands* (pp. 3–27). Marketing Science Institute.

Keller, K. L., & Lehmann, D. R. (2003). How Do Brands Create Value? *Marketing Management, 12*(3), 26–32.

Keller, K. L., & Lehmann, D. R. (2006). Brands and Branding: Research Findings and Future Priorities. *Marketing Science, 25*(6), 740–759.

Keller, K. L., & Swaminathan, V. (2020). *Strategic Brand Management: Building, Measuring, and Managing Brand Equity* (5th ed.). Pearson Education.

Kotler, P., Armstrong, G., Wong, V, & Saunders, J. (2008). Principles of marketing: Fifth European edition. London: Pearson.

Kozinets, R. V. (2002). The Field Behind the Screen: Using Netnography for Marketing Research in Online Communities. *Journal of Marketing Research, 39*(1), 61–72.

Lalaounis, S. T. (2017). *Design Management: Organisation and Marketing Perspectives*. Routledge.

Lalaounis, S. T. (2020). *Strategic Brand Management and Development: Creating and Marketing Successful Brands*. Routledge.

Liedtka, J. (2004). Design Thinking: The Role of Hypothesis Generation and Testing. In R. J. Boland & F. Collopy (Eds.), *Managing as Designing* (pp. 193–197). Stanford Business Books.

Liedtka, J. (2015). Perspective: Linking Design Thinking with Innovation Outcomes Through Cognitive Bias Reduction. *Journal of Product Innovation Management, 32*(6), 925–938.

Llamas, R., & Belk, R. W. (2013). Living in a Digital World. In R. W. Belk & R. Llamas (Eds.), *The Routledge Companion to Digital Consumption* (pp. 3–12). Routledge.

Maier, J. (2015). *The Ambidextrous Organization*. Palgrave Macmillan.

Malinowski, B. (1922). *Argonauts of the Western Pacific*. E.P. Dutton.

March, J. G. (1991). Exploration and Exploitation in Organizational Learning. *Organization Science, 2*(1), 71–87.

Margulies, W. P. (1977). Make Most of Your Corporate Identity. *Harvard Business Review, 55*(4), 66–74.

Martin, R. L. (2009). *The Design of Business: Why Design Thinking Is the Next Competitive Advantage*. Harvard Business Press.

McCracken, G. (1986). Culture and Consumption: A Theoretical Account of the Structure and Movement of the Cultural Meaning of Consumer Goods. *Journal of Consumer Research, 13*, 71–84.

Meinel, M., Eismann, T. T., Baccarella, C. V., Fixson, S. K., & Voigt, K. I. (2020). Does Applying Design Thinking Result in Better New Product Concepts Than a Traditional Innovation Approach? An Experimental Comparison Study. *European Management Journal, 38*(4), 661–671.

Michlewski, K. (2008). Uncovering Design Attitude: Inside the Culture of Designers. *Organization Studies, 29*(3), 373–392.

Moisander, J., & Valtonen, A. (2012). Interpretive Marketing Research: Using Ethnography in Strategic Market Development. In L. Peñaloza, N. Toulouse, & L. M. Visconti (Eds.), *Marketing Management: A Cultural Perspective* (pp. 246–260). Routledge.

Morris, P. (2003). *The Bakhtin Reader: Selected Writings of Bakhtin, Medvedev, Voloshinov*. Arnold.

Muñiz, A. M., Jr., & O'Guinn, T. C. (2001). Brand Community. *Journal of Consumer Research, 27*(4), 412–432.

Nagaraj, V., Berente, N., Lyytinen, K., & Gaskin, J. (2020). Team Design Thinking, Product Innovativeness, and the Moderating Role of Problem Unfamiliarity. *Journal of Product Innovation Management, 37*(4), 297–323

Peñaloza, L. (1998). Just Doing It: A Visual Ethnographic Study of Spectacular Consumption Behavior at Nike Town. *Consumption, Markets and Culture, 2*(4), 337–400.

Percy, L., Rossiter, J., & Elliott, R. (2001). *Strategic Advertising Management*. Oxford University Press.

Plowman, T. (2003). Ethnography and Critical Design Practice. In B. Laurel (Ed.), *Design Research: Methods and Perspectives*. MIT press.

Richins, M. L. (1997). Measuring Emotions in the Consumption Experience. *Journal of Consumer Research, 24*(2), 127–146.

Rosenbaum-Elliott, R., Percy, L., & Pervan, S. (2011). *Strategic Brand Management*. Oxford University Press.

Schmitt, B. H., & Simonson, A. (1997). *Marketing Aesthetics: The Strategic Management of Brands, Identity, and Image*. Simon and Schuster.

Schmitt, B. H., Simonson, A., & Marcus, J. (1995). Managing Corporate Image and Identity. *Long Range Planning, 28*(5), 82–92.

Schroeder, J. E. (2009). The Cultural Codes of Branding. *Marketing Theory, 9*(1), 123–126.

Shepherd, S., Chartrand, T. L., & Fitzsimons, G. J. (2015). When Brands Reflect Our Ideal World: The Values and Brand Preferences of Consumers Who Support Versus Reject Society's Dominant Ideology. *Journal of Consumer Research, 42*(1), 76–92.

Smith, W. K., & Tushman, M. L. (2005). Managing Strategic Contradictions: A Top Management Model for Managing Innovation Streams. *Organization Science, 16*(5), 522–536.

Solomon, M. R. (1988). Mapping Product Constellations: A Social Categorization Approach to Consumption Symbolism. *Psychology & Marketing, 5*(3), 233.

Thompson, C. J., Rindfleisch, A., & Arsel, Z. (2006). Emotional branding and the strategic value of the doppelgänger brand image. *Journal of Marketing, 70*(1), 50–64.

Tushman, M. L., & O'Reilly, C. A., III. (1996). Ambidextrous Organisations: Managing Evolutionary and Revolutionary Change. *California Management Review, 38*(4), 8–30.

Tynan, C., & McKechnie, S. (2009). Experience Marketing: A Review and Reassessment. *Journal of Marketing Management, 25*(5–6), 501–517.

Van Rekom, J., Jacobs, G., & Verlegh, P. W. (2006). Measuring and Managing the Essence of a Brand Personality. *Marketing Letters, 17*(3), 181–192.

Vargo, S. L., & Lusch, R. F. (2004). Evolving to a New Dominant Logic for Marketing. *Journal of Marketing, 68*(1), 1–17.

Vargo, S. L., & Lusch, R. F. (2008). Service-Dominant Logic: Continuing the Evolution. *Journal of the Academy of Marketing Science, 36*(1), 1–10.

Wasson, C. (2000). Ethnography in the Field of Design. *Human Organization, 59*(4), 377–388.

Wattanasupachoke, T. (2012). Design Thinking, Innovativeness and Performance: An Empirical Examination. *International Journal of Management & Innovation, 4*(1), 1–14.

Recommended Reading

Belk, R. W. (1988). Possessions and the Extended Self. *Journal of Consumer Research, 15*(2), 139–168.

Beverland, M. B., Wilner, S. J., & Micheli, P. (2015). Reconciling the Tension Between Consistency and Relevance: Design Thinking as a Mechanism for Brand Ambidexterity. *Journal of the Academy of Marketing Science, 43*(5), 589–609.

Keller, K. L. (2001). *Building Customer-Based Brand Equity: A Blueprint for Creating Strong Brands* (pp. 3–27). Marketing Science Institute.

Moisander, J., & Valtonen, A. (2012). Interpretive Marketing Research: Using Ethnography in Strategic Market Development. In L. Peñaloza, N. Toulouse, & L. M. Visconti (Eds.), *Marketing Management: A Cultural Perspective* (pp. 246–260). Routledge.

Wasson, C. (2000). Ethnography in the Field of Design. *Human Organization, 59*(4), 377–388.

Design Thinking: Practice and Applications

8

Learning Objectives

- To develop an understanding of design thinking methodologies utilised within a broad range of diverse contexts.
- To introduce the key elements of service design and how these both inform and enhance end-user experiences.
- To illustrate how design can contribute to and drive organisational innovation at a strategic level of application.
- To gain a deeper understanding of industry specific tools and how these can foster wider innovation networks.
- To provide insights as to how design thinking practices traverse organisational structures and stakeholder groups.

8.1 Introduction

This chapter focuses upon design thinking in practice; it departs away from its theoretical underpinnings touched upon and critiqued in earlier sections of this book. Three leading academics share their experiences of drawing upon and deploying a diverse range of tools and techniques that span the disciplines and design and service design. The first two cases are discussed by leading design academics, Ir Ehsan

---

Three leading academics equally contributed to this chapter (in the following alphabetical order): (1) Dr Bijan Aryana, Senior Lecturer in Design at Chalmers University of Technology, Sweden; (2) Ir Ehsan Baha, Assistant Professor in Designer Identity Development at University of Montréal, Canada; (3) Dr Radka Newton, Senior Teaching Fellow at Lancaster University, UK.

Supplementary Information The online version contains supplementary material available at [https://doi.org/10.1007/978-3-030-94206-9_8].

Y. Huang, D. Hands, *Design Thinking for New Business Contexts*, https://doi.org/10.1007/978-3-030-94206-9_8

Baha and Dr Bijan Aryana, which explores design thinking processes, methods, tools in two large organisations. Following this, Dr Radka Newton, based in Lancaster University, UK, offers the third case study, working with a broad range of stakeholders in a higher education institution. The primary aim of the project was to identify as to where improvements could be made to enhance the student learning experience as part of their degree studies. Findings from the three sets of cases offer a rich illustration as to the transformative nature of design to afford enhanced end-user experiences.

8.2 Design Processes, Methods and Tools

The authors of this section, Ir Ehsan Baha and Dr Bijan Aryana share similar professional journeys in which they explored both academia and industry for gaining a better understanding of holistic patterns of design in various applications and socio-technical contexts. Ir Ehsan Baha is an Assistant Professor at the School of Industrial Design of University of Montréal and also the founder of the design consultancy Meaningwise. Dr Bijan Aryana is a Senior Lecturer in Design at Chalmers University of Technology, Division of Design and Human Factors. The aim of this discussion is to cast light on design thinking for practice, two real world cases are used for clarifying the contents. These cases are intentionally selected from sectors that are less represented in current design thinking literature despite their impact on the society and economy.

Introduction

In his book, The Sciences of the Artificial, Herbert Simon defines design as: devising courses of action with the aim of changing existing situations into preferred ones (Simon, 1996). As one of the pioneers of Design Science, he highlights the fact that design is the core attribute of any professional activity (Simon, 1988). There have been many changes in the discipline of design ever since, and not everyone shares Simon's definition of design. Nevertheless, designers of the twenty-first century benefit a lot from scientific methods, for example, in areas like user studies and design evaluation. Despite benefiting from scientific methods, design still has a strong relationship with practice and it cannot be learned without engaging in real world practice. Research done on prominent designers shows that they benefit from their personal qualities, tacit knowledge and soft skills for the success they achieve in design projects (Cross, 2011). Hence, understanding the principles of design on an abstract level using only explicit knowledge is just the starting point of understanding design. In this section, we explore intangible aspects of the relationship between design thinking and practice, including the design process and the understanding of stakeholders' varied languages and requirements. Moreover, we explore the importance of having a reflective approach, generating collaborations, with tools and methods that emerge through design (Aryana, 2020).

The first case elaborates the unique characteristics of design in business-to-business (B2B) settings, as well as designing experiences for complex human machine systems. In this case, we will look at Hitachi ABB Power Grids, a global provider of power and digital technologies, advanced automation systems, and open digital platforms for power grids. In addition to producing physical equipment, Hitachi ABB Power Grids aims for effective digitalisation of all elements of the energy value chain. To address this, a variety of design solutions including services, digital user interfaces, and physical peripherals are required. Due to the sensitivity and complexity of power grid systems, a thorough understanding of safety and human factors is necessary. Designers must consider the requirements of individual end-users, in addition to companies and organisations as customers. Resultant designs in this industry might be in use for decades.

The second case shows the challenging task of designing and introducing a new type of service at MaaS Global. MaaS Global represents itself as the world's first true Mobility as a Service (MaaS) operator. MaaS is a service, which orchestrates various means of transport and provides its users with a single point of interaction via an integrated mobility platform. The core product of MaaS Global is a mobile application called Whim. Whim users have access to many transport options, free from timetables, fixed routes, parking worries and the costs of owning a car. This case is an example of complex services, which could be challenging for designers. The MaaS provider cannot control every touch point of the service, especially physical touch points, while it is responsible for the overall user experience throughout each journey.

8.3 Case Example 1: Hitachi ABB Power Grids

Design Process

At Hitachi ABB Power Grids, design is being viewed as combination of various activities including defining and solving problems, deciding what part of the problem to solve, and what order to follow in solving the problem, finding stakeholders, identifying methods and technologies that can address the problem, exploring the solution space, and calculating the costs and resources required for the solution. As these activities suggest, a real-world design project does not follow predefined steps. The scope of the problem and the order of design related activities are to be defined as the project proceeds. Design follows an evolutionary process in Hitachi ABB Power Grids. Clients usually plan to use these expensive systems for a relatively long period of time, which means that designers often cannot completely see what would happen at the end of the inheritance phase, when for example a second version of the system is going to be designed.

In addition, the common iterative Human Centred Design (HCD) process may not be applicable for many of the projects in high-risk industry, as it is not always affordable to prototype and test a complex and expensive system. In such cases, an in-depth cognitive task analysis increases the success chance. Cognitive task analysis aims at understanding tasks that require high level of cognitive activity including judgement, problem solving, remembering, recalling, attention and decision making (Crandall et al., 2006). By predicting the tasks and analysing them from a cognitive point of view, it would be possible to make design decisions prior to developing and testing expensive systems. Documentation of cognitive task analyses helped the design team to create their own tools that give them shortcuts for identifying design specifications such as colour perception and service design mapping templates that are adopted to this specific industry. Of course, when tests on low fidelity level are possible, for example in the case of user interface design, such tests can facilitate the decision-making process and ease the communication between the design team and management.

The complexity of systems requires small and focused teams with unique knowledge and skills for development of each part. These small teams also work in a large organisation landscape. Because of this contradiction, networks are necessary for effective information flow among these small teams and ensuring collaboration. Design can produce visible and tangible outcomes such as scenarios of use or user interfaces. These outcomes are understandable for most people regardless of their professional background. For example, a new human machine interface that improves usability and safety in a specific product that is developed by a team can trigger questions about usability and safety in other products developed by other teams, even if those products are different in terms of their core technology or area of utilisation. The design team can open a discussion and facilitate collaboration between the teams. In this case, design can act as a tool for collaborative network initiation (Baha et al., 2013).

In summary, design at Hitachi ABB Power Grids follows an emerging and evolutionary process with the following characteristics:

- Every design project is unique, and it is hard to set predefined and sequential steps for the project. Activities and decisions evolve as a project proceeds. However, certain phases and set of methods and tools are identifiable.
- The impact of design is not limited to product or service level. Inside the organisation, design can shape decision making and resource allocation. It impacts the future of the organisation, as the relationship between the client and the organisation starts and lasts for years after purchasing the system. Power grids are vital parts of the infrastructure and design of systems can have a long-term impact on areas beyond the organisation including built environment, natural environment, and the society.
- Documentation of design gradually creates industry-specific tools, for example for identifying colour perception or service design mapping. Design facilitates the collaboration and communication among small and specialised teams by representing artefacts or scenarios of use in tangible ways, beyond technical complexity. Thus, design at Hitachi ABB Power Grids does not only produce systems, but also networks, tools and ways of collaboration.

Methods and Tools

The long lifespan of systems in the power grids industry means that designers often are not able to observe the inheritance of their designs. However, it is likely that designers inherit solutions from earlier generations. Many systems from the past decades have been defined as products, while the current strategy of Hitachi ABB Power Grids is to define new systems as a part of a service. One of the common methods for initiating projects is problem reframing in which product design problems of the past are reframed as service design problems of the present. This method is often accompanied by qualitative research. For qualitative research, contextual inquiry is a common method which casts light on how system operators work with existing products. Contextual inquiry is a mix of observation and semi-structured interview in the context of use (Sleeswijk Visser et al., 2005). It starts with a set of standard questions and then participants are questioned and observed while performing their ordinary tasks. This method can produce relevant data for cognitive task analysis explained in earlier, as it gives information about the tasks, their sequences, and related decisions and perceptions of users. Designers also look at quantitative data from secondary sources, and this gives them an idea about most common incidents in similar systems in the past. Such data is available from authorities responsible for safety and standards. Qualitative and quantitative data help designers to use another tool called service map that facilitates transition from inheritance phase to variety generation. Service map is a visual representation of how design requirements of a service match the service attributes (Tomczak et al., 2012).

Visualisation is a powerful ideation tool that enables designers to show alternative processes through which a future system will work. Visualisation can empower and be empowered by with problem reframing. For example, when designers were ideating visualisation displays for electric transmission and power distribution network systems, they realised that the standard diagrams for transmission networks locate connections based on a technical logic. The line thickness in these diagrams represents the nominal voltage. In case of problems in the network, these visualisations can help the clients to understand in which connection the problem occurred and proceed with maintenance. The data from qualitative research helped designers to reframe this problem as what if the system makes the client aware of how the situation develops and maintenance in which geographic location can prevent problems? This reframed problem translated into the idea of visualising state estimator in which the user can see the power network in connection with the real geographic locations. The solution also utilises icons and colour coding to give users a dynamic understanding of how voltage and capacity are distributed in the network, which accordingly can show potential problematic connections.

In addition to generating new ideas using visualisation and problem reframing, literature review also can provide the design team with existing solutions like technologies and user interfaces, which may have potential for the current project. Although prototyping the whole system may not be possible, human machine interfaces and visual displays can be prototyped with lower fidelities at this point, so the management and the design team can make a decision about the promising ideas that can be implemented.

An effective concept pitch presentation plays a key role in justifying a design solution and attracting resources for implementation. In a large organisation where people are coming from various disciplinary backgrounds, there is a need for clear and simple presentation of concepts with minimum technical jargon. An effective pitch presentation can help management and business teams to evaluate concepts and make the right decision for further investment on implementing the concepts.

8.4 Case Example 2: Maas Global

Design Process

The core product of MaaS Global is the application called 'Whim' which is a multimodal travel platform that enables people to use different means of transport such as bikes, e-scooters, public transports, taxis, and rental cars. Everything from planning a journey to booking a trip and receiving a receipt can be done through this app. Whim can be a good example of the concept of mobility as a service (MaaS).

Service design for MaaS can be defined as advocating user perspective within the business. In other words, design translates human behaviours into design solutions. As an activity, design at MaaS Global is structured around users and aims to understand what services and artefacts are being used currently and to translate user needs into an improvement of their lifestyle. As a young digital business, business context and investors' expectations dictate a structured approach towards the design process, where certain milestones should be visible for everyone. In addition, as software technology is at the heart of the service, software development strategies impact the way the design process is organised. This means that although designers are aware of the iterative nature of human centred design, the sharp deadlines for achieving business and software development objectives sometimes direct them to a linear process. In addition, many activities that are theoretically supposed to be in sequential order can be done simultaneously to ensure such deadlines. There are many iterations between ideation and implementation phases, as immediate feedback from the market may lead to using alternative solutions that are already developed but are not used in the final product. Examples of such solutions include alternative scenarios of use, visual contents, interactions or technical features.

Designers do not often have enough freedom to explore a variety of ideas and insights due to the limited time available for completion of each project. However, they document ideas and keep them in 'parking lots' for future projects where ideas may find opportunities to grow. Such ideas are usually being collected at the end of each design sprint, or from competitor benchmarking. For example, when MaaS Global decided to enter a new market in Northern Europe, service design ideas from earlier projects were used as probes in user studies. Users' feedback to these ideas helped the consumer insight team to reframe the brief and consider an adapted way of delivering the service. In the literature, design processes often start with identifying the problem, but in MaaS Global projects, problems can be inherited. Designers may even start with something that exists now such as existing mobility services and scenarios of use. In fact, one could say that design starts in solution space with some existing prototypes. When there are already solutions, designers need to start the design process by looking at opportunities beyond the organisation's conventional solutions.

Although there is a dedicated design team within the organisation, design is strongly connected to every division within MaaS Global. Multiple groups may work on a project from research to implementation, so it is important to know if they are solving the right problem. The higher management is actively involved in problem reframing for design. A wide range of qualitative and quantitative methods are being used through a design project, which makes it impossible for the designers to deal with all data without getting help from data analytics and consumer insight teams. The consumer insight team works closely with the data analytics team to deliver a realistic idea of the existing situation, as well as projections of the future. One of the unique characteristics of design for MaaS is that the service provider does not have a full control on all service touch points. Mobility providers such as public transport, taxi companies and shared mobility providers are the ones who shape a significant part of the users' experience. Therefore, service design for MaaS requires adaptation of conventional service design tools and methods. Along with addressing the design briefs, the design team is also involved in adapting and reinventing methods and tools. Not all such adaptations are formally documented due to limited time and resources. However, few became permanent parts of the design practice at MaaS Global including a card-sorting toolkit for MaaS, and visual mobility probes for co-creation workshops.

Overall, similar to Hitachi ABB Power Grids, design at MaaS Global has an emerging and evolutionary nature that can be elaborated by following highlights:

- Design at MaaS Global has been adapted to sharp business deadlines and software development realities. Some design activities may be done in parallel, and such activities are distributed among divisions in MaaS Global. Therefore, it is hardly a predefined and sequential process.
- Design at MaaS global impacts multiple levels, ranging from the final product service to business strategy. As mentioned, design activities are distributed within the organisation. For example, higher management is actively involved in problem reframing. The business itself is structured around a digital product, which is highly influenced by design, and somehow represents the identity of MaaS global. In some cases, design ideas that are not implemented may be used for a better understanding of the use context and setting strategic goals.
- Some design projects may initiate in a solution space and not necessarily a problem space. The service cannot identify its touchpoints, but it should look at existing means of transport and mobility services.

Methods and Tools

It is interesting that like Hitachi ABB Power Grids, many projects at MaaS Global start with inheritance. Mobility as a service is a new concept, but mobility itself is not. To deliver a MaaS solution, an understanding of the solution space is necessary. The solution space includes existing experiences, technologies, and business models originated from other mobility related areas. Examples include but are not limited to available means of transport, shared mobility solutions like carpooling and ride hailing, and services around mobility like navigation services. Quantitative data which can be accessed through data analytics shape the big picture of how these solutions work together. For example, one can understand how often people in an area combine different mobility solutions in a single journey, or how they manage transitions. This data can be used in a method called behavioural mapping.

In this method, participants' behaviours are being recorded in a specific setting during a certain period. The data can be collected by looking at specific individuals or geographic areas, which can give insights to temporal or locational patterns of behaviours (Ng, 2016).

As seen in Hitachi ABB Power Grids, problem reframing can be a method for variety generation. Reframing problems provides opportunity for creative ideation and innovation. Qualitative user studies help the designers to reframe problems based on real world user scenarios. For user studies, field probing is used which is a mix of observation and semi-structured interviews in the context (Mattelmäki, 2006). Travellers are observed in locations like train stations or public transport hubs, with a focus on transitions between different means of transport and their interactions with the environment, for example when they try to get travel information from displays or similar. When they consent, they were interviewed for more details about their daily travel habits and decisions in choosing mobility options. To implement the design, only one or two high fidelity prototypes are tested. Data from the tests are more likely to convenience the management and investors to accept a new design (Baha, Ghei et al., 2021). For the test, a group of randomly selected users are offered with the new design, while others evaluate an existing design. In case there are two high fidelity prototypes, a randomly selected group will work with one of the prototypes and the rest will work with the other one. This method is called AB testing (Marsh, 2018). Metrics like number of errors, time spent on each prototype, and percentage of users who complete certain tasks can be used for comparing alternatives offered to participants.

Summary

Design thinking projects are initiated, embedded, and developed with(in) one or more organisations depending on an objective and context. In practice, the project objectives and context have an entangled relationship. A design thinking project can gain its objectives from the context. However, project objectives can also alter a project context, or in some cases initiate a new project context. In design consultancy projects for example, external designers usually perform an intake meeting with their client(s) to clarify the objectives of the project. The intake meeting functions as a dialogic inquiry where designers meet clients in order or both parties to get acquainted and negotiate one or more projects. Such a meeting is usually followed up by constructing a proposal for the project.

The intake meetings and project proposals are effective means for defining the objectives of a design thinking project. However, in practice, project objectives maybe challenged and may require several rounds of revision. These challenges are not only caused by the unfolding of the project, depending on its nature and the situation at hand, they are also inherent to the nature of design and its understanding within organisations. While design often gets pushed by business for predictability, embracing uncertainty is its strength (Stolterman, 2021; Verganti, 2017). This tension also plays a role in how professionals with a different disciplinary background understand design and design expertise within an organisation. In practice, the latter is quite a challenge. Many organisations and professionals do not understand the nature and the expertise of designers (Baha, Gokhle et al., 2021), and designers have difficulty to clearly communicate their expertise and roles in organisations. Consequently, a better understanding of design, the design thinking project and the expertise of the designers is formed through the practice of design thinking. That is, project objectives become clearer and find a better alignment with the design thinking project context in time. Furthermore, although design traditionally has an orientation around graphics and products of a single organisation, expanding in depth and reach, today design has evolved to an order of systems designed by collaborative networks consisting of multiple organizations. With the advancements of information technology, everyday products and services are increasingly becoming digitized. This digitalisation has changed the nature of products and services in multiple ways amongst which their evolving form, produced by fluctuating collaborative networks (Sturkenboom et al., 2019). Thus, rapid changes in systems and their related stakeholders also accounts for dynamic project objectives in design thinking projects.

Defining, maintaining and revising project objectives is a complex task in the practice of design thinking. Alignment is required between a number of project context aspects. The type of organisation and their offering(s) are two main project context aspects that influence the objective of a design thinking project. SMEs often need design thinking to improve the quality of their existing solutions, while enterprises often use design thinking for entering or creating new markets (Norman & Verganti, 2014). Start-ups for example, are often in a fuzzy front end of innovation where they are still searching for an appropriate identity that can bring them stability. Design thinking projects here can serve this identity search, helping starts-ups to better position itself and scale up. SMEs often need design thinking to improve the quality of their offerings while enterprises often also require design thinking for entering a market or creating new one (Norman & Verganti, 2014). In this way, design thinking is not only in service of an organisational regime, but it can also alter the regime of an organisation (Dong et al., 2021). In other words, through establishing, expanding, and creating new offerings, design thinking projects support organisations with stabilisation, growth, and maintenance. Another aspect that defines the objective of a design thinking project is timing. Design thinking projects can engage with different parts and stages of an organisation. Organisations are in the process of starting up, scaling up, existing as a small to medium enterprise or existing as an enterprise that is currently operational with a roadmap.

There are different levels where design thinking projects can have impact within an organisation. The total experience model designed by Van Erp (2011) (see Fig. 8.1), distinguishes four roles for designers: (1) Entrepreneur, (2) Strategist, (3) Conceptualist and (4) designer. Although this role taxonomy is not exhaustive, the four roles, in combination with the right column that we have added to Van Erp's model, can explain how in-house and external designers can be positioned, position themselves, navigate and influence a design thinking project. Noticeable here is that the higher designers get in the model, the fewer number of people and more decision-making power. Although the different levels indicate a hierarchy of autonomy and power in a design thinking project, all four levels are co-dependent and require a fundamental alignment.

While in the past, design within organisations was mainly on a realisation level, applied to graphics and products, today design is also applied to services, and product service systems. With the developments of design and its establishment in business, however, the realisation level was extended to conceptualisation, where the

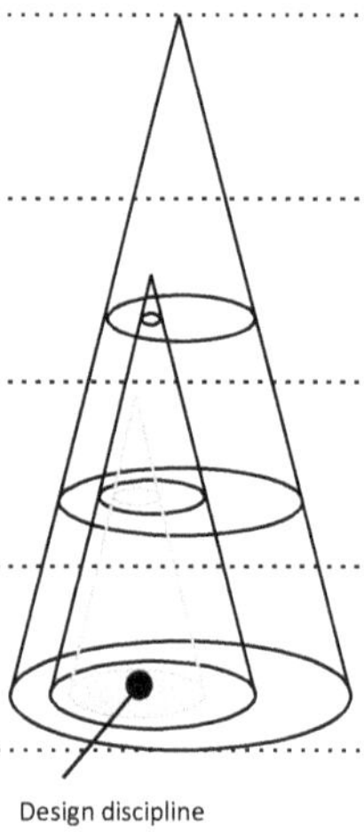

	What is being developed	*What is being experienced*	*What is being offered to the firm*
Entrepreneur	**Dreams:** vision, ambition, economic value	Meaning	Ways of working within and with other organizations
Strategist	**Direction:** the brand, product strategy, communication strategy	Meaning, emotional experience	Positioning / competing within existing and creation of new markets
Conceptualist	**Interaction:** cross medial concepts, product service systems	Aesthetics, meaning, emotional experience	Optimal use of resources, infrastructure
Designer	**Design:** products, services, communication	Aesthetics, meaning, emotional experience	Portfolio of the offerings

Fig. 8.1 Van Erp's total experience model with designer roles and the range of developments and experiences they can offer (Van Erp, 2011; adapted and elaborated by authors)

making and thinking activity in design became separate, resulting in what we know as design thinking today. Today design has expanded further to a strategic level where design thinking projects are used to explore possible futures for an organisation. In some organisations, start-ups often, the influence of design thinking is further raised to the entrepreneurial level. On this level, design thinking is used for organisational design, branding, and leading of an organisation.

8.5 Understanding the Student Learning Experience Through a Design Methods Approach

The following case study offered by Dr Radka Newton, Senior Teaching Fellow, based at Lancaster University, UK, provides a rich illustration of the application of a design-led approach to an annual degree programme review and the curriculum learning experience. The design thinking methodology incorporated systematic mapping, personas, and user journey mapping, to help educators to better understand the students' university 'experience'. In addition, special thanks go to PhD student Yueyi (Joy) Wang who provided all the figures and illustrations to accompany this case study.

Introduction

Design thinking methodology is the foundation to many branches of design activities. Service design, which is dedicated to creating meaningful human-centred interactions, is one excellent approach to achieving this activity. Over the past decade, the educational sector has started describing the student experience as a process using a variety of concepts from service operations management, and most recently service design. Service design research and its application within public services, health and social innovation (Sangiorgi & Prendiville, 2017; Kimbell, 2009) have identified the benefits of a user-centred approach to curriculum development and teaching practices. Students can easily be denominated as co-producers of their educational experience (Carey, 2013) and as such, they have active engagement in co-creating the value of that experience (Osborne et al., 2016). Universities can be perceived as networks facilitating the values and creating an environment in which the student can actively create their personalised version of the experience (Prahalad & Ramaswamy, 2004). It is a two-way process where the facilitator (university) and the student are constantly entering a dialogue through multiple interactions and touch points. Service design that encompasses the complexity described above and achieves excellent user interaction is crucial for strategic aims of any service-orientated practices, including education. Holmlid & Evenson (2008) provide a comprehensive summary of the meaning of service design putting emphasis on mapping the user journey and exploring the expectations and the reality that the customer is experiencing whilst trying to achieve the desired qualities within the resources of the organisation providing the service.

> in service design, collaborators visualise, express and choreograph what other people can't see, envisage solutions that do not yet exist, observe and interpret needs and behaviours and transform them into possible service futures, and express and evaluate, in the language of experience, the quality of design. (Holmlid & Evenson, 2008, p. 341)

Service design in education has so far been predominantly explored in the areas of student support services such as student registration and induction (Baranova et al., 2010; Kuzmina et al., 2012; Madden & Walters, 2016). It is making slow inroads to the design of the curriculum and more widely to the design of the student experience (Altay, 2014; Lilley et al., 2012; Pazell & Hamilton, 2020). There are many aspects of the education that cannot be seen, which does not mean they do not exist. Educators thrive to receive feedback from students dominated by high levels of satisfaction and fulfilment. However, often we hear frustrations, disappointment and confusion due to poorly designed programmes and courses that are centred around classroom availability, system function or administration processes that are outdated and nobody has energy to review or challenge. Most educators want to help their students reach their highest potential, similarly to service designers who simply try to create good experience for users. In business schools, we aim to educate students to be better managers and to understand continuous improvement techniques, to understand how to make strategic decisions, how to listen to their teams and how to be more engaged within their own development. Designing a good learning experience means understanding the student needs, combined with their expectations and assumptions, as well as their family pressures of their learning outputs. To be able to truly design a meaningful learning experience, the student who has embarked on this journey needs to stay at the heart of this design. Design offers the educators emotional and practical mindset to really think about the value that we are delivering to students. Design helps educators focus on the learning journey and not solely on the output.

This case study will provide an example of applying service design and user-centred design methods to understand students and their educational experience on MSc Management programme at Lancaster University, UK. The case aims to demonstrate educators an application of designerly mindset in order to achieve the goal of placing the learner into the centre of the learning process.

The Context of MSc Management Programme at Lancaster University

MSc Management Programme:

- Globally ranked and accredited postgraduate programme with an average cohort size of 50 students.
- 60% non-EU overseas students (China, India, Thailand, Taiwan)
- 20% UK students (10% already studies in Lancaster)
- 20% EU students
- 50/50 male female

Entry criteria:

- Equivalent of upper second-class honours in the first degree achieved in any academic discipline—prior knowledge of business sand management not required
- English language score IELTS 7.0
- Work experience after the first degree is limited to 2 years to enter this programme

Issue:

The programme curriculum was remodelled to align the programme with a European counterpart delivered globally. The course structure changed to one-week module delivery with an increased breadth of subjects all delivered in one-week block. Students did like the block nature of the delivery and reported that it was easier to focus on one subject at a time. However, students expressed anxiety and stress, higher level of complaints about the learning experience related to assessment. Students stopped engaging with the customised career development provision.

Based on the identified issue, service design approach was selected to address the particular issue of increased stress, complaints and lack of engagement with career provision. Data has been collected from 2018 onwards from 114 students who have participated in a design-led programme review process. The iteration of zoom in and zoom out (see Fig. 8.2) generated an understanding of wider educational ecosystems which allow educators to understand the issues within a complex network, acknowledging the barriers and bureaucracies and also identifying creative solutions and potential opportunities for change.

Mapping the Organisational Ecosystem

Placing the design of the educational experience into a wider environmental context is paramount and often forgotten. The learning occurs in a certain cultural and regulatory context with quality assurance and accreditation parameters driven by

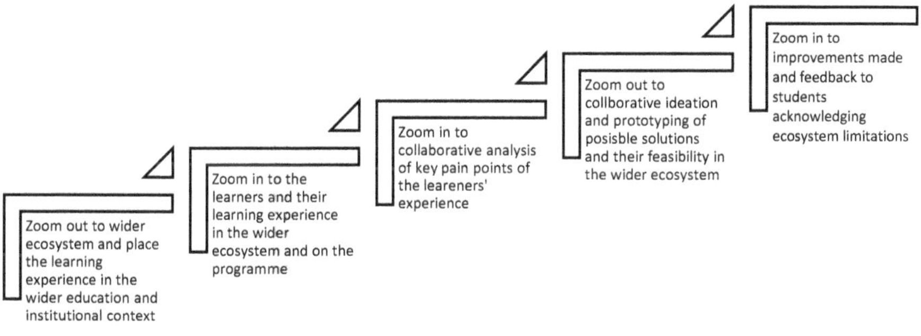

Fig. 8.2 Design-led annual programme review process (adapted by author)

multiple stakeholders, internal and external. The full educational ecosystem includes not only the human actors but also interfaces such as student record systems, accommodation, student union, places of learning and places of social interaction. Such ecosystems could be very complex, and it is useful to start with a broader visualisation that prepares a sense-making ground for understanding. Ecosystem mapping heightens the awareness of the organisational context, the limitations within that context, and unavoidable influence on educational experience designing and planning. It also allows people to pause and appreciate the culture of the organisation and encourages dialogues between the organisation and its stakeholders. University is as a complex ecosystem full of mysterious processes and dark corridors which are not always easy to get through. With the presented case, the one-year postgraduate programme MSc Management (MiM) inhabits the Management School and Lancaster University ecosystems. MiM is a small component of this vast ecosystem and yet contains many components that are reliant on the appreciation and understanding of the wider picture. Ecosystem mapping ensures pattern recognition and relationship between the MiM programme design and other components within the organisation. The university ecosystem (Fig. 8.3) provides a higher-level mapping that gives us an opportunity to see the position of MiM in the organisational network.

Questions to ask:

- How is the University governance impacting on the programme design process?
- What is the accepted process of programme design and what is the timescale?
- Who makes the final decisions about programme design?
- Who should be involved in the design process at the University level?
- What are the regulations and legal obligations that we need to incorporate into our design?
- What are the key University systems and actors that MiM students will interact with during their programme?

Key findings from the University ecosystem mapping:

- MiM students are an integral part of this large ecosystem and their experience will be impacted by their interaction with components such as the visa application process, the infrastructure in the city and its connection to the University. Within Central University systems that they will interact with registration team, accommodation, and the social activities offered through the Campus wider services. Some components at outside of the university service and yet affect the students' overall experience.
- All staff involved in the MiM programme are an integral part of this large ecosystem and they cannot always be able to carry out decisions without consulting the University counterparts. MiM design will feature in different order of prioritisation for different University level actors.

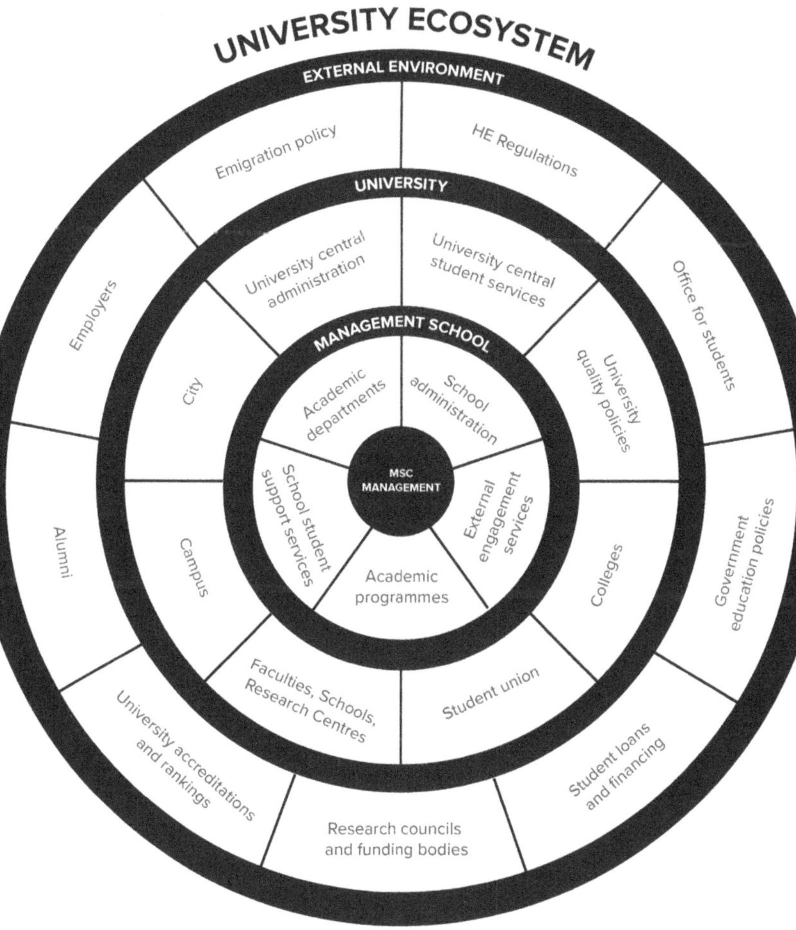

Fig. 8.3 University ecosystem (developed by author)

The ecosystem mapping can be taken to another level by zooming in to the more imminent MiM context of the Management school (Fig. 8.4), which provides further layer of information important for our sense-making stage of the design. The questions to ask will be the same as those we asked at the University level with additional curiosity about the MiM programme place within the Management school.

Key findings from the Management School ecosystem mapping:

- MiM does not belong to an academic department and is administered from a central school postgraduate office.
- MiM has multiple specific and unique resources such as its own programme team and careers support, as well as dependency on all academic departments who provide the teaching staff.
- MiM students do not interact with any other students within the curriculum that is solely delivered for them.

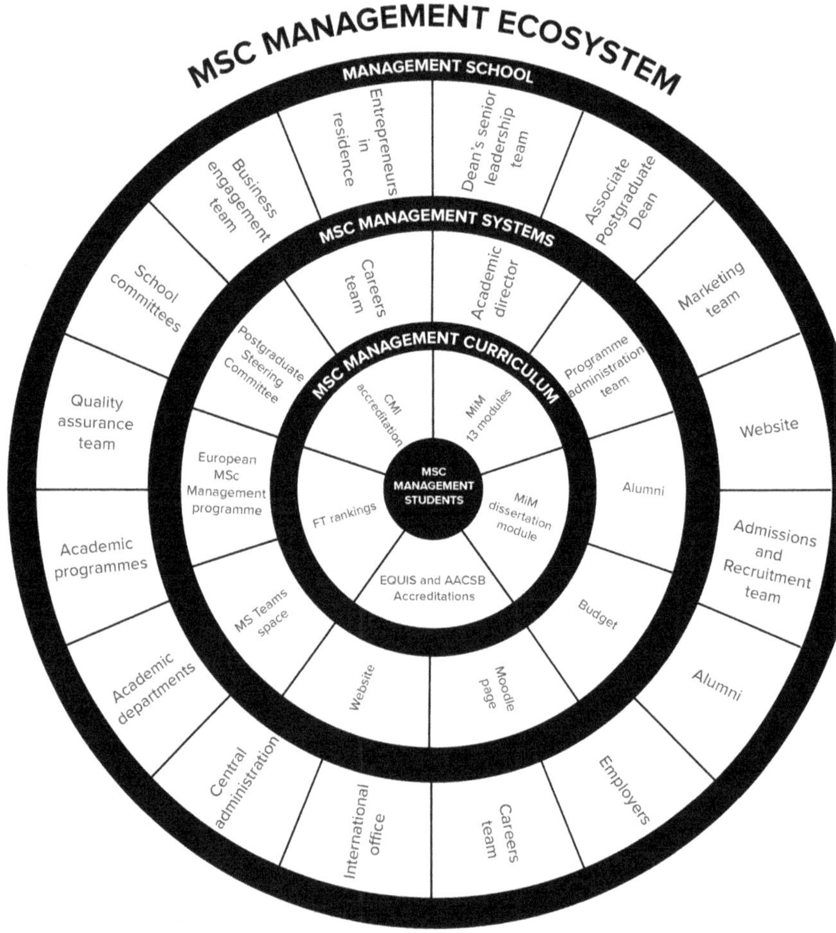

Fig. 8.4 Management school ecosystem (developed by author)

- MiM is subject to multiple accreditations and rankings and its reputation reflects the broader school, not just the programme.

The ecosystem mapping facilitates visual understanding of the context of the learners and the context of the organisational structures that programme design is based on. It helps clarify assumptions of the learners' touch points and empathise with matching of the system's benefits and limitations. Location and campus facilities of a university will determine whether students will enjoy their university life during their learning as well as enjoyment and friendships. MiM students are a part of a big university community not just the Management School. They will make new friends, new connections through accommodation colleges, sports teams and student societies. For many of them, it will be their first time away from home. All salient elements outside of teaching contents should be considered while designing the learning experience of both the programme and curriculum.

Student Personas

In education, we usually start at the point of the programme development and delivery whilst the discovery stage is quickly rushed through and neglected. The discovery stage is crucial for designing successful and meaningful learning experience and also helps avoid expensive developments that often fail and do not meet the needs of our students, bringing about more frustration to educators. There are different ways of engaging students in the discovery stage. Here we demonstrate how to involve students' participation to create personas and map their emotional learning journey. Design methods like personas, empathy mapping or journey mapping provide a complementary mechanism to gain deeper understanding of our students' needs and acknowledging the holistic nature of student learning journeys as well as the importance of emotions and empathy. The first design tool that MiM students engaged with was persona visualising and focusing on the story behind each student. Students worked in self-selected groups of five, and as a stimulus, they were encouraged to think about a typical student on their programme, using the broad parameters outlined in Fig. 8.5. It is very important that not to provide students with any pre-set templates and provide them enough freedom, yet some framework to guide their thinking and subsequent discussions.

Student groups were given an A3 card, coloured pens, a selection of stickers and various craft materials. During the process, staffs were checking around the room whilst using questions to stimulate the discussion. It started with a series of informal and light-hearted questions such as:

- What is your name?
- Where are you from?
- Do you have any pets?
- What colour of jacket do you like to wear?
- Do you visit family in back home often?

The process of creating personas was insightful to observe. The artefacts that students created underpinned by the stories developed a profound portfolio of boundary objects (Star and Griesemer, 1989) facilitating the intersection between the programme ecosystem and the students' world that they carry, from their own backgrounds as well as how it is adapted within the wider university ecosystem. The visual representation provided insights into how the students saw themselves and what they considered important to share. It provided a near to cathartic experience of portraying their expectations, needs, fears and emotions as well as some facts that afforded us better understanding of our student cohort. It also helped them create a distance from making any comments, which may be personal to them as individuals, which they found very helpful and non-threatening. For example, the story of an ambitious German student called Alex Wolf (see Fig. 8.6), who despite his active lifestyle, engagement with social media, high career motivations, and also suffers

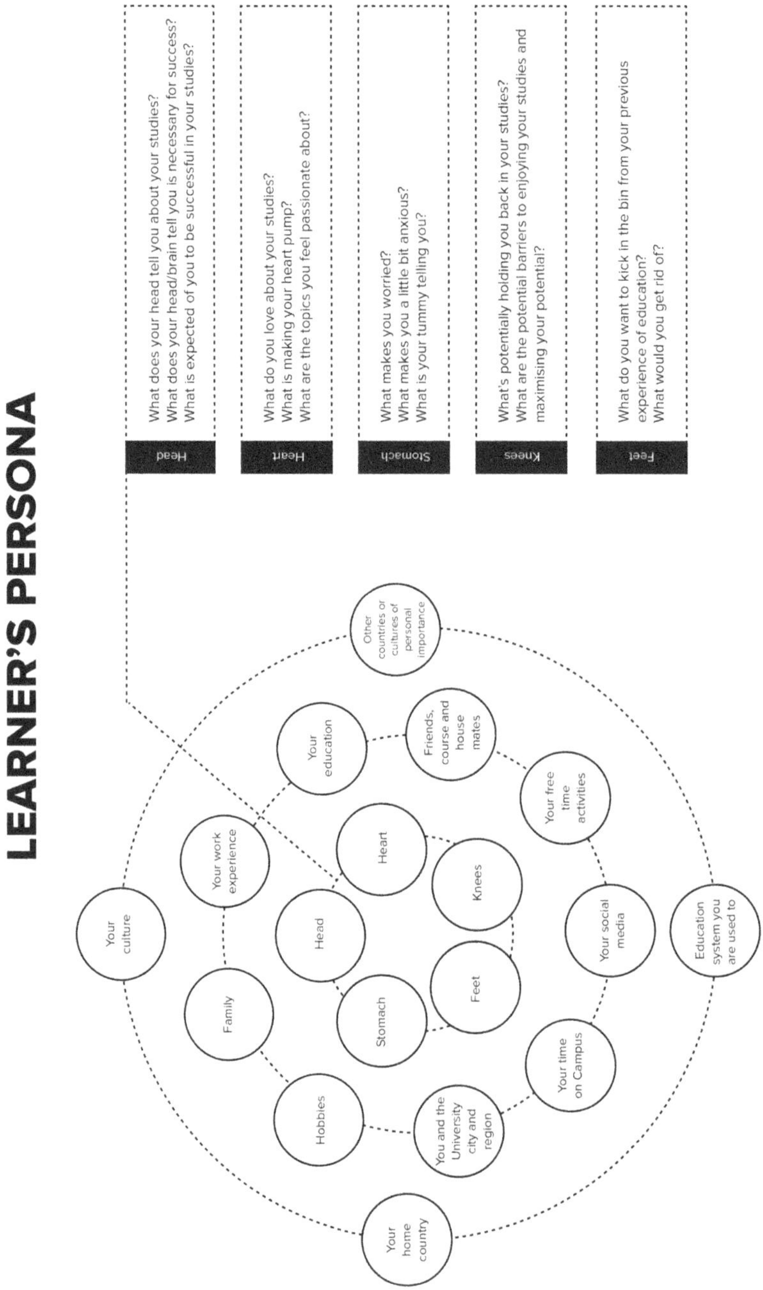

Fig. 8.5 Student persona (developed by author)

insecurities around language barrier and struggles with mental health. This particular persona helped staff and other students break down the assumptions we have about the European students who are usually high achievers and often pass through the programme without any major difficulties.

Another example was Joy from China (see Fig. 8.7), whose ambition is to become rich, have a better future and most importantly get a distinction for her studies. She doesn't have a clear career aim but comes from a business family and as the only child is prepared to go back to family business after a bit of a corporate work experience. Joy struggles with exams on the programme. She is an active person with many hobbies and enjoys being a member of student societies. Joy's persona revealed some new information about students from family business backgrounds who find it difficult to think about their career path. It also brought the focus on academic achievement in Asian students to light and their stress levels around their exams.

The students' personas were developed in a workshop by the students themselves who had directly experienced the learning process. From their stories, educators could identify key influents to improve and redesign the learning experience through both emotional and practice perspectives. The typical data review does not offer an opportunity to capture the depth of student's characteristics as design workshops do. This designerly method is complementary to the data-driven feedback informing the annual programme review bringing the involvement of students in a way

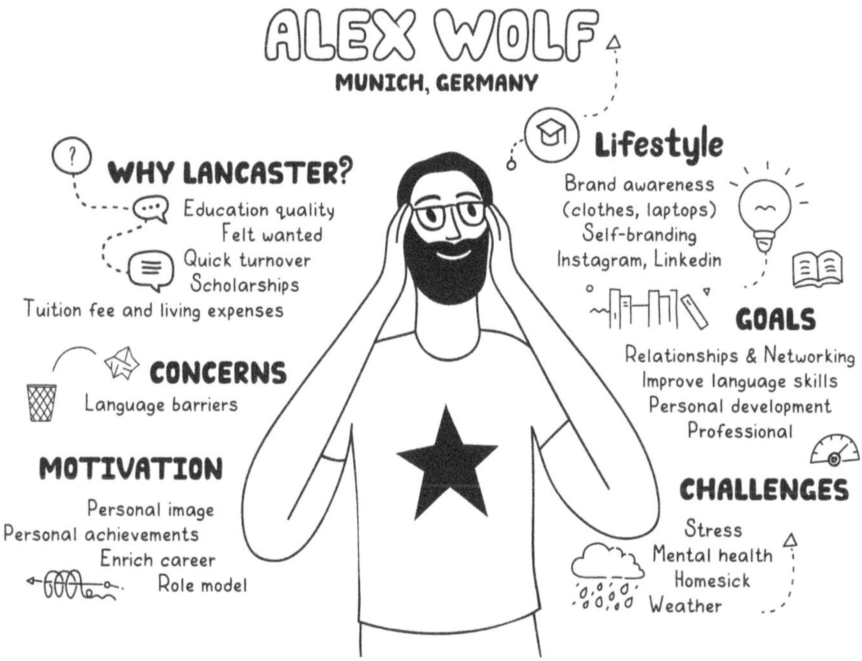

Fig. 8.6 Visual persona example—Alex Wolf (visualisation by Joy Wang)

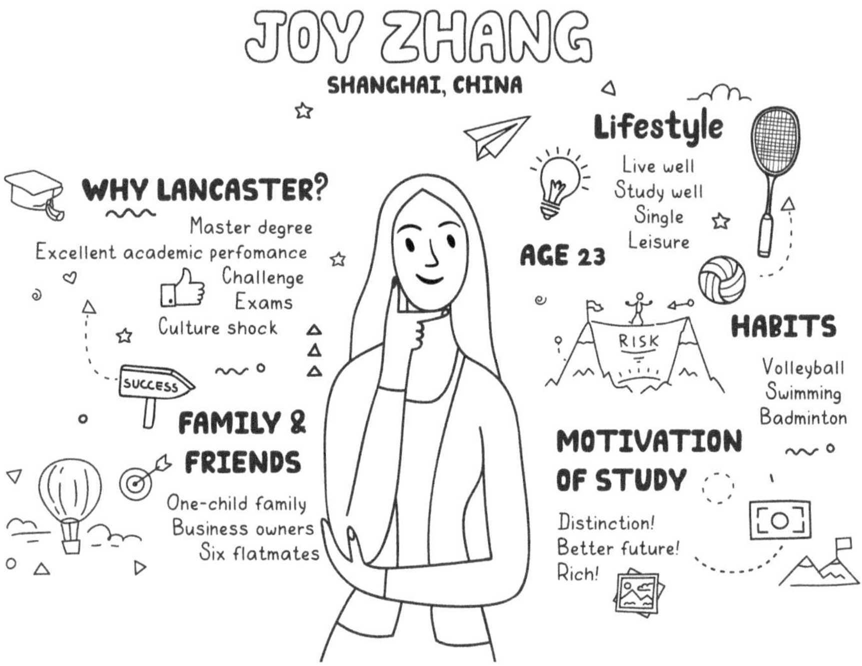

Fig. 8.7 Visual persona example Joy Zhang (visualisation by Joy Wang)

different from the usual module surveys. In addition, the design workshops on MiM programme have had the following benefits for the participants, which exceeded the planned objectives of the programme team to glean in-depth information about the cohort:

- Students learnt about the importance of understanding the customer voice in business

> The nature of the workshop was ideal. Learning by doing, from my point, is always the best. I learnt a lot about the development of a persona and then using this persona to develop a "customer" lifecycle where the persona is the customer of the university and students have needs which the uni and the programme need to address.

- Students developed greater self-awareness and deepened friendships

> even if I am an introvert, we got to know each other well. It was not like… I was among friends rather than strangers
>
> It is kind of comforting, in a way, to know that everyone is going through it together and that you're not the only person that feels sometimes, how am I going to get through this and stuff.

- Students felt included in the programme design and empowered as human beings

> I feel it positively included everyone, we were able to all of us get involved and contribute for the improvement.
>
> Like at the end of the day we're human beings, we're not just robots so you need to think about the student well-being first, which this is the most thing I liked about this university.

Emotional Journey Mapping

Journey maps visualise the user experience over a certain period and capture a sequence of steps the user goes through during their engagement with certain service (Stickdorn et al. 2011). Journey mapping or experience mapping serves as an ethnographic research method giving attention to actions and emotions that the user may find difficult to articulate otherwise. It is also telling what events or touchpoints the user chose to project onto the journey map and what emotions they associate with it. In addition, it gives more context to the information voiced in the persona. For instance, students in MiM programme pointed out anxiety around exams. The journey created a visual story of the programme experience and helped the programme team gained insights into the highs and lows of the cohort. To start the mapping activity, long rolls of white paper were placed on a wall. Coloured pens, sticky notes and emoji stickers were also provided. Students started with their persona's journey at the start of the programme and took us through to the current point of the workshop. By elaborating their feelings instead of discussing individual tasks, students were empowered to admit first exam failures, homesickness, job application rejections as these events were not personally associated with them.

The usual temptation is either to blame the students, assume that they do not access the information that is provided, or react to the lack of student engagement by either introducing more provision or making it compulsory. By adopting design approach, we have taken more empathic approach, which consequently shows the true pain points and provides an effective and efficient insight into possible areas of improvement. The involvement of the students in the reflection as well as ideation provides an opportunity of improvement by co-design. The design approach served as a non-judgemental method to focus on the areas we set out to improve and having the initial awareness of how the programme first into the university ecosystem together with understanding of potential barriers and enablers in the programme ecosystem helped he programme team take the inspiration from the students and turn it into tangible and valuable changes to the programme. In addition, it enables the programme team to listen to the voices from students and turn it into tangible and valuable changes to the programme.

The initial question to start the mapping activity was, "Why aren't the students engaging with our careers provision"? Having reviewed the journey maps, the programme team realised that the main challenge is to deliver learning events at the right time and in the right format. November stood out as the cold month with first assignments fails and job application rejections occurring at the same time. Employer campus visits and practice job interviews with our careers team became too overwhelming for students. The key points that we understood from the reflections were:

- The career sessions were scheduled in the times when the students felt lowest due to the first assessment failures, weather and homesickness
- The information overload meant the students disengaged with activities beyond their programme modules
- The focus on careers seemed too scary and distant
- Some of the students didn't want a traditional graduate career as we imagined it
- Students felt confused about what to do next
- The programme was too busy, students felt over-assessed, they found it difficult to cope with their hectic schedule with scarce downtime

The visualisation of emotional journey mapping shows patterns of the common responds and associated emotions in the cohort. The reoccurring patterns reveal more systematic issues in the programme design and provide an opportunity to address those as a priority. For instance, one of the high spike of positive emotions related to a cohort visited Manchester Career Fair that depicted in the extract of journey map below (see Fig. 8.8). In subsequent years the University decided to discontinue this particular career fair activity and funding was withdrawn. Confirmation of the value brought by this event through journey mapping has supported our appeal to keep this as a funded activity for future cohorts.

Another example is the negative emotions associated with exams. This negative pattern appeared in all journey maps, which has provided us with an opportunity to understand the context of the exam fears with a rapid prototyping of preventative actions such as providing past exam papers, scheduling exams in mid-week to give space at each side of the week to prepare and relax before the next learning event which has been followed through assessment strategy and supported by university-wide stakeholders. The last example of a pattern that need to be mentioned was related to the lack of downtime leading to lack of student engagement in societies and sport activities, which may lead to more serious mental health issues. Students prototyped a week in the programme structure and simply kept Wednesday afternoon off, which is a university designated time for sports and societies. The assumption the programme team made was that this only related to undergraduate student and postgraduate timetable never allowed for this time to be incorporated as downtime. This was a real light bulb moment for the programme team and this very simple adjustment provided the MiM programme with a unique characteristic that started attracting more University students who wanted to progress to the master's degree within our university. This feature also provides acknowledgment that 'We Care' about the students' overall university experience, not only the learning on the programme.

The value of taking time to engage with our learners though a service design methodology has facilitated a focused programme improvement strategy with understanding of what learning experience features add value and how they fit into the wider life of a student and the University ecosystem. The constant zooming in and zoom out with no judgement on single activity has been essential to this practice (see Fig. 8.2). In addition, the service design approach informed a quick and easy

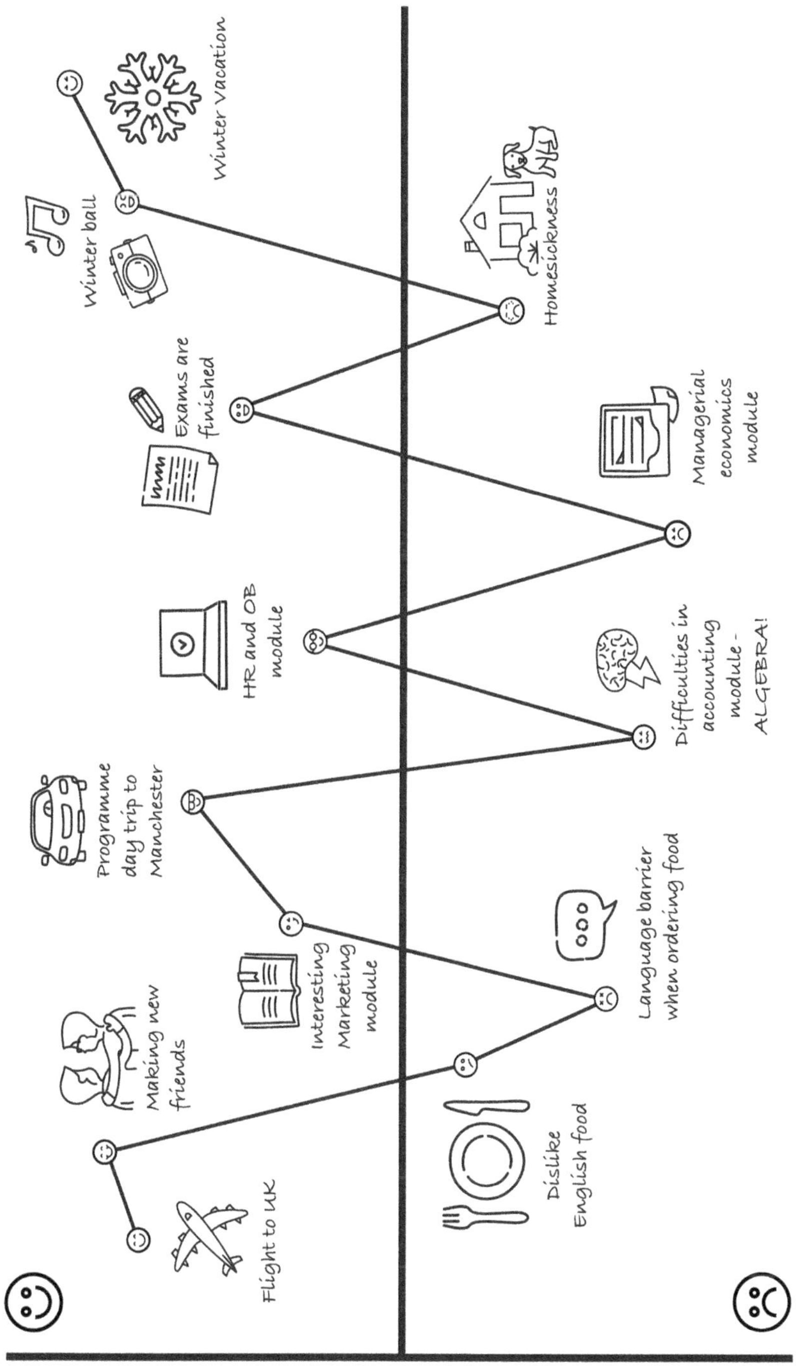

Fig. 8.8 Emotional journey map extract (visualisation by Joy Wang)

modification that systematically improved the programme design at the same time centrally placing students at the heart of this process.

Summary

The typical way of improving a university programme through student feedback usually results in collecting complaints, which is not that helpful. The average uptake of students to complete standard evaluations on the MiM programme oscillates between 10% and 30%, which does not provide a representative view of the student experience. Many students worry that providing feedback may have negative impact on their relationship with staff and impact on their grades. Design methods introduce a new way to capture many aspects of students' needs and concerns and create a non-judgemental space between staff and students where students could voice their reflections through a persona and their emotional journey map. The value of the design approach is ultimately in addressing the right problems in the right way instead of rushing into conclusions based on assumptions.

There is multiple theoretical impact of service design applying in educational context that needs to be researched further. The key concepts that ought to be explored are related to adaptability of service design to a higher education context and its impact on student engagement through partnership. The approach in this initiative was driven by improving students and staff experience and was liberated from the burden of the debate related to the concept of student as a customer. The engagement between the student and the educational institution has not been perceived as a pure supplier-customer relationship but has been superseded by a collaborative concept where the student is a co-producer of their own university experience. A testimony from one of the student participants confirms the twofold value that design methods have brought to the students on the Lancaster MiM programme:

> I really liked both activities as they allowed us to step back and have a good think about our development since starting the programme and also the people we are surrounded by, whether they be students or administrative staff. I liked how fun it was as it made it easier for us to take part and share ideas, and to be more relaxed with each other. I think being in groups was also good as we could all add our own ideas and reflect upon them based on what others thought and said.

Chapter Summary To demonstrate the breadth of the practical application of design thinking, this chapter has carefully chosen three diverse case examples drawn from industry practice. In a way, the rationale for their selection was to illustrate the different approaches and methods that were applied and the unique challenges that each case encountered. Using service design principles underpinned by design thinking methodologies in the higher education sector is rarely explored in design literature; even less so in the realm of business and management. The cases offered by Aryana and Baha further lend credence to the elasticity and applicability of designerly approaches when seeking competitive advantage. In the near future and beyond, the field of design thinking will feature and critically debate the distinct advantages of utilising design approaches to often insoluble problems. It is heartening to see cases of this nature, testament to the increasing confidence of organisations to adopt alternative approaches to solving the wicked and complex challenges that lie ahead.

Review Questions

1. The first case study focused on placing students as central to the research process. What other tools and techniques would you additionally draw upon to identify their current educational experiences and how could these be enhanced?
2. Hitachi ABB Power Grids use the full range of design to develop complex interactive systems. What other ways do they use design?
3. MaaS Global often uses insights and ideas in identified from earlier projects that are 'parked'. What mechanisms would you put in place where these ideas could be widely shared amongst the extended design team?

Project Questions

1. Learning persona is an incredibly powerful tool to gain deeper insights into student's values and interests. Based on Fig. 8.5, create your own learning persona in connection with your previous or current educational experience.
2. Create an evaluation strategy that can be used to test complex systems where design is a key element of your approach.
3. Identify a multimodal travel platform (ranging from bikes to public transport) and then document the critical areas where the user interfaces with its main touchpoints.

Chapter Tasks

1. Form a small group of no more than six people, and then give each person a box of paper clip; in this activity try and find as many uses for them as possible, apart from holding papers. After 60 minutes, share ideas with the rest of the group to see if there are any unifying principles or designs.
2. Storyboarding can be a particularly useful creative exercise for developing new procedures or improving existing processes. Rather than writing out the steps of the procedure, draw each step in a series of small, rectangular boxes, like. You might discover a useful new step in the process that you had not considered.

3. Based on your own shopping habits, create a visual journey map of a regular trip to your local supermarket, identify key points that you find important and pain points that you would improve upon to enhance your shopping experience.

References

Altay, B. (2014). User-Centered Design Through Learner-Centered Instruction. *Teaching in Higher Education, 19*(2), 138–155.

Aryana, B. (2020). Emerging Design: Integrating Learning, Practice and Research. *Journal of Design, Business & Society, 6*(1), 71–107.

Baha, S. E., Ghei, T., & Kranzbühler, A. M. (2021). Mitigating Company Adoption Barriers of Design-Driven Innovation with Human Centered Design. In *The 23rd International Conference on Engineering Design—Design in Motion (ICED 21)* (vol. 1, pp. 2097–2106).

Baha, S. E., Gokhle, S., Sturkenboom, N., Price, R. A., & Snelders, H. M. J. J. (2021). *What Is the Designer in Me?* Manuscript submitted for publication.

Baha, S.E., Sturkenboom, N., Lu, Y., & Raijmakers, B. (2013). Using Design to Initiate Collaborative Networks. In *The 2nd Cambridge Academic Design Management Conference (CADMC 2013)* (vol. 1, pp. 1–15).

Baranova, P., Morrison, S., & Mutton, J. (2010). Service Design in Higher and Further Education. *JISC CETIS, 6*.

Carey, P. (2013). Student as Co-producer in a Marketised Higher Education System: A Case Study of Students' Experience of Participation in Curriculum Design. *Innovations in Education and Teaching International, 50*(3), 250–260.

Crandall, B., Klein, G., Hoffman, R. R., & Senior Research Scientist. (2006). *Working Minds: A Practitioner's Guide to Cognitive Task Analysis*. MIT Press.

Cross, N. (2011). *Design Thinking: Understanding How Designers Think and Work*. Berg.

Dong, A., Kleinsmann, M., & Snelders, D. (2021). The Design of Firms: Part 1—Theory of the Firm. *Design Issues, 37*(2), 60–76.

Holmlid, S., & Evenson, S. (2008). Bringing Service Design to Service Sciences, Management and Engineering. *Service Science, Management and Engineering—Education for the 21st Century*, 341–345.

Kimbell, L. (2009). Insights from Service Design Practice. In *The 8th European Academy of Design Conference (EAD08)* (pp. 249–253).

Kuzmina, K., Bhamra, T., & Triminghan, R. (2012). *Service Design and Its Role in Changing Education* (pp. 27–36, S. Miettinen & A. Valtonen, Eds.). Lapland University Press.

Lilley, M., Pyper, A., & Attwood, S. (2012). Understanding the Student Experience Through the Use of Personas. *Innovation in Teaching and Learning in Information and Computer Sciences, 11*(1), 4–13.

Madden, H., & Walters, A. (2016). Using an Action Research Approach to Embed Service Design in a Higher Education Institution. *Swedish Design Research Journal, 14*(1), pp. 40–50.

Marsh, S. (2018). *User Research: A Practical Guide to Designing Better Products and Services*. Kogan Page Publishers.

Mattelmäki, T. (2006). *Design Probes*. PhD thesis, Aalto University. https://aaltodoc.aalto.fi/handle/123456789/11829

Ng, C. F. (2016). Behavioral Mapping and Tracking. *Research Methods for Environmental Psychology, 29*. https://books.google.com/books?hl=en&lr=&id=8mi-CgAAQBAJ&oi=fnd&pg=PA29&dq=%22Behavioral+Mapping+and+Tracking%22&ots=Losbi_6GXQ&sig=FQSaTmwmnkALB4ZgY_Lbpp99yJQ

Norman, D. A., & Verganti, R. (2014). Incremental and Radical Innovation: Design Research vs. Technology and Meaning Change. *Design Issues, 30*(1), 78–96. https://doi.org/10.1162/desi_a_00250

Osborne, S. P., Radnor, Z., & Strokosch, K. (2016). Co-production and the Co-creation of Value in Public Services: A Suitable Case for Treatment?. *Public Management Review, 18*(5), 639–653.

Pazell, S., & Hamilton, A. (2020). A Student-Centred Approach to Undergraduate Course Design in Occupational Therapy. *Higher Education Research & Development, 40*, 1–18.

Prahalad, C. K., & Ramaswamy, V. (2004). Co-creation Experiences: The Next Practice in Value Creation. *Journal of Interactive Marketing, 18*(3), 5–14.

Sangiorgi, D., & Prendiville, A. (Eds.). (2017). *Designing for Service: Key Issues and New Directions*. Bloomsbury Publishing.

Simon, H. A. (1988). The Science of Design: Creating the Artificial. *Design Issues, 4*(1/2), 67–82.

Simon, H. A. (1996). *The Sciences of the Artificial*. MIT Press.

Sleeswijk Visser, F., Stappers, P. J., Van der Lugt, R., & Sanders, E. B. N. (2005). Contextmapping: Experiences from Practice. *CoDesign, 1*(2), 119–149.

Star, S. L., & Griesemer, J. R. (1989). Institutional Ecology, Translations' and Boundary Objects: Amateurs and Professionals in Berkeley's Museum of Vertebrate Zoology, 1907–39. *Social Studies of Science, 19*(3), 387–420.

Stickdorn, M., Schneider, J., Andrews, K., & Lawrence, A. (2011). *This Is Service Design Thinking: Basics, Tools, Cases* (Vol. 1). Wiley.

Stolterman, E. (2021). The Challenge of Improving Designing. *International Journal of Design, 15*(1), 65–74.

Sturkenboom, N., Baha, S. E., Price, R. A., Kleinsmann, M., & Snelders, H. M. J. J. (2019). A CHAT Approach to Understand Framing in Digital Service Innovation. *Proceedings of the Design Society: International Conference on Engineering Design, 1*(1), 3031–3040.

Tomczak, J. M., Cieślińska, K., & Pleszkun, M. (2012). Development of Service Composition by Applying ICT Service Mapping. In *Computer Networks* (pp. 45–54). Springer.

Van Erp, J. (2011). Designing the Total Experience—A Model for the Changing Role of the Designer. *In The 4th World Conference on Design Research (IASDR 2011)* (p. 9).

Verganti, R. (2017). Design Thinkers Think Like Managers. *She Ji: The Journal of Design, Economics, and Innovation, 3*(2), 100–102.

9 Design Directions and Future Trajectories

Learning Objectives

- To introduce and examine the role and application of design within a broad range of dynamic future-orientated contexts.
- To examine the diverse range of international [DESIS / Living Lab] networks and understand their primary remit in the desire to fostering social innovation.
- To provide an understanding of design democracy and its commitment to the co-creation of user centred values.
- To critically examine the emergence of data driven innovation offered through the Internet of Things (IoT).
- To identify emergent macro trends and developments within the broad themes of technology, demographics and the environment.

9.1 Introduction

Design is in a continual state of perpetual change: this is a given; but what is contested is understanding the factors that are driving this perpetual and transformational change. In an attempt to understand and reflect upon these (and often) invisible forces driving change, it is timely to pause for a moment and take stock of the current situation and then focus our energies to the near future as to where design wants to go and what it wants to be. To begin answering these challenging set of

Supplementary Information The online version contains supplementary material available at [https://doi.org/10.1007/978-3-030-94206-9_9].

Y. Huang, D. Hands, *Design Thinking for New Business Contexts*,
https://doi.org/10.1007/978-3-030-94206-9_9

interrelated questions, Chap. 9 begins with a brief reflection as to the current state of design, especially its role beyond the traditional design studio and the limited confines of aesthetic application and promotional activities. One could argue that "design has come of age" being widely acknowledged and respected by its more mature partners and their respective disciplines active in the world of commerce and industry. Furthermore, design is transcending the boundaries of industry practice and application, being invited into the higher echelons of local and national policy making; exploring and informing policy that is shaping the infrastructure of urban environments, national healthcare delivery and transportation amongst many other aspects of government responsibility.

Alongside policy making, design is increasingly playing a greater role in society, and one such initiative is the DESIS Lab network, founded by Ezio Manzini in 2009, an international network of design schools and related organisations working on initiatives in the design for social innovation and sustainability fields. In the complexity of contemporary society, social innovation is gaining wider attention and especially the design profession is increasingly recognising its potential, as a driver of sustainable change. Change cannot be imposed, meaningful change is facilitated through inclusivity, mutual respect and understanding, in a way democratising the process of transformational change via design. One such approach is participatory design where all stakeholders contribute to this process on an equitable footing, where no one holds the definitive view—empowering participants through meaningful 'involvement' and 'empathetic' understanding. The concept of Living labs is introduced, which in a way, takes action research to a higher level, where ideas, abstract concepts are prototyped and tested in complex real world settings. What makes these labs successful is the commitment to the non-judgemental sharing of ideas and values in socially orientated 'experimental' spaces brokered by shared value stakeholders and participants. In terms of exponential innovative growth potential, one has to look no further than the internet of things (IoT) and its capacity to disrupt not only mature markets, but every aspect and nuance of our everyday lives. Some say 'data is the new oil' but one could argue that IoT is by far greater an industry movement than oil. The total installed base of Internet of Things (IoT) connected devices worldwide is projected to amount to 30.9 billion units by 2025, a sharp jump from the 13.8 billion units that are expected in 2021 (Statista, 2021).

The role of design as a conduit between the realms of data and innovation is an important one, and this contested territory is ripe for negotiation and respectful cooperation. This chapter concludes by focusing attention towards the future, identifying three significant and mutually interconnected areas of activity that embrace technological advancements, people and society and the environment, in particular climate change. These vast and critically important 'terrains' of activity coupled with the onset of globalisation are indeed the new 'Steppe' plains that can be meaningfully navigated through the footsteps of design.

9.2 Design Influences and Contested Territories

This section sets out the pervasive and influential role that design can offer to perennial wicked problems; problems well beyond the established boundaries of design activities. Challenges in contemporary society, such as population growth, political, economic and environmental factors and social divisions, are creating drivers for innovation (Kimbell, 2011). As such, language and terminology (such as innovation and design thinking) that have historically been attributed to design, are finding their way into other domains and becoming socialised as a means of practice (Carlgren, 2013). Consequently, designers and the profession of design is finding a meaningful role beyond the conventional 'design studio', and working in increasingly diverse settings such as local, regional and national policymaking, healthcare provision and delivery and education, in order to address a varied range of complex problems.

In today's globalised society, the world is fast becoming complex and interdependent; as such, we are witnessing transformational changes in every aspect of our lives, leading to the formation of new wicked challenges for the design profession. These complex and emergent challenges are not isolated to one particular sector, but across a whole range of interrelated domains where simple design solutions are unfeasible. Typically, these challenges and associated problems can often be characterised as emergent phenomena with non-linear uncertainties. Collectively, these are having a detrimental impact on a wide variety of key aspects of our planet, our society, our health and at a deeply personal level, our spirit as to how we perceive and understand the world around us. Human beings are depleting the planet's natural resources and standards of living will begin to decline by 2030 unless immediate action is taken. The World Wide Fund for Nature (WWF, 2018) warns that the current overexploitation of natural resources is generating an enormous deficit, as 20% more than can be regenerated is consumed each year and this percentage is growing steadily.

The current ecological crisis, wherein we continue to deplete our natural capital on a massive scale will inevitably lead to food supply shortages and subsequent price increases by 2030, leading to increasing sections of society encountering food poverty. The World Health Organisation has identified that

> The largest number of undernourished people (more than 500 million) live in Asia, mostly in southern Asian countries. Together, Africa and Asia bear the greatest share of all forms of malnutrition, accounting for more than nine out of ten of all stunted children and over nine out of ten of all wasted children worldwide. In southern Asia and sub-Saharan Africa, one child in three is stunted. (WHO, 2019)

Furthermore, our social crisis sees nearly 2.5 billion people on our planet living in abject poverty. With the rise of Covid-19 continuing unabated, in the 'Poverty and Shared Prosperity Report' by the World Bank (2020), "the pandemic is estimated to push an additional 88 million to 115 million people into extreme poverty this year, with the total rising to as many as 150 million by 2021, depending on the severity of the economic contraction. Extreme poverty, defined as living on less than $1.90 a day, is likely to affect between 9.1% and 9.4% of the world's population in 2020". Given these appalling statistics, these arguably constitute the most significant failure of our time. These crises, however, present significant challenges and opportunities for design. It is now timely for design (in its broadest sense of application) to face these challenges and envision and realise alternative directions for the planet.

Given its complexity, design is continually reflecting upon its historical development as a driver for change; on the present, as a discipline seeking dynamic cross-disciplinary horizons far beyond its current boundaries; and the future, becoming an alternative means of engaging with emergent global challenges. Design is a balance between the technological and humanistic aspects of society and culture. Its primary aim is to make the industrialised world both human, habitable and importantly, equitable, a means to evenly share prosperity to everyone. In fact, it has been widely acknowledged that design is now the best tool we have available to us in making sense of the increasingly complex and challenging situation that we currently find ourselves in. The growing trend to use design as a transformational tool has also brought more focus on the disciple of design, requiring design practitioners to be more open and co-operative in how they work. In particular, demonstrate talent and expertise with both quantitative and qualitative research methods; have the ability to analyse and synthesise often complex data sets, and subsequently communicate findings and solutions in objective and compelling ways. If design is the best available tool at our disposal in order to shape desired futures, how might the designer best critically reflect, collaborate, create and articulate new visions for local, regional, national and international contexts? How can designers effectively develop news of wider participation to create these truly desirable futures?

Designers are equipped with a set of inherent skills and attributes that they offer to any given problem (regardless of context) is that they possess non-tangible skills; those that cannot be seen or do not have a physical manifestation. Some of these non-tangible skills relate to the confidence, approaches and mindset of the designer; their ability to ask 'what if' questions and to take risks, their comfort in ambiguity and confidence in their own creative abilities (Cross, 2006; Campbell, 2009). These types of skills are often tacit, come naturally through experience (Cross, 2011; Wood et al., 2009).

Hargraves (2018, p. 78) argues, "For most of the nineteenth and twentieth centuries, designers thought of themselves as having subject matter expertise. Furniture designers were experts in the construction of chairs, tables, cupboards, and other furniture. Graphic designers understood themselves as masters of two-dimensional communicative form. This conception has shifted significantly during the past 40 years. Design, in large measure, no longer understands itself through the classes of artefacts it produces. Instead, design commonly conceives of itself and promotes itself as a general approach for innovative change as having no subject matter that is properly its own. This conception leads to an anxiety that manifests in questions commonly asked of designers: 'What exactly do you design?'"

Design is becoming further diverse in its meaningful application, forming a new approach to policymaking, healthcare delivery and crime reduction activities. We are also witnessing the emergence of sub-fields within the discipline of design, seeing the growing prominence of service design, social innovation, radical co-design and so forth. Primarily, these developments have been largely brought about by the changing roles and contexts of design and of how it is used within highly contextualised settings. By building purposeful relationships, the designer (working with other disciplines, professionals and citizens) will enhance their own and others abilities to challenge existing economic, social, environmental, and political models. This will help to foster a deeper understanding and strengthen the interrelationship between the design profession and other specialist domains of practice. As such, this could for instance, lead to more sustainable products, services and processes, whilst rethinking how policy could work better. Collaboration alone, however, will not be enough. It requires shifts in the culture and practices of co-designing, co-innovation and co-production to collectively decide and socially organise a future world that affords a wider means of prosperity to everyone.

In 2020, the UK Design Council (2021) launched an initiative as to how a systematic design approach can contribute to achieving net zero within sustainable development; in particular, working across business, public and the third sector, in alignment with the UK government's target outcome of net zero emissions by 2050. What was particularly interesting with this ambitious initiative is that their approach and central role within the project was twofold:

- To provide greater awareness and credibility to the growing practice of systemic design and create a framework that allows designers from different disciplines to come together with non-design professions and communities to undertake this work.
- To use our position to influence policy, regulation, standards and the design commissioning system to make it easier for designers to work in this way.

Turning our attention away from the UK, a noteworthy international initiative that positions design as a central agent for change is the DESIS Network. DESIS is the acronym for 'Design for Social Innovation and Sustainability' which features an international network of design schools or departments of design (DESIS Labs) within larger higher educational institutions. The primary remit of the DESIS association is *to use design to trigger, enable and scale-up social innovation through design thinking and design knowledge* (DESIS, 2021). Academics within the Labs (be it lecturers, researchers or a combination of both) are committed to advancing the role of design to foster societal change through design theory and practice. "Design schools (DESIS Labs) aim to participate and empower these processes, being one of these centres or by being connected with other existing centres. In this, DESIS Labs, being based in universities have the flexibility to explore and consolidate new frontiers, but at the same time stimulates universities to be open to society" (Cipolla et al., 2015, p. 6). A notable example would include the DSU-DESIS Lab, (Dongseo University) located in Busan, South Korea, which devotes particular emphasis working with local communities in cooperation with industry, small business owners, and regional governments. In Curitiba, Brazil, the Design & Sustainability Research Center at Federal University of Paraná (UFPR) hosts a DESIS Lab that focuses on the development of protocols for projects in Design for Sustainability through open innovation platforms (Crowd-Design, Crowd-Funding, Crowd Voting, Crowd Sourcing).

9.3 Democratic Design

The development and marketization of commercial products and services intended for mass-market consumers, offers many unique challenges to both the organisation and design/marketing functions. One primary challenge is the adoption of collaborative approaches to truly understand 'who' exactly they are designing for, in particular, the specific end-users of their product offerings. When designing products that have mass appeal, finding representative participants is of primary importance. In order to achieve this, designers need to work beyond the confines of the organisation, reaching out into the wider marketplace where specific representation of the ideal user can be sought. However, one major obstacle that is frequently encountered is that external parties have little incentive to actively participate, especially within tight schedules set out by the company. One further benefit of identifying and understanding 'lead' users is that they could provide vital user insights that could then initiate the development of subsequent innovative products. Effectively undertaken, this in a way could change a company product-centric approach to one that engages with the co-creation of value between the company and their users.

While the view of the individual innovator prevails, it is becoming increasingly challenged by the collaborative business environment as a basis for innovation (Prahalad & Krishnan, 2008). One notable advocate for user driven innovation is Eric von Hippel, American economist and Professor at the MIT Sloan School of Management, who was the inventor of the 'Lead User Method' that places primary emphasis on the end-user to drive product innovation(s). In essence, "the method is based on the empirical knowledge that innovations are often not initiated by manufacturers, but users stand often as the propelling strength behind developments" (Hengsberger, 2019; von Hippel, 2005). This advocacy for external input(s) into the design development process, leads us to the theme of 'participatory' design, where this approach is an inclusive method to co-design, co-create and co-operate with numerous stakeholders (as opposed to just end-users). Designers use an extensive range of tools and techniques to understand users; as such, the designer moves into the bounded realm of the user. However, participatory design turns this approach around, where end users move into the realm of design and design research.

Worthwhile to point out here, that although the end-users are an invaluable part of this approach, ultimately, the commissioner of design decides the final decision regarding product attributes and its position within the marketplace. In a way, the user is the main passenger in the vehicle, but the designer is the one who is driving the vehicle to its ultimate destination. This then begs the question, "so what is the main role of the end-user in this particular research approach?" Firstly, users would take part in extensive activities whereby they would form a central part in developing low fidelity mock-ups of the products (be it soft or physical) that would be tested in a variety of hypothetical scenarios. This then, would allow users to share invaluable insights as to why the product was developed in a particular way to suit their specific needs. Through this sharing of ideas and rich personal insights, the (design) researcher can then gain a deeper understanding of what they need. In essence, it is an effective means of validation, to see a product in use as opposed to gaining written or spoken feedback; in short, research through design. There is a point of caution here that needs to be highlighted; that this intensive and time-consuming process is more expensive than non-participatory design methods. However, in particular contexts of product use, the benefits of this approach far outweigh the disadvantages. As touched upon, participatory design should be used when companies want a particular set of users to act as opposed to speak. As the old adage rings true, 'actions speak louder than words.'

Due to the rich and broad nature of participatory design as an inclusive approach to yielding detailed user insights, context is highly important; in both the way, the designer would create a democratic framework for the research study and the tools in which to collect data. There is a vast array of tools and techniques available to the designer, so it is important to understand and define as to what are the ultimate aims of the project. Sanders et al. (2010) offer an interesting approach to the selection of tools available and their particular merits when collecting specific user requirements. Their framework has three distinct elements that include: (1) form; (2) purpose; (3) context, which should be equally considered when planning a PD project.

Firstly, form articulates what particular type of activity is going to take place; this may entail making prototypes, talking where participants would recount experiences or be involved in detailed discussions about how they use a particular product or service. Purpose, outline why tools and techniques are going to be drawn upon and used; in particular—tools to glean detailed information through probing; for priming, as in preparing participants for the research study; understanding, as in developing a deeper understanding of their experiences; and fiction exploration, to develop conceptual propositions for preferred fictional futures. Finally, context focuses on the overarching PD study in terms of cohort size of participants, and whether online or in-person (which is particularly pertinent given the ongoing Covid-19 restrictions). It is worthwhile to point out here that there is a distinct difference between 'Participatory' design and 'User-centred' design, where they are commonly misunderstood as being the same. Robertson and Simonsen (2012) articulate the key differences, arguing, "Participatory Design is not the same as 'user-centered design;' though the two can have much in common and some design tools and techniques are used in both. While many areas of design now pay at least lip service to people's participation, the question of how participation is being negotiated and defined (and by whom) is fundamental to distinguishing Participatory Design from the more common user-centered approaches."

Living Labs: Co-Creative Potentialities?

Following on from participatory design, the emergence of the living lab movement, places participatory design central to its role within the co-creation of innovative solutions. In essence, the concept of living labs is widely attributed to the late William (Bill) Mitchell, Dean of the School of Architecture and Planning at the Massachusetts Institute of Technology, was considered one of the world's leading urban theorists. Through the work of his Smart Cities research group at the MIT Media Lab, he pioneered new approaches to integrating design and technology to make cities more responsive to their citizens and more efficient in their use of resources. Before we discuss the movement in further detail, the Living Labs phenomenon is very limited to the point that there is a lack of a widely recognised definition (Kviselius & Andersson, 2009; Tang et al., 2012). However, two primary characteristics form the essence of a living lab; firstly, they are bounded environments that facilitate real-life testing and experimentation; and secondly, participants and users are knowingly involved within the process of innovation. Here, the term 'knowingly' is an important point, where users actively engage with the sharing of ideas and experiences. Claudia Dell' Era and Paolo Landoni (2014) undertook a lengthy examination of living labs, and from their research study, they defined a living lab as "a design research methodology aimed at co-creating innovation through the involvement of aware users in a real-life setting". Their definition accords with the findings of Eriksson et al. (2005) and Schuurman et al. (2012), who describe Living Labs as a user-centric research methodology to sense, prototype, validate and refine complex solutions in multiple and evolving real-life contexts. Due to both the popularity and relevance of living labs as engines for stimulating innovation, we are witnessing the global emergence of living labs. One main umbrella organisation driving the growth of living labs is the 'European Network of Living Labs' (ENoLL) in Europe and now expanding its remit worldwide. Since its early formation in 2006, ENoLL has labelled over 460 living labs to date. ENoLL is active in many different areas of work and funded projects to strengthen the impact that living labs can generate, focusing on capacity building and scaling-up of solutions and services.

Primary areas of activity include:

- Smart Cities
- Future Internet
- Education
- Design
- Big Data
- Climate
- Creative Industries

Not only do the living labs focus upon specific themes, they also base themselves around particular areas of investigation. 'Research' labs conduct research on a host of activities based around the innovation process. 'Corporate' labs extensively involve users and other stakeholders to co-create innovations within a physical environment. 'Organisational' labs are where members of the organisation co-creatively develop innovations. 'Intermediary' labs accommodate a diverse range of partners to innovate in a central (but neutral) environment. Often you will find that living labs comprise of four main partners—(1) researchers; (2) public organisations; (3) companies; (4) end-users. Benefits to each partners are diverse; companies can gain access to and generate novel ideas for commercialisation. Public sector organisations can identify opportunities for an increased return on investment on innovation research and users can initiate innovations that they seek which are not currently available. A pre-requisite for living labs is that they should have access to multi-contextual environments alongside cutting-edge technologies and infrastructure to facilitate and support user involvement and testing. Furthermore, to underpin these activities, the labs need the involvement of experts drawn from the different partners in order to succeed. The following examples illustrate the different areas of focus of the labs in Table 9.1. Provide a snapshot of the range of activities currently being undertaken across the ENoLL network of living labs.

9.4 Data and Design

Data driven innovation is becoming widely recognised as a means of securing competitive advantage, however, due to its ambiguous nature, data driven innovation (DDI) can feature in a wide variety of forms and applications. Due to its emergent nature and commercial sensitivity, it is often difficult for organisations and individuals to understand its application in commercial practice. In essence, DDI is an innovative idea that has its origins arising from correlations in data, which could then go on to filling a measurable need or marketplace opportunity. A succinct definition of DDI refers to the innovation process that relies on digital technologies to provide new processes, services and products (e.g., Martínez-López & Casillas, 2013; Nambisan et al., 2017). However, DDI is a far more complex area of practice, where many thousands of innovative products draw upon big data to function; furthermore, many processes and sub-systems are optimised through data. The smartphone is a simple example of a ubiquitous product that relies heavily upon real-time data to provide the user with added value features through its interactive functionality. This process creates instantaneous data at each step, which forges a continuous data chain production system.

The role of big data in innovation is a huge area of discussion, as such, this section will focus on one particular aspect, that of the 'Internet of Things' (IoT) which deserves particular attention. IoT coined by British entrepreneur Kevin Ashton in 1999, primarily refers to the billions of physical devices that are connected to the internet, sharing and collecting data; due to the availability of cheap computing devices and global wireless networks, it is now possible to transform everyday objects into a part of the internet of things. Through connecting all these devices and adding sensors to them, you can now add many layers of digital intelligence, thus enabling them to communicate real-time data without the need of human

Table 9.1 ENoLL living labs—examples of living labs by area of focus

Name	Country	Area of focus
LivingLab SHANGHAI'	China	An educational platform based on the open approach and environment of Sino-Finnish Centre, located in Tongji University. It promotes open innovation for generating social construction of knowledge, bridging top-down and bottom-up social innovation process in real world contexts by involving relevant stakeholders.
Basaksehir Living Lab	Turkey	The Living Lab has aimed to increase the life standards of the local society, the quality of Basaksehir city and consciousness of urbanisation by means of taking into consideration desires of the local citizen and society by a set of high and standardised innovative services for the local public as well as private organisations. Basaksehir Municipality, in accordance to these purposes regarding applying the quality, provide unconditioned customer satisfaction, education and control to all of its citizen and employees, by continuously improving and applying development facilities.
TIE-LL Technology Innovation Ecosystem	Italy	TIE Living Lab aims at operating as a *smart platform* to stimulate technology innovation and innovative entrepreneurship for local development in the global scenarios, by leveraging on talents, technology, collaboration, collective intelligence, and networking, in the strategic perspective to exploit and valorise research outcomes, technological assets and scientific results. Thus, TIE Living Lab acts as a bridge that connects civil society, academy, businesses, markets, government and institutions, aiming at helping entrepreneurs overcome the *valley of death*, and at fostering innovation and entrepreneurship.
Lahti Living Lab	Finland	The special focus of the Lahti Living Lab is to develop and study innovativeness and productivity in the public sector. The main activity is to integrate the users into the innovation processes of public sector service development. For this purpose, the methods and tools are developed and studied. The methods of involving and activating the users vary, there are methods based on ICT but also on face-to-face communication. The Lahti Living Lab concept consists of different research and development projects, which all have a common nominator, that is, the users as innovators.

Source: enoll.org (2021)

intervention. As such, it allows the super fluid connection between both physical and digital universes. Not only devices can feature within this dynamic system, but also smart cities, where entire urban environments are embedded with sensors to enable city planners and urbanists to understand and manage complex living environments. The Internet of Things comprises four key elements:

- *People*: using hardware devices in a network to share information and usage data. Common examples include fitness sensors and social networks.
- *Things*: physical sensors, devices, actuators, and other items generating data or receiving information from other sources.

- *Data*: raw data analysed and processed into meaningful information to support intelligent decisions and control mechanisms.
- *Processes*: leveraging connectivity among data, things and people to add value to the user.

IoT has come some way from its original application within the realm of manufacturing, where its nascent means of usage was 'machine-to-machine' via radio frequency identification (RFID). Moving away from an industrial setting, IoT is turning its attention towards our everyday living and working environment, filling homes and offices with interconnected smart devices. Tech analyst company IDC predicts that in total there will be 41.6 billion connected IoT devices by 2025, or "things". It also suggests industrial and automotive equipment represent the largest opportunity of connected "things", but it also sees strong adoption of smart home and wearable devices in the near term. (Ranger, 2020). The benefits of IoT to business are extensive; however, it does depend on specific application—usually based around the themes of efficiency and agility. For instance, organisations would have greater access to detailed data about their own products in use and their internal operating systems and therefore, develop a stronger ability to make swift changes as a result.

Alongside the IoT, new terms are being coined given its wider application; these include the 'Internet of Everything' "is bringing together people, process, data, and things to make networked connections more relevant and valuable than ever before-turning information into actions that create new capabilities, richer experiences, and unprecedented economic opportunity for businesses, individuals, and countries" (Cisco, 2013). Then we have the 'Industrial Internet of Things' (IIoT) which goes beyond the normal consumer devices and internetworking of physical devices usually associated with the IoT. What makes it distinct is the intersection of information technology (IT) and operational technology (OT). Finally, 'Enterprise IoT' is the next advancement in technology that enables physical 'things' with embedded computing devices (tiny computers) to participate in business processes for reducing manual work and increasing overall business efficiencies. IoT allows devices and people to work more seamlessly together, offering the following distinct benefits to the company:

- *Enhanced productivity*: it is a given that machines are far superior to humans when it comes to producing and managing complex data. With the exponential growth of IoT within the factory, products and systems can smoothly operate on a regular and consistent basis. This enhanced means of operation can lead to the creation of better products whilst also delivering enhanced customer service experiences. The collection of real time data can enable service refinements based on user-generated information.
- *Increased automation*: following on from enhanced productivity, the IoT can allow organisations and manufacturers to automate repetitive tasks that would otherwise be conducted by people. IoT systems connected to the cloud and AI algorithms will enable machines to do much more work than they could ever

have done before. This frees human beings to focus on more creative value-added work, rather than just crunching numbers.

- *Improved efficiency*: regardless of business operation, the more data that can be collected can be used to improve efficiencies. For instance, IoT is an important component of predictive maintenance, which is a technique that uses condition-monitoring tools and techniques to monitor the performance of a structure or a piece of equipment during operation. The recorded information enables an engineer to predict the future failure point of the asset being monitored, allowing the asset to be fixed or replaced just before it fails.
- *Augmented customer experiences*: IoT is beginning to feature heavily in the development and delivery of enhanced customer experiences. The mantra 'the customer is king' is placing greater emphasis on the organisation to continually refine and develop how they interact with their customers, and indeed a wider range of their stakeholders. The internet of things in conjunction with artificial intelligence can provide greater insights into customer requirements and behaviours.

With IoT offering the huge potential to disrupt established markets, companies need to re-think their business models and operating procedures to exploit fully this new technology. This places greater emphasis on the way companies conceive, create and commercialise IoT offerings to often-unfamiliar customer audiences wary of new technologies. In essence, companies need to be strategic in the way they promote and market IoT products in order to survive. To be successful, companies need to be careful in the way they convince potential new customers to the benefits that their products offer, thus justifying either premium prices or taking the time and trouble to familiarise themselves with how they use this new technology. As such, this takes us back to the critical business functions of design and marketing when devising a heavily reliant IoT marketing strategy. Firstly, beginning with the customer (or end user or both) who initially are reticent to purchase an unfamiliar premium product, the benefits need to be articulated in a manner where value in use to them is clearly explicit. For instance, customers could save on their monthly domestic energy bills by being more energy efficient, or improving home security, offering peace of mind whilst away on vacation. Connected IoT devices provide a wider range of benefits (both monetary and non-monetary) which could result in a series of unique value propositions. However, these need to be carefully crafted in all marketing and promotional materials in order to win over sceptical consumers. The Internet Society (2019) conducted extensive research into customer perceptions and attitudes towards IoT devices, with main findings that included:

- 63% of people surveyed find connected devices 'creepy' in the way they collect data about people and their behaviours.
- This sentiment is echoed throughout the survey, with half of people across markets distrusting their connected devices to protect their privacy and handle their information in a respectful manner (53%).

- On top of not trusting the device itself to keep data secure, 75% of people agree there is reason for concern about their data being used by other organisations without their permission.
- The security concerns are serious enough to deter almost a third (28%) of people who do not own smart devices from buying one; security concerns are as strong a deterrent as the price of a device.
- People have concerns about security and privacy but do not know how to adapt and adjust device settings in a way that might allay these fears. 80% of people surveyed are aware of how to set and reset passwords, but only 50% are aware of how to disable the collection of data about users and their behaviours.

The above set of findings is widely held across many consumer groups regarding IoT, and as such, these perceptions can be overcome through intelligently planned and executed marketing strategies. Consultancy firm L.E.K. (2015) offers an interesting set of marketing strategies based around the introduction of IoT to both new and existing customers (Table 9.2). As can be seen, the different approaches between traditional and IoT marketing strategies is markedly different in both planning and implementation.

Alongside marketing IoT products to companies and individuals, the internet of things can also make a huge contribution to marketing activities in its own right. It is particularly relevant to bridging the physical and digital worlds within high street retailing where enhanced customer experiences are crucial in ensuring customer engagement and retention. IoT allows marketers to offer highly personalised and context specific tailored messages to the consumer, for example, digital signage and wayfinding in physical retail environments via mobile applications or other devices in digital interactions. With more retailers adopting IoT technologies, advanced personalised digital interactions will become the norm on the high street; retailers who do not keep up with this growing trend will soon obsolete. Research undertaken by the forecasting consultancy Juniper (2015) found that leading retailers using the IoT to generate an 'ecosystem' are poised to gain market advantage and capitalise on the

Table 9.2 Marketing traditional products versus Marketing IoT devices

	Stand-alone box	Connected device
Target profile	Open to purchase	Open to change
Sales touchpoints	B2C: Established channels	B2C: Established and new channels
	B2B: Limited touchpoints, typically technical/functional experts	B2B: Multiple touchpoints; cross-functional and C-suite stakeholders
Sales approach	Identifying and meeting existing needs	Sharing insights and bringing awareness of new needs
	Product expertise	Customer expertise
	Price versus quality trade-off	Transformation
	Focus on meeting specs and known needs	'Nonobvious' benefits; focus on value (monetary and nonmonetary) of benefits.

Source: L.E.K. Consulting

opportunity. Linking the hardware elements of RFID tags, beacons and connected consumer electronics, such as wearables, with software analytics promises in-depth business insight and an enhanced customer experience. "Retailers such as Zara and Target are already taking advantage of the benefits offered by RFID asset tracking" noted author Steffen Sorrell. "Meanwhile the beacon industry is expanding rapidly; used as a method to provide consumers with contextually relevant information in conjunction with their smartphone or wearable will enormously enhance the in-store experience".

As IoT innovation advances and permeates our daily lives, it will disrupt entire industries and has a profound impact on business. Despite a number of companies considering incorporating IoT components to their products and service portfolios, there is still a lack of understanding on the developmental processes of IoT products and services as well. Traditional design processes are fast becoming redundant when used to create IoT products, as such; organisations now need to take into account real-time data flows during the design process throughout product development, which in turn, could shape commercial outcomes. Lee et al. (2019, 2020) have conducted extensive research into IoT NPD processes that require radical re-thinking as to how organisations embark upon digitally orientated business strategies.

9.5 Design Directions in an Era of Uncertainty

Design as we know is a discipline that exists between two worlds—'the here and now' and the 'where we could be' offering endless possibilities for curious minds. It is worth pointing out that this section does not attempt to predict the future, more so to reflect upon where design is now and its potential evolutionary 'next step' as a means to enhancing our daily lives set against the backdrop of social and technical change. In essence, design thinking is a driver for meaningful change within a globalised world. Design is and will always be considered an invisible resource? Often the term 'design' is commonly, and sadly, used to articulate how either a product or object looks, mainly at a very superficial level of understanding. With this rather limited definition of usage, it is regarded as a frivolous activity offering no real worth to the organisation. However, enlightened organisations regardless of size, really understand its 'value' not just at a tactical level of engagement, but as a vital ingredient and source of both inspiration and opportunity. When carefully managed and orchestrated, design has the innate ability to offer a distinct range of value-propositions that are desirable in the eyes of the consumer and end-users alike. With the advent of globalisation in full force, competition between companies is becoming increasingly fierce, and as such, design is now becoming the commercial 'imperative' in the continual struggle towards long-term survival and continued sustainable success. Here, we are going to turn our attention to three increasingly critical developments that organisations of all sizes, needs to plan for and respond to in order to survive. Aspects of these developments have been touched upon within preceding chapters of this book, however, due to their growing importance, they do warrant closer investigation. The following will shape the contours of the world we will live in during the coming decades:

- Technology
- Demographics
- Environment

Building on the progress of human development, numerous countries and nation states will encounter many structural challenges to build on and augment earlier successes, especially set against the backdrop of climate change and economic uncertainty. Furthermore, the damaging consequences of extreme weather events and rising sea levels will disproportionately affect poorer countries and developing economies even further. Alongside environmental challenges, the exponential rise of technological developments will accelerate and improve human experiences, however, there is an increasing possibility that these developments could open up new fissures and tensions between industries, and society as a whole, leading to socio-economic inequalities. To further exacerbate economic and social disparities, demographic changes could lead to global migration, a potential pressure that will increase friction between states. The rise of Asian economies is challenging established rules and institutions as, combined with their large population size and densities, they create new and unforeseen challenges to western economies.

Technology

A confluence of diverse trends is providing fertile conditions for a perfect storm over the next few decades and beyond. However, it is widely accepted that these new technologies will not come to fruition evenly or predictably, they will more than likely to share a set of common drivers and associated dynamics. Digital experience continues to be a critical driver of enterprise transformation in fact, 64% of participants in Deloitte's global CIO survey say digital technologies will affect their businesses in the next three years. (Deloitte, 2020). With the wider dissemination of technological expertise, the drive to the setting of common standards to promote one solution over another and faster product development processes will inform long-term strategies to ensure continued commercial success. With timelines shrinking, the ability to develop, commercialise and withdraw technologies from the marketplace is now measured in years as opposed to decades. Multiple partners and international joint ventures (IJV) are driving technological developments that can be offered to the marketplace before rival companies. With this growing imbalance of technological knowledge, developing countries are becoming dependent on adopting technologies without understanding the implications of these choices being fully considered.

A good example of this comes from a recently published study (Poliquin, 2020) from the University of California, Los Angeles, which explores how technology (in the broadest sense) has affected wages over the years. The research examined the introduction of something as relatively mundane as broadband into Brazil between 2000 and 2009. It revealed that the technology coincided with an increase in wages across the labour market, but whereas the average employee saw wages rise by just 2.3%, those in managerial positions saw a 9% rise, and those in the boardroom saw an even more impressive 19% boost to the income. The hypothesis proposed by the researchers is that the new technology allowed the more productive workers to be even more productive, thus widening the income gap between them. Martin Ford issues an equally strong warning. In his book, *The Lights in the Tunnel* (2009), he argues, "as technology accelerates, machine automation may ultimately penetrate the economy to the extent that wages no longer provide the bulk of consumers with adequate discretionary income and confidence in the future. If this issue is not addressed, the result will be a downward economic spiral".

Demographics

According to a report published by the National Intelligence Council (NIC, 2021) it estimates that during the next 20 years, the world's population will continue to increase every year, adding approximately 1.4 billion people to reach an estimated 9.2 billion by 2040, but the rate of population growth will slow in all regions. However, this growth will quickly decline from 2040. Population growth in China will plateau, being overtaken by India as the most populous country around 2027. As widely acknowledged, the global population will age, rising from a median of around 31 years in 2020 to 35 in 2040. This ageing population will bring associated challenges, in particular affecting Eastern Europe and China. One such development will include the reduction in productivity as older workers show reduced productivity gains and a greater reliance on healthcare provision and access to affordable pension schemes. A report produced by UNECE (2007) points out, "the number and proportion of older persons in society increases, so the total resources required to meet their needs are growing. Literally all spheres of society need to adapt to this change".

The World Health Organisation (2018) predicts that:

- Between 2015 and 2050, the proportion of the world's population over 60 years will nearly double from 12% to 22%.
- By 2020, the number of people aged 60 years and older will outnumber children younger than 5 years.
- In 2050, 80% of older people will be living in low- and middle-income countries.
- The pace of population ageing is much faster than in the past.
- All countries face major challenges to ensure that their health and social systems are ready to make the most of this demographic shift.

Environment

Since the start of the industrial revolution in the eighteenth century, there has been a significant change to the earth's atmosphere due to increased emissions of greenhouse gases, primarily caused by humans. Consequently, this has led to global warming which has effected noticeable change in the climate. Through the burning of fossil fuels (coal, natural gas and oil) combined with large-scale land use and urbanisation, these contributing factors have further intensified greenhouse emissions. According to the scientific reports of the Intergovernmental Panel on Climate Change (IPCC, 2018), "the average global surface temperature has increased by 1.04 °C in the last 130 years, the sharp increase in global warming since 1950 can no longer be explained by natural climate fluctuations. Greenhouse gases such as carbon dioxide (CO_2) are almost certainly responsible for this". Alongside the physical effects of climate change, nation states and geographic regions will encounter challenges and tensions regarding reducing emissions of greenhouse gases and the implementation of adaptive measures. The burden of these measures will not be shared equally across the globe, thus making it challenging when applying these stringent commitments. There is also a growing movement towards reducing global warming, with youth activists like Greta Thunberg, giving voice to the concerns of young people across the world.

In a report released by UNICEF (2021), Thunberg argues, "We are not just victims, we are also leading the fight. But [the world] is still not treating the climate crisis like an emergency. We are still just talking and greenwashing things instead of taking real action. But, on the other hand, there have been many millions of people mobilised, especially young people, and that is a very important step in the right direction". Policymakers continually have to devise policies that are deeply unpopular amongst the general public, drawing protests against their implementation, such as all new conventional petrol and diesel cars and vans are set to be banned from sale in the UK from 2030. New hybrids will be given a stay of execution until 2035, on the condition they are capable of covering a "significant distance" in zero-emission mode, announced the UK government (gov.uk, 2020). Luke Murphy, head of the influential Institute for Public Policy Research's Environmental Justice Commission, points out, that "The phase-out of new petrol and diesel vehicles by 2030 is an important step, but it won't be enough just to switch to electric vehicles. If we attempt to replace vehicles one-for-one, it will be a huge draw on other environmental resources. We need to reduce car use overall, which means greater investment in sustainable public transport options, including rail and bus services, as well as more support for cycling and walking". (Forbes, 2020).

Chapter Summary Design could be considered a rebellious child constantly questioning things and long-held, widely accepted assumptions. The following oft-quoted remark reflects the contrarian nature of design that "the important thing is not to stop questioning. Curiosity has its own reason for existing" (Einstein, 1955). Following on from this maxim, this broad ranging chapter has introduced a plethora of emergent themes and topics that both capture and reflect the continual progression of design as an agent of change. However, the forces that influence and shape the contours of design are complex and often invisible, thus making any predictions as to its next evolutionary steps almost impossible to predict. Regarding the present day, design has travelled a considerable journey since its primary role as a stylistic and perfunctory element of industry and commerce from the seeds of the eighteenth century industrial revolution. Fast forward to the twenty-first century where disruption and creative renewal are a given, design has finally found a safe harbour to reflect and reappraise its next evolutionary journey over unchartered horizons and turbulent seas of meaningful engagement. The themes of digital, technological advancement and IoT present many significant challenges to both the individual and organisations alike. The bifurcation between these two respective domains is becoming increasingly blurred, even more so with the emergence of democratic design and the rising empowerment of the end-user within the design development process. Taking these inclusive principles further, we are witnessing the rise of collaborative research centres and departments such as the DESIS network and Living Labs reaching out into new and unchartered territories of socially orientated modes of engagement.

In today's hyper-connected world, one country's societal problems can become ours. Nations are facing stagnating economic growth, financial instability, political turmoil, hunger, poverty and the consequences of the Covid-19 pandemic. These are all social issues that have to be addressed, one way or the other, and as such, these wicked problems generate many opportunities for ambitious entrepreneurial minds. In fact, more than 80% of economic growth comes from innovation and application of this new knowledge. However, it should be acknowledged that social innovation is actually adding an extra dimension to the field and practice of innovation, sustaining economic and social growth and indeed wider prosperity to a whole range of individuals and communities. Uncertainty and unpredictability are recurrent themes frequently discussed by industry and policymakers alike, and the positioning of design to plan for, accommodate and respond to global challenges that include, technology, demographics and climate change are becoming the new imperatives that demand urgent critical attention. To conclude Chap. 9, future challenges potentially have their inherent solutions inspired from the past, and in respect of these emergent global challenges, the prescient Chinese proverb poetically suggests, "when the winds of change blow, some people build walls and others build windmills".

Review Questions

1. What are classed as 'wicked' problems and how is the design profession addressing these perennial problems?
2. DESIS Labs is an international network of design research centres; what types of research themes are they critically engaging with?
3. Participatory design is an inclusive approach to yielding information rich user centred data, what are the three main elements of participatory design?
4. Living Labs focus upon a diverse range of specific research themes; who are the four main partners that feature within Living Labs projects?
5. What are the numerous benefits to the company when embarking on IoT developmental strategies?

Project Questions

1. Identify two diverse 'wicked' problems and discuss where and how design could contribute to addressing them.
2. Identify and list a series of tools and techniques widely used within participatory design and list out factors that make them particularly unique to gleaning user-centred insights.
3. Select one commonly used domestic appliance within the home and consider ways in which it could be transformed into a digitally enable IoT product system.
4. Devise a marketing strategy for an IoT related device to new customers who are unfamiliar with IoT outlining its two primary benefits.
5. It is widely forecast that population growth will significantly increase over the next 60 years; identify a series of implications where design can minimise the impact of this development.

Chapter Tasks

1. Develop a simple 500 word proposal outlining your research interests and how they could be turned into a DESIS Lab.
2. Based on this proposal, which partner organisations would be instrumental in turning your idea into a viable proposition and what benefits would they offer to your Lab?
3. Identify five IoT products currently on the marketplace and list the key similarities and differences between them.
4. List three main advantages and disadvantages of establishing an International Joint Venture. What other aspects of an IJV do you think need to be taken into account?
5. Form a small group of no more than four people; then identify a current partnership between two leading international brands, examining the pros and cons for each brand within that partnership.

References

Campbell, E. (2009). *You Know More Than You Think You Do: Design as Resourcefulness and Self-reliance*. RSA Design & Society, RSA.

Carlgren, L. (2013). *Design Thinking as an Enabler of Innovation: Exploring the Concept and Its Relation to Building Innovation Capabilities*. PhD dissertation, Chalmers University of Technology.

Cipolla, C., Afonso, R., & Joly, M. P. (2015). *Transformative Social Innovation Narrative of the DESIS Network*. TRANSIT: EU SSH.2013.3.2-1 Grant Agreement No: 613169 | 31st of March 2015.

Cisco. (2013). *What Is the Internet of Everything (Ioe)?* Retrieved August 16, 2021, from https://www.cisco.com/c/dam/en_us/about/business-insights/docs/ioe-value-index-faq.pdf

Cross, N. (2006). *Designerly Ways of Knowing*. Springer.

Cross, N. (2011). *Design Thinking: Understanding How Designers Think and Work*. Berg.

Dell' Era, C., & Landoni, P. (2014). Living Lab: A Methodology Between User-Centred Design and Participatory Design. *Creativity and Innovation Management, 23*(2), 137–154.

Deloitte. (2020). Tech Trends 2020. *Deloitte Insights*. Retrieved August 19, 2021, from https://www2.deloitte.com/content/dam/Deloitte/pt/Documents/tech-trends/TechTrends2020.pdf

Design Council. (2021, April). *Beyond Net Zero—A Systematic Design Approach*. UK Design Council.

DESIS Network. (2021). About. [Online]. https://www.desisnetwork.org/about/

Einstein, A. (1955, May 2). Old Man's Advice to Youth: 'Never Lose a Holy Curiosity'. *LIFE Magazine*, p. 64.

enoll.org. (2021). LivingLab SHANGHAI. Retrieved August 5, 2021, from https://enoll.org/network/living-labs/?livinglab=livinglab-shanghai#description

Eriksson, M., Niitamo, V. P., & Kulkki, S. (2005). *State-of-the-Art in Utilizing Living Labs Approach to User-centric ICT Innovation—A European Approach*. Working Paper. Luleå University of Technology.

Forbes. (2020). Britain Will Ban Gasoline Cars in 2030. Why Are Experts Not Impressed? Retrieved August 20, 2021, from https://www.forbes.com/sites/davidrvetter/2020/11/18/britain-will-ban-gasoline-cars-in-2030-why-are-experts-not-impressed/?sh=2b98728536e4

Ford, M. (2009). *The Lights in the Tunnel: Automation, Accelerating Technology, and the Economy of the Future: Volume 1*. CreateSpace Independent Publishing Platform.

Gov.uk. (2020). Government Takes Historic Step Towards Net-Zero with End of Sale of New Petrol and Diesel Cars by 2030. Retrieved August 20, 2021, from https://www.gov.uk/government/news/government-takes-historic-step-towards-net-zero-with-end-of-sale-of-new-petrol-and-diesel-cars-by-2030

Hargraves, I. (2018). Care and Capacities of Human-Centered Design. *Design Issues, 34*(3), 76–88.

Hengsberger, A. (2019). LEAD User Method: An Interview with Eric von Hippel. Retrieved July 29, 2021, from https://www.lead-innovation.com/english-blog/lead-user-method-an-interview-with-eric-von-hippel

Internet Society. (2019). The Trust Opportunity: Exploring Consumer Attitudes to the Internet of Things. Retrieved August 17, 2021, from https://www.internetsociety.org/resources/doc/2019/trust-opportunity-exploring-consumer-attitudes-to-iot/

IPCC. (2018). *Special Report Global Warming of 1.5° C*. FAU Florida Atlantic University 2018. Retrieved August 19, 2021, from https://www.ipcc.ch/sr15/

Juniper Research. (2015). Retail Spend on 'Internet of Things' to Reach $2.5bn by 2020. Retrieved August 17, 2021, from https://www.juniperresearch.com/press/retail-spend-on-iot-to-reach-2-5bn-by-2020

Kimbell, L. (2011). Rethinking Design Thinking: Part I. *Design and Culture, 3*(3), 285–306.

Kviselius, N. Z., & Andersson, P. (2009). Living Labs as Tools for Open Innovation. *Communications & Strategies, 74*, 75–94.
L.E.K. (2015). The IoT Opportunity: Is Your Go-to-Market Strategy as Smart as Your Product? *Executive Insights, XVII*, 22. Retrieved August 17, 2021, from https://www.lek.com/sites/default/files/insights/pdf-attachments/IoT_InternetofThings_IoT-Preparedness_LEK-ExecutiveInsights-1722_0.pdf
Lee, B., Cooper, R., Hands, D., & Coulton, P. (2019). Value Creation for IoT: Challenges and Opportunities Within the Design and Development Process. In *Living in the Internet of Things (IoT 2019)* (p. 8). IET.
Lee, B., Cooper, R., Hands, D., & Coulton, P. (2020, August 11–14). Designing for the Internet of Things: A Critical Interrogation of IoT Processes and Principles. In *Conference Proceedings 'Tangible, Embedded, Networked—DRS SIG TentSIG', DRS 2020.*
Martínez-López, F. J., & Casillas, J. (2013). Artificial Intelligence-Based Systems Applied in Industrial Marketing: An Historical Overview, Current and Future Insights. *Industrial Marketing Management, 42*(4), 489–495.
Nambisan, S., Lyytinen, K., Majchrzak, A., & Song, M. (2017). Digital Innovation Management: Reinventing Innovation Management Research in a Digital World. *MIS Quarterly, 41*(1), 223–238.
NIC. (2021, March). *Global Trends 2040: A More Contested World.* Retrieved August 19, 2021, from https://www.dni.gov/nic/globaltrends
Poliquin, C. (2020). *The Wage and Inequality Impacts of Broadband Internet.* University of California. Retrieved August 19, 2021, from https://www.poliquin.xyz/files/poliquin_jmp.pdf
Prahalad, C. K., & Krishnan, M. S. (2008). *The New Age of Innovation. Driving Co-created Value Through Global Networks.* McGraw Hill.
Ranger, S. (2020). What Is the IoT? Everything You Need to Know about the Internet of Things Right Now. Retrieved August 16, 2021, from https://www.zdnet.com/article/what-is-the-internet-of-things-everything-you-need-to-know-about-the-iot-right-now/
Robertson, T., & Simonsen, J. (2012). Challenges and Opportunities in Contemporary Participatory Design. *Design Issues, 28*(3), 3–9.
Sanders, E. B.-N., Brandt, E., & Binder, T. (2010, November). A Framework for Organizing the Tools and Techniques of Participatory Design. In *PDC '10: Proceedings of the 11th Biennial Participatory Design Conference* (pp. 195–198).
Schuurman, D., Lievens, B., De Marez, L., & Ballon, P. (2012). Towards Optimal User Involvement in Innovation Processes: A Panel-Centered Living Lab Approach. In *Technology Management for Emerging Technologies (PICMET), 2012 Proceedings of PICMET'12* (pp. 2046–2054). IEEE.
Statista. (2021). Internet of Things (IoT) and Non-IoT Active Device Connections Worldwide from 2010 to 2025. Retrieved August 22, 2021, from https://www.statista.com/statistics/1101442/iot-number-of-connected-devices-worldwide
Tang, T., Wu, Z., Hamalainen, M., & Ji, Y. (2012). From Web 2.0 to Living Lab: An Exploration of the Evolved Innovation Principles. *Journal of Emerging Technologies in Web Intelligence, 4*, 379–385.
UNECE. (2007). Challenges and Opportunities of Population Ageing. Retrieved August 19, 2021, from https://unece.org/DAM/highlights/what_ECE_does/English/0726054_UNECE_AGEING.pdf
UNICEF. (2021). The Climate Crisis Is a Child Rights Crisis: Introducing the Children's Climate Risk Index. Retrieved August 20, 2021, from https://www.unicef.org/reports/climate-crisis-child-rights-crisis
Von Hippel, E. (2005). *Democratizing Innovation.* MIT Press.

WHO. (2018). *Ageing and Health*. Retrieved August 18, 2021, from https://www.who.int/news-room/fact-sheets/detail/ageing-and-health

WHO. (2019). World Hunger Is Still Not Going Down after Three Years and Obesity Is Still Growing—UN Report. Retrieved July 21, 2021, from https://www.who.int/news/item/15-07-2019-world-hunger-is-still-not-going-down-after-three-years-and-obesity-is-still-growing-un-report

Wood, N., Rust, C., & Horne, G. (2009). A Tacit Understanding: The Designers Role in Capturing and Passing on the Skilled Knowledge of Master Craftsmen. *International Journal of Design, 3*(3), 65–78.

World Bank. (2020). *Poverty and Shared Prosperity 2020: Reversals of Fortune*. Retrieved July 21, 2021, from https://www.worldbank.org/en/publication/poverty-and-shared-prosperity

WWF. (2018). WWF Report Reveals Staggering Extent of Human Impact on Planet. Retrieved July 21, 2021, from https://www.worldwildlife.org/press-releases/wwf-report-reveals-staggering-extent-of-human-impact-on-planet

Summary 10

10.1 The Design Nexus: Reflections and Reorganisation

Over the last decade, design thinking has moved considerably into many facets of organisational life. It has also been widely drawn upon and utilised to address deep-rooted social and global challenges. Its evolutionary development continues to inform its character and value as a highly creative problem-solving approach to often complex problems. Many regard it as a panacea to solve all known ills and wicked problems with one prescribed dose of application; then magically, solutions and desired endpoints are successfully achieved. Sadly, however, this is not the case. We strike a strong cautionary note here to argue that design thinking does have a leading role in effecting meaningful change, but, (here is the caveat) it does have limitations as to what and how it can contribute to leading this 'change.' Complex problems, by their very definition, are complex, and as such, demand the input and voice of many different stakeholders, many of whom are drawn from a diverse range of disciplinary backgrounds. In addition to these, a further layer of complexity is that of context—the very specific conditions and surrounding phenomena—in which it is applied. When these two factors are not taken fully into account, design thinking often over-promises and under-delivers to expectant and subsequently, disappointed audiences.

Going back to the issue of complex problems, these are widely recognised as multi-dimensional and non-linear, which cannot be properly addressed by a 'traditional' design thinking approach. In a way, design thinking needs to become more 'messy' and fluid without its demarcated boundaries of application in use. In essence, it needs to become more 'design' as opposed to a philosophy based on key design principles, more akin to a design 'related' approach. This aspect could be connected to its inherent ambiguous nature, where design thinking needs to

Y. Huang, D. Hands, *Design Thinking for New Business Contexts*, https://doi.org/10.1007/978-3-030-94206-9_10

demonstrate its true value as an agent for change. Like it or not, design thinking is here to stay, but it needs to move onto its next evolutionary stage of development. Both authors are from traditional design backgrounds, and have carefully scrutinised the development of design thinking as a nascent approach to engaging with complex problems. In order to move it forward, the authors here, aim to carefully nudge, cajole and coax design thinking back to its original roots—the discipline of design. As such, we have identified five distinct characteristics of its nature (Fig. 10.1) that are shrouded within its veil of ambiguity (although some characteristics are less ambiguous than others); however, let's draw our attention to the following five key elements that could strengthen the value of design thinking to its most ardent critics (many of whom reside in the discipline of design). Firstly, the five dimensions have differing levels of influence and impact; these align with Richard Buchanan's '4 orders of design' that in Chap. 4. Design thinking cuts across the four orders to foster transformational change, ranging from behavioural 'interactions' at an individual level, right through to systemic change when applied at a macro level of strategic engagement.

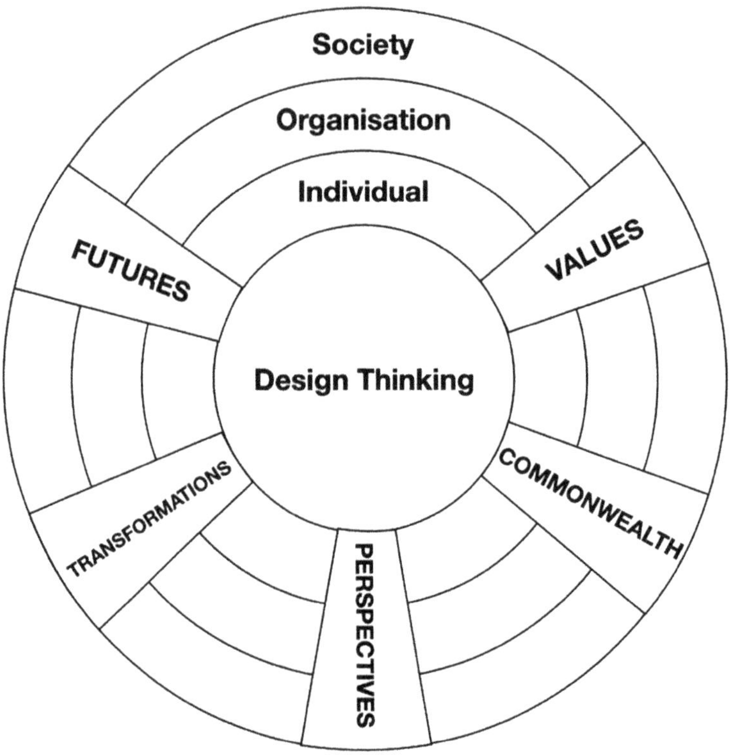

Fig. 10.1 The five interrelated dimensions of design thinking (developed by authors)

10.2 Design Values

Design values investigating the value of design is not a new endeavour; this has been ongoing since the late 1960s (in particular with the emergence of the Design Research Society in 1966 to advance design as a recognised discipline in its own right). Design Councils around the globe have been strong advocates for design, promoting it to many industry sectors, over the last two decades. Furthermore, with the emergence of sub-disciplines that sits within design (for instance, UX design; participatory design and so forth), its reach and value have entered into new domains of application. Chapters within this book have demonstrated the immense value that design can create, when utilised as both a problem and decision making framework that is embedded into the DNA of the organisation. Chapter 2 discussed how design thinking could inform business strategy, whilst cementing stronger customer relationships. It introduced Fraser's 'Three Gears of Design' methodology where end-user insights can identify new business opportunities via the development of innovative new products and services that are truly user centred.

Furthermore, the chapter explored how SMEs could adopt design thinking practices to scale-up ambitious growth plans, taking them from stage 1 to stage 4 on the Danish Design Ladder. To assist the strategic growth ambitions of SMEs, governments around the world are creating local and national design support programmes to drive long-term economic growth and industry competitiveness. Chapter 6 featured an interesting and an in-depth account of young Gaming start-up companies based in Dundee in the UK, that are contributing to the development of the high growth video game industry. However, as the author (Dr Xinya You) points out, these small companies faced many critical challenges in the formative stages of company development. Three high level risks that the fledgling companies faced (and continue to face) include the huge financial risks associated with the development of IP in the long term. Secondly, technological innovation risks often leads to missed commercial opportunities that are vital to SME growth. To overcome the many inherent risks across the gaming sector, the author was instrumental in creating two design tools that led to the development of an InGAME Business model design booklet to support and increase the value of the Dundee games cluster to the region. Chapter 8 explored the intangible aspects of the relationship between design thinking and practice, in particular, the creation of user value through design thinking tools and methods. The two case examples offered both a powerful and pervasive argument as to the role of design thinking and how it could be used to explore both possible and potential futures for strategic direction and growth.

10.3 Design Commonwealth

Design commonwealth is a traditional English term for a political community founded for the common 'good'. In this sense, we view common good as democratic design process, where design thinking is embraced as a powerful vehicle to create meaningful participation and inclusivity amongst individuals and wider communities. Chapter 9 places great emphasis on the democratisation of the design decision-making process. It touches upon and traverses the vast expanse of end-user participation and the many diverse tools and techniques to capture the 'voices' of the user. Eric von Hippel is a leading advocate who has devoted his career to developing methods and frameworks to drive user inspired innovation via his 'Lead User Method' that places primary emphasis on the end-user to foster product innovation. The chapter then turns its attention to the 'Living Labs' movement, that places participatory design central to its role within the co-creation of innovative solutions. What makes the Living Labs particularly unique is that they are bounded environments that facilitate real-life testing and experimentation.

In addition to this, participants and users are explicitly involved within this activity, generating and offering highly personalised insights and observations, rather than mere passive participants. Chapter 4 explores the complex issue of organisational change management, offering a series of well recognised and commonly used change management frameworks to foster transformational change. However, given the strengths and merits of each adopted route to change, Chap. 4 introduces an alternative design orientated approach based on Richard Buchannan's four orders of design. Moving through the four orders, the fourth and final order is primarily focused upon systems and organisational design. It focuses more upon the psychological and cultural contexts that give meaning to design and the wider system that supports it. IBM is a noteworthy example of how a leading international organisation is radically implementing cultural change across its organisational divisions, with design thinking at the heart of this ongoing process. Chapter 5 critically interrogates the theme of design commonwealth through the perspective of creative confidence, where it focuses on promoting an innovation mindset to engage employees with a new set of approaches, practices and methodologies to foster innovation and change. The author of Chap. 5 (Dr Beatriz Itzel Cruz Megchun) offers a wide variety of contexts and applications of design thinking that demonstrates its applicability to a range of diverse contexts. Highlighted throughout the discussion were the different types of economic systems and business structures that warrant very specific approaches to the usage of design thinking practices. What may be appropriate and suitable for one business type may not be suitable to another business with a completely different organisational structure. This takes us back to the earlier discussion where context is critical when embarking on a set of design thinking interventions.

10.4 Design Perspectives

Design perspectives is a particularly prescient and recurrent theme given the ongoing impact and uncertainty of Covid-19 to national and local economies. Chapter 4 takes a closer look at the rise of business uncertainty and the need to plan ahead in order to remain commercially viable in the shifting landscape of enterprise. CEO's and business leaders rely upon established structures and processes to navigate corporate turbulence, which in a way mitigate risk and financial impact to profit margins. What we are witnessing throughout the globe, is how well prepared and agile businesses are, given the ongoing seismic events since spring 2020. This leads us to explore the skill sets and competencies of tomorrow's business leaders and the leadership qualities required in order to provide vision and agency to companies operating in complex international markets. Chapter 3 examines business curricula within the higher education sector, and how does it equip business leaders with the abilities to lead and deliver projects through instilling a sense of common purpose to their employees. Uncertainty can be commonly measured by both magnitude and duration, challenging even the most resilient entrepreneurial minds. Readers can draw upon local examples of companies struggling or flourishing within these challenging times, where firm leadership saved many companies as others fell by the wayside and declined.

New and alternative perspectives have risen to the fore, none more so in business and management education. Traditional curricula and methods of teaching are continually being re-appraised, undergoing continual scrutiny for industry relevance, both for today and tomorrows dynamic commercial landscapes. Chapter 3 compared and contrasted the key pedagogical approaches between design and business education, identifying how shared approaches could go some way to equip students with T-shaped skills that offer them deep knowledge of their subject area alongside a broad base of general supporting skills. With the advent of design thinking modules and short courses growing in prominence in business schools, design is slowly becoming recognised as a key element and driver of organisational creativity and innovation. New technologies and educational systems are being developed to support continuous professional development to business executives. We are seeing the emergence of leading universities and industry partners offering a wide range of design thinking short courses to prepare participants for the future challenges that lie ahead when striving for organisational competitiveness and success.

10.5 Design Transformations

Design transformations primarily involves the development of robust and highly flexible business strategies that embrace ongoing technological developments and shifting consumer demographics. Chapter 9 carefully examines the exponential growth of IoT and its disruptive potential to established business models. To re-affirm this, the often quoted adage "data is the new oil" perfectly captures the huge growth potential of the internet of things and its vast untapped potential to revolutionise business and our everyday lives. For example, Airbiquity is a software and engineering company that provides real-time data to users of connected motor vehicles, in addition to lifecycle management support services. The impact of this service offering is contributing to profound changes in the way we use and maintain motor vehicles on a daily basis. JOSH.AI provides voice controlled home automation using a wide variety of connected devices. This technology allows users with physical or cognitive impairments to lead independent lives that would have been unthinkable only a few years ago. At an urban scale of application, the rise of smart cities allows planners, urbanists and architects to design integrated and networked environments that can radically re-shape the way we conceive and develop transport infrastructure, water supply and waste disposal facilities. Combined, it allows for a more interactive and responsive approach to uniform city administration and governance.

Chapter 8 featured a comprehensive discussion by Dr Radka Newton whereupon a small team of academics utilised a vast array of design thinking tools to elicit a deeper understanding of the student learning experience at Lancaster University. Service design is a closely related discipline to design thinking that shares many similarities in the way it utilises creative processes to capture the intangible experiences by the user, in this particular case, the users were students who freely shared their experiences with the academic team in order to improve upon the existing education provision within the department. Chapter 2 introduced and debated the value of design support programmes to SMEs by the UK Design Council. It is widely acknowledged that SMEs are the engine of growth for regional and national economies, however in order to flourish, SMEs require tailored 'support' programmes to remain competitive. Support could take the form of knowledge transfer, capacity building and employee skills development. In this case, it touched upon the 'Design Leadership Programme' where SMEs could add meaningful value to their customers and clients via the development of fluid design strategies to create new business opportunities.

10.6 Design Futures

Design futures explores the proactive nature of design thinking where attention is devoted towards imaginary and preferred futures for the organisation. Within the advent of rapid globalisation, intelligent technologies, and new demographic trends, changes in overall business activity are leading to cross-industry and cross-sectoral cooperation. In order to develop more flexible business models, design thinking has become the new focus towards new business model development within contemporary organisational practice. In a traditional organisational structure, two important elements in business activities, design and management are often undertaken in isolation; however, it is commonly agreed that this binary model is no longer sufficient to both create and foster meaningful values in the development of strategic planning business activities. Key design decision makers need to understand and embrace the basic logic of business practices. Similarly, CEOs and business managers need to be aware of the impact of design on the enterprise against the backdrop of emergent future trends in order to secure long-term sustainable success.

Chapter 7 provides a detailed account of implementing a three-stage process to achieve brand ambidexterity in order to ensure brand relevance in a contemporary post-modern world. The first stage of the change process centres upon re-framing organisational routes to innovation (destabilisation) via problem interrogation and contextual immersion. Then, stage two (define and develop) involves the designers working closely with brand managers to scope potential problems that could be encountered in the solution implementation phases. Finally stage three (transformation) culminates in the refreshed brand identity that aligns with corporate objectives moving into the future. Chapter 6 introduces and explores sustainable futures, set against the backdrop of climate change and global environmental challenges that are forcing organisations to change their current business practices. Policymakers and businesses have to reappraise their existing understanding and approaches to sustainability issues that include the 'Triple Bottom Line' (TBL) when measuring impact and metrics for success. Central to this ongoing and crucial debate is design, where the design profession can draw upon its vast repertoire of skills and methodologies to embrace and overcome these critical challenges.

10.7 Final Reflections

The themes introduced within this book highlight a plethora of critical roles and applications of design throughout a variety of complex and demanding contexts. These challenges span and traverse established boundaries that are continually being redefined in a contemporary era of great uncertainty and ambiguity. Design continues its relentless journey of development, entering into new domains of influence, ranging from healthcare delivery, policymaking and reducing social inequality. Climate change, sustainable development goals and globalisation amongst many more emergent causes are forcing individuals, organisations and national governments to seek new ways to address these urgent challenges. Design is one such tool that could be deployed to re-think and engage with these interconnected context-sensitive challenges. The five dimensions of design thinking offered by the authors provide agency to the role and understanding of design thinking as one such powerful means to facilitate meaningful change for people and the planet, both now and in the future.

> Spend eighty percent of your time focusing on the opportunities of tomorrow rather than the problems of yesterday.
>
> —Brian Tracy, motivational speaker and writer

Index

Y. Huang, D. Hands, *Design Thinking for New Business Contexts*,
https://doi.org/10.1007/978-3-030-94206-9

www.ingramcontent.com/pod-product-compliance
Ingram Content Group UK Ltd.
Pitfield, Milton Keynes, MK11 3LW, UK
UKHW020053040925
462575UK00013B/628

9783030942052